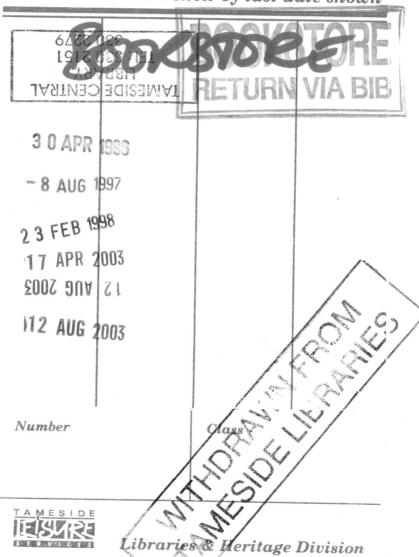

ALSO BY GARY CAREY

All the Stars in Heaven
Doug and Mary
Katharine Hepburn: A Hollywood Yankee
Marlon Brando: The Only Contender
Judy Holliday: An Intimate Life Story

ANITA LOOS

A BIOGRAPHY

Gary Carey

BLOOMSBURY

First published in Great Britain 1988
Copyright ©1988 by Gary Carey

Bloomsbury Publishing Ltd., 2 Soho Square, London WIV 5DE

British Library Cataloging in Publication Data

Carey, Gary.
  Anita Loos : a biography.
  1. Fiction in English. American writers
  Loos, Anita, 1888–1981
  I. Title.   3662
  813'.52
  ISBN 0-7475-0294-3

IN MEMORY OF
Ruth and Ted Carey

Contents

Illustrations   ix
Acknowledgments   xv

PART ONE: *Eastward, Ho!*

1 *Vital Statistics*   3
2 *Daddy's Mascot*   10
3 *Cérébrale*   23
4 *Triangle Days*   31
5 *Excursion*   38
6 *Fairbanks and Company*   43
7 *Getting Married*   53

PART TWO: *Marriage à la Mode*

8 *Mrs. E.*   73
9 *Broadway Transfer*   82
10 *Diary of a Professional Lady*   93
11 *Stage Whispers*   103
12 *A Cure for Mr. E.*   116
13 *Palm Beach Story*   122
14 *Altered States*   134

PART THREE: *Westward, Woe!*

15 *Hello and Goodbye*   145
16 *Studio Politics*   156

17 *The Toughest Year*   169
18 *House Guests*   175
19 *Genius and Goddesses*   184
20 *Lull Before the Storm*   194
21 *Fort Loos*   200
22 *Bicoastal*   205

P A R T   F O U R : *Playbills*

23 *Happy Birthday, Lousy Christmas*   213
24 *Siren's Song*   223
25 *From the French*   232
26 *Unity and Disharmony*   243
27 *Writer's Cramp*   252

P A R T   F I V E : *A Lady of Memoirs*

28 *A Strange Exhilaration*   265
29 *The Needle's Eye*   273
30 *Walpurgis Nights*   279
31 *A Girl Like I*   283
32 *Mining the Past*   289
33 *Friendship*   294
34 *Striving for Transcendence*   301
35 *Gladys*   307

    Epilogue   314

    Index   317

Illustrations

Anita's maternal grandparents (*Courtesy of the Anita Loos Estate*)   6

The Smith House (*Courtesy of the Anita Loos Estate*)   6

Anita's parents (*Courtesy of The Lester Glassner Collection*)   8

Anita Loos, age four (*Courtesy of the Anita Loos Estate*)   11

Anita and her sister Gladys, 1894 (*Both Courtesy of The Lester Glassner Collection*)   14, 15

Anita's Aunt Nina (*Courtesy of The Lester Glassner Collection*)   18

Horace Robinson, Aunt Nina's husband (*Courtesy of The Lester Glassner Collection*)   18

Mary Pickford and Lionel Barrymore, 1912 (*Courtesy of the Museum of Modern Art Film Stills Archive*)   24

Mary Pickford in *The New York Hat* (*Courtesy of The Lester Glassner Collection*)   24

Anita at Coronado, 1914 (*Courtesy of The Lester Glassner Collection*)   27

Mae Marsh (*Courtesy of the Museum of Modern Art Film Stills Archive*)   36

Anita with Douglas Fairbanks, 1917 (*Courtesy of the Anita Loos Estate*)   45

Douglas Fairbanks, *Wild and Wooly* (*Courtesy of the Museum of Modern Art Film Stills Archive*)   45

Anita and John Emerson, 1918 (*Courtesy of the Anita Loos Estate*)   51

Emerson with stuffed crocodile (*Courtesy of the Anita Loos Estate*)   51

Anita, 1914–15 (*Courtesy of the Museum of Modern Art Film Stills Archive*)   52

Louise Huff and Ernest Truex in *Oh, You Women!* (1919) (*Courtesy of the Museum of Modern Art Film Stills Archive*)   54

Constance Talmadge, 1916 (*Courtesy of the Anita Loos Estate*)   57

Constance Talmadge in evening dress (*Courtesy of the Anita Loos Estate*)   58

Norma Talmadge (*Courtesy of the Anita Loos Estate*)   59

Joe Schenck and Norma Talmadge at Long Island, 1919 (*Courtesy of the Anita Loos Estate*)   60

Emerson, Anita, Constance Talmadge, Sidney Franklin, and Oliver Marsh, 1919 (*Courtesy of the Anita Loos Estate*)   62

Constance Talmadge in *A Virtuous Vamp* (*Courtesy of the Anita Loos Estate*)   62

From the script of *A Virtuous Vamp* (*Courtesy of the Anita Loos Estate*)   63

Nathan Gibson Clark (*Courtesy of the Anita Loos Estate*)   66

Anita and Emerson on their wedding day, June 21, 1920 (*Courtesy of the Museum of Modern Art Film Stills Archive*)   69

Anita and Emerson on Long Island (*Courtesy of the Anita Loos Estate*)   76

Norma and Constance Talmadge and Anita, 1920 (*Courtesy of the Anita Loos Estate*)   77

Emerson and Anita at Malmaison (*Courtesy of the Anita Loos Estate*)   78

Emerson with soprano Dorothy Jordan (*Courtesy of the Anita Loos Estate*)   83

Mae Clarke and James Cagney in *Public Enemy* (1931) (*Courtesy of the Museum of Modern Art Film Stills Archive*)   89

Minnie Loos in the late 1920s (*Courtesy of the Museum of Modern Art Film Stills Archive*)   90

Ruth Gordon, 1925 (*Courtesy of the Anita Loos Estate*)   91

Illustration and title page from an original edition of *Gentlemen Prefer Blondes*, 1925 (*Courtesy of Boni & Liveright*)   96, 97

Anita, Joseph Hergesheimer, Aileen Pringle, and H. L. Mencken, 1925 (*Courtesy of the Museum of Modern Art Film Stills Archive*)   101

Adele Astaire and her husband Charles, Lord Cavendish (*Courtesy of the Anita Loos Estate*)   107

Marjorie Oelrichs, Ruth Dubonnet, and Anita in Paris, 1925 (*Courtesy of The Lester Glassner Collection*)   110

June Walker and Frank Morgan (*Courtesy of The Lester Glassner Collection*)   112

Ruth Taylor and Alice White, 1928 (*Courtesy of the Museum of Modern Art Film Stills Archive*)   113

Pages from playbill for the 1927 stage production of *Gentlemen Prefer Blondes* (*Courtesy of the author*)   114, 115

Anita, 1927 (*Courtesy of the Anita Loos Collection*)   118

Benito Mussolini, 1927 (*Courtesy of the Anita Loos Estate*)   119

Anita and Emerson, 1927 (*All courtesy of the Anita Loos Collection*)   124, 125

Anita and Addison Mizner, 1927 (*Courtesy of the Anita Loos Estate*)   126

Mizner, Anita, actor Richard Barthelmess, and his wife, Jessica, 1927 (*Courtesy of the Anita Loos Estate*)   127

Wilson Mizner, Addison's brother, and Anita, 1927 (*Courtesy of the Anita Loos Estate*)   128

The Count and Countess Paul de Vallambrosa, 1927 (*Courtesy of the Anita Loos Estate*)   129

Anita in costume for Palm Beach ball (*Courtesy of the Anita Loos Estate*)   131

Anita and Emerson dressed as Mr. and Mrs. Stolesbury for a Palm Beach costume party (*Courtesy of the Anita Loos Estate*)   132

Irving Thalberg and his wife, Norma Shearer (*Courtesy of the Museum of Modern Art Film Stills Archive*)   146

Publicity still of Anita, Chester Morris, and Jean Harlow (*Courtesy of The Lester Glassner Collection*)   149

Chester Morris and Jean Harlow (*Courtesy of The Lester Glassner Collection*)   149

Anita and her Pomeranian, Cagney (*Courtesy of The Lester Glassner Collection*)   151

Anita and her brother, Clifford, in the early 1930s (*Courtesy of the Anita Loos Estate*)   152

Minnie and R. Beers Loos in the early 1930s (*Courtesy of the Anita Loos Estate*)   153

Tilly Losch in California, 1937 (*Courtesy of the Anita Loos Estate*)   154

Anita, Emerson, artist Kees Van Dongen, and Tilly Losch, 1937 (*Courtesy of the Museum of Modern Art Film Stills Archive*)   155

Clark Gable and Jean Harlow, 1933 (*Courtesy of the Museum of Modern Art Film Stills Archive*)   157

Edwin Hubble and Aldous Huxley, 1938 (*Courtesy of the Anita Loos Collection*)   160

Spencer Tracy and Jean Harlow, 1935 (*Courtesy of the Museum of Modern Art Film Stills Archive*)   161

Robert Hopkins, 1936 (*Courtesy of the Anita Loos Collection*)   163

Clark Gable and Jeanette MacDonald, 1936 (*Courtesy of the Museum of Modern Art Film Stills Archive*)   166

Earthquake sequence from *San Francisco* (*Courtesy of the Museum of Modern Art Film Stills Archive*)   167

Anita's beachfront house in Santa Monica (*Courtesy of the Anita Loos Estate*)   176

Marjorie Oelrichs, Leopold Stokowski, and Anita in Santa Monica, 1937 (*Courtesy of the Anita Loos Estate*)   177

Betty and Sandy Wendel with Anita (*Courtesy of the Anita Loos Estate*)   179

Robert Hopkins, Anita, Eddy Duchin, Marjorie Oelrichs, and Emerson, 1936 (*Courtesy of the Anita Loos Estate*)   180

Peter Duchin (*Courtesy of the Anita Loos Estate*)   183

George Cukor and the cast on the set of *The Women,* 1939 (*Courtesy of the Museum of Modern Art Film Stills Archive*)   186

Anita and Norma Shearer on the set of *The Women* (*Courtesy of the Anita Loos Estate*)   187

Paulette Goddard, 1936 (*Courtesy of the Museum of Modern Art Film Stills Archive*)   188

Aldous and Maria Huxley and Anita (*All courtesy of the Anita Loos Estate*) 190, 191

Louis B. Mayer, Paulette Goddard, Joan Crawford, and Hunt Stromberg at the premiere of *The Women* (*Courtesy of the Museum of Modern Art Film Stills Archive*)   195

Nelson Eddy, Jeanette MacDonald, and director W. S. Van Dyke, 1942 (*Courtesy of the Museum of Modern Art Film Stills Archive*)   198

Helen Hayes, Grace Valentine, and Enid Markey, 1946 (*Courtesy of The Lester Glassner Collection*)   214

Page from *Happy Birthday* playbill (*Courtesy of the author*)   216

Anita with Richard and Mary Sale, 1947 (*Courtesy of the Anita Loos Estate*)   218

ZaSu Pitts (*Courtesy of the Museum of Modern Art Film Stills Archive*)   220

Frances Marion (*Courtesy of the Museum of Modern Art Film Stills Archive*) 221

Natasha Wilson (*Courtesy of The Lester Glassner Collection*)   226

Anita and Carol Channing, 1950 (*Courtesy of the Museum of Modern Art Film Stills Archive*)   230

Lismore, the Cavendish castle in Ireland (*Courtesy of the Anita Loos Estate*)   233

From *A Mouse Is Born* (*Courtesy of the artist, Federico Pallavicini*)   235

Playbill for *Gigi,* 1951 (*Courtesy of the author*)   238

Audrey Hepburn in 1950 (*Courtesy of the Museum of Modern Art Film Stills Archive*)   239

Anita and Colette in Paris (*Courtesy of The Lester Glassner Collection*)   240

Pierre Barillet with Anita (*Courtesy of The Lester Glassner Collection*)   246

Anita and Gladys, 1952 (*Courtesy of The Lester Glassner Collection*)   249

Lady Mendl's home, After All (*Courtesy of the Anita Loos Estate*)   253

Anita, Horst Buchholz, and Robert Lewis, 1959 (*Courtesy of The Lester Glassner Collection*)   259

Playbill for *Chéri* (*Courtesy of the author*)   260

Cris Alexander, Anita, Miss Moore, and Gladys, 1960 (*Courtesy of The Lester Glassner Collection*)   275

Anita dressed for the Capote ball, 1966 (*Courtesy of The Lester Glassner Collection*)   285

Miss Moore, Christmas 1966 (*Courtesy of The Lester Glassner Collection*)   286

Pages from the playbill for *Lorelei (Courtesy of the author)*   298, 299

Acknowledgments

A N I T A   L O O S wrote two memoirs before her death in 1981. Autobiographi-cal references abound in many of her other writings—her film scripts, plays, and countless magazine articles. She was a born storyteller, and was always in peak form when reshaping a real-life encounter to make an amusing anecdote.

There are discrepancies between what she selected to remember in print and what is related in this biography, which is based largely on the diaries which she began keeping in 1926 and went on with until a few months before her death. She never jotted down her daily life with an eye toward future publication; her journals were an *aide-memoire,* written when an event was fresh in her mind, with no regard to literary style. They present an Anita far different from the one who emerges when she chose to write as an ironic, slightly detached observer of the follies of her times.

I met Anita in 1966 when I was working in the film department of the Museum of Modern Art and suggested to her that the Museum present a retrospective of her films. We remained friends after that event and spoke often, frequently off-the-record. Anita spoke frankly, often outrageously, about the many celebrities she had known, but also cautioned me, "Don't repeat that! It's true, but it might hurt him [or her]." I held my tongue, but I kept notes, and now that the people in question and Anita are gone, I feel free to tell some of the tales.

This book would not have been possible without the cooperation of Mary Loos, Anita's niece. I am also indebted to the following for their help and participation: Cris Alexander, Don Bachardy, Joan Berg, Carol Channing, Richard Coe, Ray Pierre Corsini, the late George Cukor, Ruth Dubonnet, Lillian Gish, Lester Glassner, Morton Gottlieb, Timothy Gray, Tammy Grimes, James Hatcher, Helen Hayes, Charles Hollereith, the late Christopher Isherwood, Avis Klein, Herman Levin, Charles Lowe, the late Rouben Mamoulian, the late Margo, Sam Marx, the late Grete Mosheim, the late Cathleen Nesbitt, Federico Pallavicini, Ted Peckham, Edward Sale, Richard Sale, Esta Silsbee, Stanley Simmons, Oliver Smith, Betty Wendel, Miles White.

The comments made by Louise Huff Stillman are taken from a 1970 interview with the author, previously unpublished. I have also drawn on tributes made by Ruth Gordon and Joshua Logan at a memorial service for Anita in August 1981.

Finally, I salaam with affection and gratitude to my wife, Carol; my agent, Ray Corsini; and my editor, Vicky Wilson, for their patience and encouragement. Who says a gentleman can't prefer both blondes and brunettes?

PART
One

EASTWARD, HO!

1

Vital Statistics

*A*NITA LOOS'S comic masterpiece, *Gentlemen Prefer Blondes,* is the story of a golddigger's progress in the bathtub-gin era of American history. In its inimitable way, it is as evocative of the 1920s as Fitzgerald's novels, *No, No, Nanette,* a Clara Bow movie, or one of those Cecil Beaton photographs of the likes of Emerald Cunard posed against a cascade of polka dots.

The sense of a bygone era conveyed by *Blondes* is so intense that many readers assume that Anita was herself a jazz baby, a petite, bobbed-hair flapper, as high-stepping as any of the heroines of the lighthearted, slightly naughty novels, plays, and films she seemingly dashed off between afternoon tea at the Plaza and pretheater dinner at Delmonico's.

This assumption is not entirely false. Anita was a participant in as well as a chronicler of the revels of that dizzy era in which she first achieved international fame. She liked to have fun, and she selected her playmates from the rich, the celebrated, and the notorious, with a special affection for shady ladies, con men, and charlatans of both sexes. For many years, she led a plush life, moving between New York and Hollywood, Paris and London, with stopovers at all the fashionable spas at home and abroad.

She had no time for pretense, snobbery, or sanctimony; she was leery of politicians, do-gooders, and promulgators of high culture. She was doubtful that the world would improve as it got older.

Suspicious and skeptical but too smart to sing the twentieth-century blues herself: this is the self-portrait that emerges from Anita's autobiographical writings. In the memoirs she wrote late in her life, she presents herself as a blithe and independent spirit who learned early that you should laugh when you can—otherwise you might die without laughing at all.

But there was another side to Anita, one barely hinted at in the memoirs and fully revealed only in the diaries she started keeping in the mid-1920s. From them comes the portrait of a woman who was extraordinarily disciplined, resilient, and morally fastidious. There were no flaming affairs in her life—a few flirtations, yes, but no extramarital arrangements. She was one of a vanishing breed, a woman who prided herself on being a lady. She had a strong awareness of what was proper, and while her code was perhaps too liberal-minded for homebodies, it was definitely too conventional to suit her more raffish friends.

She liked the company of hustlers and kept women, laughed at their tales of con games and romantic imbroglios; and her laughter—accurately described by a friend as "coming not so much from the heart as the gut," so rich and full-bodied it was out of proportion with her small frame— perhaps made them conclude that she was on their side. But this was not always so. Writing in her diary, she would often disapprove of what had made her laugh. She was not a prude, but there was a deep reserve about her, a touch of the puritan in her makeup that might well surprise anyone who knew her only through her published works.

The divergent sides of Anita's personality can be interpreted in two ways, neither necessarily excluding the other. The first centers on a vital statistic that Anita preferred to keep offstage: her date of birth. She usually implied that she started writing for the movies when she was twelve or fourteen, that she was still in her twenties when *Blondes* was written. The truth is that she was twenty-four when she sold her first scenario and close to forty when *Blondes* appeared in 1925. To be precise, Anita was born in 1888, reaching her teens before Queen Victoria had died, and consequently was as much a product of the American version of Saxe-Coburgian propriety as she was a child of the promiscuous 1920s.

Anita came of age at a turning point between two dramatically different eras of American life, and she was also the offspring of almost farcically mismatched parents, who pulled her in different directions, one toward cakes and ale, the other toward sobriety and perseverance. She loved both, though not with equal warmth, and certainly not in accordance with their individual merits. Her mother she respected but never felt close to; her "Pop" she adored, much more than he deserved.

More is known about Anita's maternal ancestry than about her father's forebears, which suggests that Pop didn't have much family history to pass along—otherwise he would have served it up, with dressing. Mom's folks, on the other hand, noted births and departures in their Bible and held on to documents and legal records that commemorated their progress in the New World.

Anita's mother was one of five children born to George Smith, who came to America from England at age seventeen, settling first in Connecticut as a farmhand. A few years after his arrival, Smith went west, like thousands of others who had heard about the gold found in California in 1848. George was one of the lucky ones: he didn't make a big strike, but neither did he go away emptyhanded. He discovered enough to buy several thousand acres of land in Siskiyou County, about two hundred miles north of San Francisco, where he went back to his first and abiding love, farming.

Then Smith married a girl he had met back east, the daughter of a Shaker family, living in Vermont, with the peculiarly half-pagan, half-Puritan name of Cleopatra Fairbrother. It was not a happy marriage. Anita remembered her grandmother as an opium-addicted recluse, propped up by many pillows in an oversized brass bed, dreamy-eyed and redolent with the scent of lavender.

Years later, when Anita saw *Long Day's Journey into Night*, she recognized her grandmother as a distant cousin of Mary Tyrone, though it wasn't childbirth that had led Cleopatra to dope. Cleopatra, Anita decided, was merely trying to escape Siskiyou County and her husband. The local landscape was enthralling for nature lovers; George Smith, a kind man and good provider, was a model husband. But neither George nor the vista offered Cleopatra the adventure she craved. She had married George to get out of New England only to stand by as George turned their bit of California into a facsimile of New England, starting with a house that would have looked proud on any Connecticut or Massachusetts lawn. Cleopatra found herself entombed in a house that represented everything she had wanted to escape by marrying George—or so Anita came to believe.

What George wanted in a wife he found in his firstborn and favorite child, Minerva, who was Anita's mother. Possibly Cleopatra chose the name, but George reduced it to "Minnie," and Minnie lived up to the diminutive: she was obedient, quiet, pretty, and yet without vanity—until R. Beers Loos came along.

Anita's parents met at a dance, and after several waltzes George Smith decided that this fortune hunter should be put at a distance from his daughter. Minnie was sent to a finishing school in Delaware, and after

LEFT: George Smith and Cleopatr[a]
Fairbrother, Anita's maternal grand-
parents, in the 1860s
BELOW: The Smith house in
Siskiyou County, California

graduation, with her father as escort, she made a grand tour of Europe. Along the way, Minnie bought a Worth gown in Paris and wore it for the first time when she married Mr. Loos, sometime in 1882.

"Beers Loos" suggests a Belgian, Flemish, or German heritage. (The name is pronounced Lōōs.) What the "R" stood for is anyone's guess— maybe Robert or Richard or a similar name, too prosaic for a young man as colorful as R. Beers imagined himself to be. Born in Ohio, he had studied journalism at a state college, then made his way to California, opening and shuttering newspaper offices along the way. Some folded for lack of a literate audience; others were burned out.

Definitely he was flamboyant—"a good-looking devil," Anita called him—and he loved anything theatrical; he was a virtuoso of the banjo, could keep his footing on a slack wire, and was ready to challenge anyone who denied he was the Edwin Booth of amateur theater circles. As he drifted along, he opened drama societies as often as newspaper offices, the former frequently flourishing while the latter foundered.

But at the time of his marriage, R. Beers was doing well with the *Etna Weekly Post,* Etna being Minnie's hometown. The *Post,* its owner boasted, had a circulation "of five hundred paying subscribers at three dollars a year" plus a readership extending beyond California. "Because of its spicy matter," R. Beers wrote in an autobiographical essay, "the *Post* circulates widely in the East." This is braggadocio, though possibly R. Beers did have a local reputation as a wit, thanks to the sometimes salty cornpone jokes and anecdotes he invented. Around this time he definitely started thinking of himself as a humorist, and later he claimed his daughter had inherited her wit and wisdom from him. Certainly they weren't a bequest from Minnie, who, being George Smith's favorite child, wasn't inclined to smile at life—not the life *she* led, anyway.

Within a year of her marriage Minnie gave birth to a son, Harry Clifford, always known to friends by his second name. Then R. Beers caught another dose of wanderlust and soon was moving his family from one town to the next, opening and shuttering offices two or three times a year.

Throughout all this, he told an interviewer, Minnie was "a true help-mate . . . all mechanical and editorial duties are divided between myself and my bride." But R. Beers was taking too much credit. Family history has it that Minnie, with baby Clifford strapped to her hip and sometimes with the help of a printer's devil, got the paper printed somewhere close to time while her bridegroom lazed at home, swigging beer and thumbing through the latest East Coast publications for "inspiration."

Minerva Smith, Anita's mother, at the time of her marriage in 1881

R. Beers Loos, Anita's father, in the late 1870s

Minnie didn't have much time or (Anita claimed) talent for housekeeping, though she tried to keep things neat and tidy. Not that R. Beers ever noticed or cared: clutter and grime were of no importance when new towns were waiting to be conquered, another batch of ladies ready to succumb to his charms. Minnie learned soon enough that neither marriage nor fatherhood was going to housebreak her husband.

Five years passed between the first and second of the Loos children, a long stretch at a time when birth control was both controversial and far from foolproof. The quick conception of Clifford and the fact that no miscarriages, stillbirths, or infant deaths occurred in the interval suggests that Minnie stayed away from her husband's bed until she found a reason to go on building a family.

Early in 1887 the Looses settled in Sissons, California (today Mount Shasta), where R. Beers started a new paper, *The Mascot*, which caught on immediately. He was so happy with *The Mascot* that Minnie may have deluded herself into thinking he was going to stay in Sissons for a while, maybe establish himself as a pillar of the community. As a newspaper editor, he was highly regarded, and for the first time Minnie could remember, he seemed to take some responsibility in the management of his publication. So perhaps to encourage him, perhaps only by accident, Minnie conceived a second child in Sissons, and on April 26, 1888, gave birth to a daughter, Corinne Anita Loos.

"Anita" was in honor of a family friend. Nobody knows anything about the "Corinne"—possibly she was a heroine from a French farce R. Beers once performed. His daughter didn't like it, and as soon as she could reason, she refused to respond to "Corinne." She was Anita, or "Nita."

2

Daddy's
Mascot

T H E F I R S T surviving photograph of Anita shows an impish child of about two or three years old, with wide, lambent eyes and a mop of brown hair cut in a Dutch bob. R. Beers was so proud of his daughter that he wanted to share her with the world. He handed out hundreds of postcards showing Anita pushing her head through the front page of *The Mascot.* She was, a slogan read, "*The Mascot*'s mascot."

Around the time Anita made her postcard debut, Minnie gave birth to a third child, another girl, named Gladys. Though blond, Gladys bore a striking resemblance to her sister, and by her second birthday she and the four-year-old Anita were often mistaken for twins. "I was destined to be the runt of the family," Anita said.

The two sisters were very close, though temperamentally they were far apart: Gladys was outgoing while Anita held herself aloof. Her reserve, she later explained, was her response to the limited amusements offered by Sissons—picnics, fishing, hopscotch, helping Pop at the office. Ennui with small-town life seems implausibly precocious for a five- or six-year-old; but in writing about her early years, Anita tended to present herself as a nearly fully developed, if miniature, version of the woman she later became.

Her discontent with Sissons may also have been a reflection of what R. Beers was feeling. Wanderlust had struck again; and recognizing the symptoms, Minnie must have felt alarmed. But when R. Beers announced that he had heard about a San Francisco weekly, *Music and Drama,* that

Anita, age four, as *The Mascot*'s mascot

was available for a small fee, Minnie gave up arguing, even though the fee wasn't modest enough for R. Beers to meet on his own. Minnie borrowed money from her father, and in 1893 the Loos family settled in a nice neighborhood in San Francisco.

While Minnie struggled to put together a household, R. Beers overhauled *Music and Drama* to suit his personality. Highbrow music wasn't his specialty, so he scrapped concert and opera coverage and renamed the weekly *The Dramatic Event*. Soon theater was taking second place to its publisher's two specialties, humor and spice. He, of course, supplied the jokes; the risqué matter was provided by Barbary Coast "hostesses," provocatively posed on top of trolley cars or feeding sea lions at the beach. In no time at all, *The Dramatic Event* looked a lot like a West Coast cousin of the *Police Gazette,* which is precisely what R. Beers intended.

Minnie longed for the quiet existence she had left behind, while her husband thrived on the frontier spirit of his adopted city. He quickly made friends with its sporting ladies, theater people, artists, and writers, among them Jack London, then eking out a living by pirating oysters and selling them beneath market price. Anita felt London's novels suffered because he wrote them when sober; they didn't suggest the London she remembered, who "when drunk, was *a poet.*"

Anita was her father's companion as he explored San Francisco. "He and I used to go fishing several times a week," she later told an interviewer. "We used to sit on the waterfront making friends with sailors and all sorts of riffraff. Fishing gave everyone a terrible thirst, so around noon, we'd go to a saloon, where I ate the hard boiled eggs and pickled beets on the counter while Pop and his companions tanked up on beer."

Minnie took a dim view of Anita's outings with her father. It wasn't proper for a child to mix with all kinds of lowlifes. Anita took Pop's side, and against the two of them Minnie didn't stand a chance. Early on, Anita had started favoring her father, which was understandable, since he provided entertainment while Minnie dished up lessons on responsibility and rectitude. How could she win when after preparing a well-balanced meal and almost getting the children to eat it, R. Beers would burst in with spring rolls or enchiladas?

One afternoon R. Beers announced that Anita and Gladys were going to be actresses. One of his friends, the manager of the Alcazar Stock Company, was looking for two youngsters for a stage version of *Quo Vadis?*: they were to be among a group of Christians about to be fed to the lions—no dialogue was involved, just a little mewling. Minnie was horrified at the idea, but the girls were delighted. The Loos girls whimpered so well in *Quo Vadis?* that they were cast in a production of *A Doll's House* starring the celebrated Blanche Bates.

After that, Gladys appears to have retired from the stage while Anita went on as a solo. She appeared in *East Lynne* as William, the wayward heroine's son, a brief but showy role: one drawn-out death scene accompanied by harp and celestial lighting. Young girls were then frequently cast as boys, and Anita's next important role was Little Lord Fauntleroy. Minnie, a good seamstress, created knickers and jacket from a maroon-velvet ballgown found in a secondhand store. From *Fauntleroy*, Anita went on to play with Henry Miller, one of the great leading men of the period, and was selected by David Belasco, "the high priest of American theater," for the first production in his native San Francisco in over ten years.

Anita's progress was a mixed blessing for the family. R. Beers alone enjoyed his daughter's small triumphs. Minnie stitched away at Anita's costumes and accompanied her to rehearsals, but she let everyone know that she was a stage mother only by coercion. And Anita didn't like being an actress: it was hard work, not magical or fun, as R. Beers had promised.

Later she realized that he was living out his ambitions through her—in the Loos family, it was the father who was the stage mother. But right then, she didn't protest; she didn't want to disappoint her Pop.

Her allegiance to R. Beers was soon tested in a dramatic, very ugly way. Perhaps she had already heard backstage gossip about his romance with Alice Nielsen, a popular soprano and star of Victor Herbert's first great success, *The Fortune Teller*. This was a lengthy affair, but R. Beers didn't limit himself to one mistress, and one of Nielsen's temporary stand-ins confronted Minnie and Anita with the disagreeable fact that R. Beers was a philanderer.

One day Minnie opened the door to a young woman who asked to speak to Mrs. Loos. Thinking she might be a bill collector, Minnie asked, "About what?" "Well, surely you know who I am!" the girl exclaimed. Minnie looked confused, so the girl blurted out that R. Beers had promised to marry her as soon as Minnie released him from their unhappy union.

"Young lady, I think you've made a terrible mistake," Minnie replied. "If my husband wants a divorce, I wouldn't stand in his way." She then explained that for years she had suffered from other women throwing themselves at her husband. "Reconsider," she warned, "or you may end up like me."

Upset that Anita was witness to this scene, Minnie told her that R. Beers couldn't help being irresistible to women. This sounded sensible to Anita, though later she wondered if Minnie perhaps wasn't too forgiving. "My mother was an earthbound angel," she wrote in her first memoir, "which may have been the reason Pop was a scamp."

This is a charming and delicately phrased summation of both parents' shortcomings, but exactly what does it mean? Does Anita feel that if Minnie had put her foot down, R. Beers wouldn't have strayed? Or is she suggesting that Minnie was too ethereal to satisfy her husband's sexual needs? The ambiguity of the statement is the more intriguing since Anita was to go through roughly the same experience with her second husband, and there is reason to believe that what she wrote about Minnie and R. Beers was also a veiled comment on the failure of her own marriage.

R. Beers kept his place in his daughter's heart for several months after the visit of his mistress. Then something happened that hurt too much to be pushed aside. Every so often R. Beers and some friends went off on a "fishing" expedition. They made a show of assembling rods and creels, then left San Francisco for a neighboring town where they spent two days drinking and whoring. On their way home, they stopped at a market to pick up some fish to take back to their wives.

ABOVE AND OPPOSITE: Anita and sister Gladys in a stock
production of *Quo Vadis?* in 1894

The women weren't fooled by this, certainly not Minnie, but she went along with it until a crisis occurred during one of his absences. Eight-year-old Gladys woke up one morning with dreadful stomach pains. Minnie sent for a doctor; an emergency appendectomy was performed on the kitchen table, and then Gladys was rushed to the nearest hospital. Later that day the child died, and she was buried before R. Beers returned home. Shouldn't they wait for Pop? Anita asked. No, Minnie snapped; they wouldn't wait. Then she told Anita what her father had been doing while Gladys was dying.

Gladys's death was the first and worst of the many misfortunes that

started to fall on the Loos family. *The Dramatic Event* went under because of poor supervision, and R. Beers took to managing stock companies and, as a last resort, a carnival. He didn't bring home much money, and often Anita was the family's main means of support. Out of necessity, she continued to act in a touring company playing one-night stands throughout northern California. Each time she returned home, home was a different apartment, each grubbier than the last.

Then George Smith died and left a sizable legacy to Minnie, who spent part of her inheritance on a newly built house near the Presidio. Another part of the money was put aside for Clifford's education. Before his death George Smith had paid his grandson's tuition to Stanford University, where Clifford, now a sophomore, had settled on medicine as a career.

What remained of the legacy was frittered away by R. Beers. By early 1903, he was reduced to accepting an offer to manage a theater in San Diego. Minnie was dismayed at abandoning her new home; but if they didn't go south, her house would probably be lost, anyway.

THE CINEOGRAPH, R. Beers's theater, was located in a Mexican neighborhood and was an early example of what was soon called a "combo theater." Stage entertainment was mixed with a one-reel film, *The Life of Christ*. The live portion of the show consisted of a comedy team, a juggler, and a trio of dancing girls.

R. Beers tried to make innovations, but the Mexican clientele wasn't receptive. They were devoted to both *The Life of Christ* and one of the live acts, a baggy-pants comic named Fritz Fields and his soubrette sidekick, Maxie Mitchell, who had been playing the Cineograph almost as long as Jesus. Fritz and Maxie opened the bill; then came Christ; and as a finale, Fritz strummed a guitar while Maxie executed splits. It made for a peculiar blend of the sacred and the profane, but it sold tickets.

One of R. Beers's variations did please the patrons. He started closing the show with a short play or skit, patterned after those featured on the best vaudeville circuits. These one-acters R. Beers wrote himself, fashioning the leading roles for Fritz and Maxie, the author and his daughter taking supporting roles, with walk-ons commandeered from whoever else happened to be around.

During one summer vacation, Clifford was pushed on stage, and much to his surprise, he enjoyed it very much, especially the proximity to Maxie. She took a shine to him too—only natural, since he was six feet tall and even better looking than his father. But in September Clifford went back to Stanford with fond memories, but no second thoughts about the theater as a career.

Inspired perhaps by Clifford's romance with Maxie, Anita developed a crush on Fritz. She was now over sixteen and could pass as a baby vamp with the added elevation of French heels and a pompadour. But offstage in braids, a middy blouse, and Mary Janes, she looked like a sixth-grader: though perfectly proportioned, she was only four foot ten, and with the kind of boyish figure that wasn't to be modish until many years later. Fritz was kind, but he never noticed her in the way she wanted.

She did have one admirer: her uncle Horace, the husband of her aunt Nina, her mother's wayward older sister. When the teen-aged Nina had taken to romping with farmhands in the hayloft, George Smith had packed her off to a San Francisco boarding school noted for its Carmelite discipline. On the train she met Horace Robinson, and after a brief tête-à-tête they eloped several stops before San Francisco. Months later they actually were married—or so they told George Smith.

Aunt Nina was the first of the many tarnished ladies who fascinated Anita; quite possibly, as Anita suggests in her memoirs, Aunt Nina was the source of that fascination. Uncle Horace had glamour, too. He was a big spender but followed no profession. But whatever he was—a gambler? a swindler?—he provided a lush life for Nina and himself.

Once a year, like birds of passage, the Robinsons flew in from exotic ports of call to dazzle the Loos household. Brilliantly attired, they arrived bearing expensive gifts wrapped in gold and silver paper. Anita was enthralled by these visitations until Uncle Horace, with a wink and a pinch, surreptitiously handed her a small diamond and sapphire ring, and then asked for a kiss. Anita was frightened by the mixed emotions she felt, and later said the experience taught her the value of "self-restraint."

Shortly after this, the Robinsons left California. Later they separated, and Nina embarked on a career of gin and easy virtue; but she stayed in touch with Minnie through parcels of discarded gowns, redolent of far-away places and expensive scent. A note was always enclosed: Maybe the dresses could be cut down for Nita.

• • •

Aunt Nina, perhaps the prototype of the many "fallen women" who figure prominently in Anita's work

Horace Robinson, Aunt Nina's husband

TWO YEARS after taking over the Cineograph, R. Beers was doing so well he felt the need of a new challenge. Living in the same apartment building was a common-law couple, Fred Meade and Margaret Iles, also feeling an itch to get on with their careers. They had come west with a touring company that had folded in Los Angeles. Fred, with a couple of Belasco credits behind him, had picked up some local stage jobs, while Margaret made pocket money by reading tarot cards and charting horoscopes. She had been born with the gift of foresight, she claimed, and the cards told her that Fred and she should open a stock company in southern California. There was a vacant stable in San Diego that could be converted into a theater, but their savings couldn't begin to cover the costs. They needed a partner, and R. Beers, thanks to Minnie's frugality, was in a position to help.

SAN DIEGO in 1905 was just big enough to be called a city. The shopping district was six blocks long; there was a large park and a sizable waterfront, the harbor crowded with yachts and U.S. Navy ships. It was, in Anita's words, "both cozy and festive." Across the harbor on a small island called Coronado stood the Hotel Del Coronado, which recently had become a fashionable winter retreat for the Eastern socialites already earmarked by R. Beers and his partners as potential customers for their stock company.

The Lyceum opened with an advertisement promising "All the Latest Metropolitan Successes." The rights to Broadway hits did not come cheap, and the managers of the Lyceum resorted to chicanery to get their scripts, as did most stock companies. At every hit Broadway show was a shorthand wizard transcribing whatever dialogue he could, inventing what he missed. His garbled record was then distributed by an agency specializing in gypping dramatists out of their royalties by offering scripts and performance rights at a fraction of what they legitimately would have cost.

The system looked foolproof, but R. Beers and his partners forgot that San Diego boasted a rival stock company which subscribed to the same service; and as bad luck would have it, one week the Lyceum and the Empire both chose the same play. The Lyceum managers suggested that henceforth the Empire check with them before scheduling a production, but the Empire looked on the Lyceum as an upstart. Animosity prevailed until the Empire decided to stage *The Prince Chap,* a tour de force for an actress who could look eight years old in Act One and eighteen in Act Five. In all of San Diego only the Lyceum favorite Anita Loos had such versatility. R. Beers agreed to loan out his daughter provided that the Empire give the Lyceum first choice on pirated scripts.

R. Beers was soon managing both companies, and Anita acted at the Lyceum under her own name while at the Empire, in a blond wig and high heels, she was billed as Cleopatra Fairbrother. This double identity was so deftly carried off that stock company patrons never suspected Cleopatra and Anita were one and the same.

A N I T A graduated from a San Diego high school in 1907 at age nineteen, two years older than the average student. It is unlikely that she was kept back by want of intelligence; probably she lost a few semesters while she was trouping. And possibly to bring her age into line with her status as a recent high-school graduate, at this time she may have started shaving years off her birth date.

At nineteen, if she had claimed to be sixteen or even fourteen, no one would have challenged her. Her size and her profession made her an oddity among her fellow students. She didn't fit in with girls who were taught that actresses were little better than prostitutes; and boys, who might have been attracted to a schoolmate actress, were disappointed in Anita, who offstage looked pretty much like their kid sisters.

"I was always standing on the sidelines, making impudent comments," Anita said of herself at this time. "I was destined to be an outsider, too much the observer to ever be deeply involved in anything but my work."

Now that she was out of school, what was to happen? Minnie wanted her to find a nice, steady husband. R. Beers assumed that she would go on acting until she fell over on the boards. Anita wasn't keen on either plan. The marriages she observed didn't encourage her to rush into matrimony; and as for acting, it was a profession for numbskulls and narcissists.

She wanted to be a writer. She had thought about this ever since, at age six in San Francisco, she had entered and won a limerick contest in a children's magazine. Since then, she had started and given up on several short stories and a play modeled on a modern French tragedy she discovered in a theater magazine: halfway through the final act, she tore it up—it looked dead even to her eyes.

Books were a luxury, so she spent most of her offstage hours at the San Diego public library, reading what she could on the spot, checking out the rest and taking it to her dressing room. The library subscribed to East Coast periodicals lavishly illustrated with pictures of socialites who wintered at the Del Coronado, and these Anita devoured as soon as they arrived.

R. Beers took her to dinner at the hotel as a nineteenth birthday present. In one of Aunt Nina's cast-off gowns, Anita felt bedraggled as the elegant ladies promenaded in their cool lawn frocks. What heaven it must be, she thought, to move confidently through such worldly surroundings! Anita resolved that somehow she was going to get out of San Diego and live as an equal with this race of demigods. Thinking it over, she realized that her second ambition depended on achieving the first: only by becoming a successful writer was she ever going to be able to free herself from stock-company California.

One way out might be through the local papers. They were supported by the tourist trade, and yet not one had a New York correspondent. The Del Coronado guests weren't interested in San Diego social notes; they wanted to know what was happening in New York while they were on vacation. Anita wasn't naive enough to think that a paper would hire her for the job; she knew she lacked the necessary qualifications. But she was clever enough to come up with a plan to overcome that disadvantage.

Culling items from East Coast publications, she pasted together a Manhattan bulletin and mailed it to one of Margaret Iles's Broadway friends, who sent it to a San Diego paper, which printed it under his name.

Profits were split seventy-five–twenty-five, Anita getting the larger share. It wasn't much, but there was the added recompense of knowing that she was the only New York correspondent never to have set foot on Fifth Avenue.

She started looking for other outlets for her writing. The *New York Morning Telegraph,* which specialized in sports and entertainment news, ran a column called "Town Talk." Readers were invited to send in anecdotes and received ten cents for every word printed. Nearly everything Anita sent the *Telegraph* was accepted, which inflated her ego but did little for her purse. At ten cents a word, she would be eighty and still playing *Lady Audley's Secret* before she got out of San Diego.

R. Beers suggested that she extend her range to include the drama: he would pass on to her his mastery of playwriting. For the Lyceum he had dashed off several one-acters, and his greatest success, *In Colorado,* was then touring the Orpheum circuit. And so, quite possibly with her father's guidance, Anita wrote *The Soul Sinners.* Since the script has vanished, there's no way of determining whether that title and a heroine named Fiamma La Flamme were intended as parody or bold-faced melodrama — probably the latter if R. Beers had a hand in it. Margaret Iles played the fiery heroine at the first performance so successfully that later, when she and Fred Meade advanced to big-time vaudeville, they took Anita's play with them. Thanks to them, she received periodic small royalties for *The Soul Sinners,* a piece of juvenilia she otherwise would have preferred to have forgotten.

B Y 1 9 1 1 all stock companies were starting to hurt from the competition of the movies. The guests at the Del Coronado didn't frequent the nickelodeons, but once the season was over and they had returned to the East Coast, R. Beers had to cater to the less sophisticated taste of the locals. Reverting to his Cineograph policy, he mixed stage entertainment with the "galloping tintypes." Every performance was made up of two short plays and one film.

Business picked up immediately. Crude as they were, the one-reelers were far livelier than the live portion of the bill. After every performance, Anita took a perfunctory curtain call, then rushed to the back of the house to catch the canned section of the show. The best of what she saw came from the Biograph Company, whose little films were better acted, and more succinctly and dynamically developed, than anything presented on the Lyceum or Empire stages.

She decided to concoct a film play herself. Knowing nothing of screen technique, she concentrated on telling a brief story whose main points came across visually. After weeks of trial and error, she had a five-page scenario that might be suitable for Biograph. Called *The Road to Plaindale,* it was about a world-weary couple who move to the hinterland only to discover that urban is better.

She mailed it to the Biograph Company in New York with a covering letter which she signed "A. Loos." An "authoress," she had heard, was frequently paid less than an author, so she decided to be ambiguous about her gender. In a few weeks she received a letter from Biograph containing a check for twenty-five dollars and a release form for A. Loos to sign and return.

Anita had found the path that would eventually lead her out of San Diego. It took another three years, during which she occasionally lost her direction; but she was already on her way.

3

Cérébrale

WITHIN six months, Anita, now twenty-four, sold three more scripts to Biograph and a fourth to the Lubin Company. For 1912 her film earnings added up to $105, a very respectable beginning.

Her third Biograph scenario was the first to go into production; and so *The New York Hat* has erroneously been accepted as her initial effort, a mistake Anita never bothered to correct: it's only human to want to start off with a classic.

The New York Hat is a one-reeler, running about twelve minutes. It opens in a small Vermont town as a dying widow hands her clergyman her savings, asking him to buy something special for her daughter. The clergyman notices the girl admiring a plumed hat in a millinery shop. He buys it and sends it anonymously to the girl, who wears it to church on Easter Sunday. Scandal! The local busybodies know she's too poor to have bought it herself, so who's her fancy man?

The milliner reveals that it's the clergyman. He's about to be defrocked and the girl branded with a scarlet letter when the clergyman explains the facts in an *honi soit qui mal y pense* sermon. Then he escorts the girl out of church with more than ministerial protectiveness.

The New York Hat was directed by D. W. Griffith, and it is particularly outstanding example of his pre-*Birth of a Nation* work. The girl is played by Mary Pickford, and she's charming, with none of the simpering, star mannerisms that mar many of her later performances.

Mary Pickford and Lionel Barrymore in *The New York Hat* (1912), the first of Anita's scenarios to be filmed

Mary Pickford in *The New York Hat*

Griffith's and Pickford's contributions are important, but they have tended to overshadow that in its themes and attitudes *The New York Hat* is pure Anita Loos. It strikes out at provincialism and pursed-lipped morality without becoming preachy or solemn, as do many Griffith films of this period. And there's a whiff of autobiography about it. The hat Mary Pickford longs for is a *New York* hat, and her yearning for it may express what Anita felt as she thumbed through *Vogue* and other fashion periodicals. Anita said she chose New England as a setting in tribute to her maternal grandmother, Cleopatra Fairbrother, who left Vermont only to find herself a prisoner in Yreka.

Possibly the town busybodies in *The New York Hat* were patterned after Anita's paternal grandmother, a sour-natured old lady who had recently come to live with R. Beers following the death of her husband. From the start Grandma Loos spread gloom wherever she turned. She disapproved of her son's "gypsy" profession, of Minnie's inept household management, of her granddaughter's modern ways. The girl was too sassy, Grandma declared, too fast with the lip and too slow about finding herself a husband.

Never one to hold motherhood sacred, R. Beers was the first to admit that the old lady must return to Ohio posthaste. An opportunity came along that allowed him to say truthfully that he and his family were about to relocate in surroundings she would find uncomfortable. She emphatically agreed. After living like gypsies, they were now going to set themselves up as beachcombers! As it turned out, Grandma Loos wasn't so far off the mark.

During the off-season summer months, the Hotel Del Coronado shut down and its beachfront was taken over by transients who lived in a colony of tents. The cool sea breeze compensated for the primitive living conditions. And for those who could afford the rent, there were thatched-roof bungalows, larger than the tents but still rudimentary as to plumbing.

Called "Tent City," this pauper's retreat started to attract vacationers who could afford a fashionable resort but instead chose to rough it on Coronado. Soon the community organized its own weekly paper and started looking for an editor. Someone suggested R. Beers, who welcomed a little added income. By taking the ferry between Coronado and San Diego, a short ride, he could edit the paper and still look after stock company business.

One perquisite of the job was a rent-free bungalow. Minnie sniffed suspiciously at her new home, but Anita was enthralled. This was *la vie de bohème,* outdoor style—sun, sea, al fresco concerts and dances. And for those who preferred fresh water to salt, the Coronado pool was available at a two-dollar admission fee.

That was a little steep for Anita, so she latched on to a young man who could just barely afford it: by convincing him that the Pacific was infested with poisonous jellyfish, she became his guest at the Coronado pool for the entire summer. He was a sweet boy, but it was the pool that was the major attraction. More precisely, it was the affluent playboys she imagined lounging around that pool.

Grandma Loos may have been right when she advised looking for a husband. But Grandma's qualifications for eligibility weren't hers; Anita wasn't looking for moral fiber or character any more than she expected romance. All she wanted was a one-way ticket out of California. Maybe she could do it on her own, but the acquisition of a rich husband would certainly speed things up.

She had come to realize that men were attracted to her. Her size was now a source of provocation, Mary Pickford and other screen actresses having set a vogue for the child-woman that challenged the supremacy of the statuesque Gibson Girl. Striving to appeal to both masculine tastes, Anita would be girlish in a sailor outfit one afternoon, worldly in a resplendent tea gown the next. One day her hair hung loose; the next, it was piled high on her head in a coronet braid, which she felt added sophistication as well as inches to her bearing.

The Coronado pool was crowded with unattached men, but most were sailors on leave from the San Diego naval base, and certainly not worth the notice of a girl who was looking for more than muscle. She had her eye out for the nonathletic types wearing blazers bulging from the weight of hefty billfolds.

Two such gentlemen fell into her hands. One was a member of a Detroit automobile family; the other, the son of the proprietor of Nevada's most productive silver mine. Both proposed, the silver heir first. Anita turned him down when she learned he was devoted to his native state: growing old in Nevada was worse than lifelong grubbery in California.

The Detroit suitor presented another problem. In choosing Anita, he was abandoning a fiancée back in Michigan. This disloyalty led to a "bare-fisted duel" on the Coronado beach between the automobile heir and the brother of the girl he had spurned. It was a scene straight out of Victor Hugo or one of the lesser Romantic dramatists, and Anita's response was derisive laughter. Chivalry was nothing more than piqued male vanity, she told her beau, who promptly returned to Detroit.

Anita at Coronado, 1914

"Therein lay my tragedy," Anita commented. "I was generally going to laugh romance away." One hundred years earlier Jane Austen had said much the same thing in *Northanger Abbey:* "A woman, especially if she has the misfortune of knowing anything, should conceal it as well as she can." The woman who wants to please men must never appear to be too bright and must never, *never* speak her mind. Anita recognized the wisdom of this lesson but couldn't follow it herself. In her memoir, *A Girl Like I,* she ends her account of her Coronado romances by saying she was "too much the *cérébrale* to find happiness as a Cinderella."

. . .

E V E N *cérébrales* must work for a living, so Anita left the Coronado and went back to her writing. During 1913 she sold thirty-six scripts to various film companies. Biograph didn't pay as well as its competitors, but she continued to give them first refusal as their pictures continued to be the best. Biograph produced nineteen of her scripts and came to rely on Anita for material for Dorothy Gish and Fay Tincher, the company's leading comediennes.

Biograph had started sending a troupe of actors to southern California during the winter months and recently had established a studio in Los Angeles. Anita never thought of paying a visit until she received a letter addressed to Miss Loos—by this time she had told her employers she was a woman—asking her to stop by when she was in Los Angeles. Earlier she had received a similar request from Reliance-Mutual, a rival company, and it seemed foolish to pass up this double invitation. Minnie wouldn't hear of her going off on her own—unmarried women didn't travel without a chaperone—and neither Anita nor R. Beers could laugh her out of such conventionality.

Arriving in Los Angeles in January 1914, Anita and Minnie went to a cheap but respectable hotel, unpacked, and arranged their clothes for the following day. Anita selected a stylish outfit. Fashion magazines were promoting middy blouses and flannel skirts, the favorite leisure wear at Tsarskoe Selo, now mass-produced in America by entrepreneur Peter Thompson. When she put on her "Peter Tom" the next morning, Anita decided to let her braid hang loose and tied an oversized taffeta bow at the end. Topping it off was a straw hat with a matching ribbon dangling jauntily from the side.

After visiting Reliance-Mutual, Anita and Minnie boarded a trolley for the Biograph studio, a block-long, ramshackle complex of one-story buildings. Just off the main entrance was a small office where they found T. E. Dougherty, Biograph's business manager. Dougherty thought Minnie was the writer until Anita corrected him. He stared in disbelief. "How did a snippet like you dream up those clever plots?"

Dougherty invited them to watch Mr. Griffith shooting his new picture, *Judith of Bethulia,* today recognized as a precursor of the Babylon section of *Intolerance.* Off-duty houris were lounging about outside camera range, and Minnie stiffened at the sight of so much bare flesh. But Anita was too exhilarated to notice her mother's disapproval.

Griffith was as amazed as Dougherty to discover Miss Loos in a pigtail. And she was terrified—and intrigued—by Griffith's dignity; he was so unlike the flashy theater people she had met in the past. Tall, gaunt, with hooded eyes and a long, beaked nose, he reminded her of "an Egyptian god," half-man, half-falcon.

Over tea Griffith asked Anita what she read. She could barely find her voice. "I wanted to impress him," she recalled, "so I prattled on about Kant, Schopenhauer, Nietzsche, and other people I barely knew anything about." Griffith mentioned Walt Whitman. Anita dismissed the poet as "hysterical," an impertinence she regretted when Griffith's reply showed he was a Whitman fan.

He kept staring at her in the most unnerving way. Finally he asked if she would be interested in playing a small role in *Judith of Bethulia*. She had resolved to put acting behind her, but that was before she was invited to be a Griffith actress. "When would you need me?" she asked.

"Tomorrow morning," he replied. She promised to be there. But Minnie wouldn't hear of it. The Biograph Company was no place for a decent girl; she wasn't going to leave her daughter alone in Los Angeles with that Mr. Griffith. "The peculiar way he looked at you!" Minnie concluded. "Almost brazen!" Anita didn't argue. She packed her bag and went back to San Diego.

Why would a self-supporting woman of twenty-five, a proclaimed enemy of parochialism, give in so easily? Anita never liked a fuss. All too often she let people have their own way until, pushed too far, she rebelled, but by then it was usually too late: a pattern had been too firmly established to be altered.

Minnie meant well; she was just overprotective. She didn't want Anita to make the same mistake she and Nina had, falling for the first good-looking man who crossed her path. Anita understood that behind all her rules and regulations was a desperate desire to make contact with her daughter, so she tried to play the role of obedient child; but her obedience served only to widen the gulf between Minnie and herself.

Back in San Diego, Anita continued to contribute to Biograph while wondering how she would ever escape her smothering mother. Only through the conventional route of marriage, she decided: with a husband to guide her daughter, Minnie just might let her lead her own life.

The problem was to find a prospective husband conventional enough for Minnie and yet willing to live with an unconventional wife: Anita wanted a mate who would look kindly on her career. There was one candidate. A few years earlier, Clifford had set himself up as a doctor in San

Diego, where he fell in love with one of the city's leading socialites, a Miss Anita Johnson. Soon Anita had a sister-in-law with the same name and a brother-in-law who kept flashing an engagement ring in her direction. Charlie Johnson was handsome and easygoing, but too fast on the draw when the cocktails were being passed around.

The only other immediate prospect was an unencouraged yet persistent suitor named Frank Pallma. About the same age as Anita, Pallma was born in New York and came to California with his family when still a child. His father, a band conductor, was in charge of the open-air concerts on Coronado Island. Frank Jr. also had a small musical talent: according to a biographical newspaper sketch of 1914, he was "composer of song and light operetta," but even "My Rose, My Rose," singled out as his "best-loved composition," faded into oblivion fairly quickly.

Anita met Pallma when she was a resident of Tent City in the summer of 1913, and just as probably she wasn't much impressed by him—he was, according to the only one of Anita's friends known to have met him, "a nice but colorless man—today I suppose he'd be called a wimp." But when Pallma proposed in the spring of 1915, Anita accepted. She wasn't in love, but Frank was steady, good-natured, and devoted, qualities that counted with Minnie.

The closer she got to the wedding, the more regrets Anita felt. It was all a setup, "a larcenous arrangement." On the night before the ceremony, she told Minnie she couldn't go through with it. Thinking she was jittery with last-minute doubts, Minnie tried to joke her out of it. "You can't call it off," she protested. "I've already ordered the wedding cake!"

Anita's only memory of the wedding was her father's pained expression. Bitter experience had taught R. Beers that marriage was a mistake for artists like himself and his daughter. For both their sakes, Anita tried to wipe out the ceremony with a quip. "Look, Pop, it didn't count. I kept my fingers crossed the whole time."

After the wedding night Anita awoke convinced that "married life was a clumsy, messy business." But the farce went on for several weeks until she realized Pallma wasn't going to take her to New York, though he had promised that as a wedding present. Poor Frank didn't have enough cash for two tickets to Sacramento.

Six months later she sent Frank out to buy some hairpins. Then she packed up and went home to Minnie. "I'm leaving Frank forever," she sobbed. Imagining the liberties Pallma must have taken with her daughter, Minnie agreed to take Anita to Los Angeles and Mr. Griffith. The movies could be no worse a fate than an insensitive husband.

4

Triangle
Days

L O C A T I N G Griffith was harder than Anita had imagined. She knew he was no longer with Biograph and had been moving about a lot since making his first masterpiece, *The Birth of a Nation.* Recently he had merged with two other film giants, Thomas Ince and Mack Sennett, to form Triangle Pictures. Each man had his own specialty, and together they could offer the public a more diversified program than anyone could have provided on his own. Ince's forte was the western; Sennett's, slapstick. Griffith's were comedies and dramas of a more elevated nature, and to set them apart, they were released as Fine Arts–Triangle productions.

Each member of the triumvirate kept separate quarters. Ince's studio was located in Culver City; Sennett's unit worked in what is today West Hollywood; Griffith rented space in Edendale. It was here that Anita expected to find him, but he wasn't on the premises. Before taking up his Triangle chores, he was working on an independent project too massive for the limited Edendale lot. "Take the trolley to Sunset Boulevard," she was told. "Keep an eye out for a Babylonian temple."

Griffith's film was *Intolerance,* and the Babylonian temple was then the largest set ever constructed in Hollywood. Anita milled among the extras until she spotted Griffith. Much to her pleasure, he remembered her. "How good to see you, Miss *Looze.*" Usually Anita was miffed when people stumbled over her name, but since Griffith was notorious for such lapses—the Gish sisters were always "the Geeshes" to him—she let it pass. "Miss Loose, where have you been hiding yourself?"

"In San Diego—but now I feel I should be closer to my work." Then, impulsively, she added, "I was married, but I've left my husband."

"Good," Griffith said. "Now maybe those plots of yours will get a little better."

He went on to outline his plans for Fine Arts–Triangle. Many Biograph actors had come with him to the new studio, including the Gish sisters, Mae Marsh, and Robert Harron; and such new players as Douglas Fairbanks and Constance and Norma Talmadge were under contract. Besides turning out his own productions, Griffith was also responsible for guiding the work of second-file directors, a promising crew that included Lloyd Ingraham, Christy Cabanne, and John Emerson.

To keep all these people busy, there was an urgent need of material. If Anita was looking for steady employment, Griffith was ready to offer her seventy-five dollars a week, plus a bonus whenever one of her scripts went into production.

M I N N I E had stayed at the hotel while Anita went in search of Griffith. When she heard the happy outcome, she said, "Wonderful, honeybunch. Tomorrow I'll start looking for a nice place for us."

Anita gasped. Wasn't she planning on returning to San Diego?

Minnie answered that she thought she'd stay on till her little girl was settled.

Anita had a sinking feeling that it was going to be a distant tomorrow before Minnie said good-bye.

They moved to the Hollywood Hotel, at the northwest intersection of Hollywood Boulevard and Highland Avenue. It was a haven for young actors who couldn't yet afford homes of their own and a sanctuary for the parents they left behind once they could. The front veranda of the Hollywood Hotel was occupied by proud mothers, knitting as they lolled in rocking chairs, boasting of their children's accomplishments. Anita hoped Minnie would join them, get so caught up in the gossip and needlework that she'd pay little attention to what her daughter was up to.

In the meantime she had the pleasure of earning steady money for work she really enjoyed. The Fine Arts–Triangle script department was supervised by Frank Woods, credited with calling Griffith's attention to *The Clansman,* the novel that served as source material for *Birth of a*

Nation. He was, Anita remembered, "a shaggy old boy with a mop of white hair and a paternal manner." He was called Daddy even by Griffith, who disapproved of any form of informality.

Woods kept a fatherly eye on Anita, and she was thankful for his protection when Frank Pallma showed up at the studio. Clifford had warned her that Pallma had taken the news of her desertion badly and insisted that he'd track her down, no matter where she was hiding. He knew she had sold scenarios to Biograph, so he inquired about her there. No, he was told, she wasn't at Biograph, but try Fine Arts; someone remembered hearing she had joined Griffith's staff.

One morning as she came to work, Anita spotted Pallma lurking around the main entrance. With her heart pounding, she scuttled down an alley and got on the lot through a side gate. Entering the office, she was so visibly upset that Daddy Woods insisted on knowing what had happened. Anita explained that her estranged husband was hounding her, possibly with violent intentions. Did she really believe that meek Frank Pallma wanted anything more than an explanation, at the most a reconciliation? Anita abhorred confrontations and possibly poured on the melodramatics to avoid a showdown with Frank.

Daddy Woods chose to believe her life was in danger. He warned all studio personnel to be on the alert for Pallma and to inform Woods personally whenever he showed up. Then he arranged various methods of getting Anita out of the studio unnoticed. The intrigue made for a fascinating game; but Pallma kept his vigil nearly every day, and it soon became disruptive and wearisome. The next time Frank appeared at the studio, Woods faced him out. Anita never knew what he said, but he was persuasive: Pallma was not there the next morning.

While Frank was on the prowl, Daddy Woods had kept Anita busy with minor rewriting jobs. Now he gave her a major assignment, though not for Griffith, who was still deeply involved with *Intolerance.* It was an adaptation of *Macbeth,* to star Sir Herbert Beerbohm Tree and planned to be Fine Arts–Triangle's most prestigious picture for the forthcoming year.

Anita swiftly reread the play, and within a week she had finished a script continuity eliminating all scenes except those dealing directly with the bloodthirsty Macbeths. Then came the major task, reducing the dialogue so that it could be printed as titles so succinct they wouldn't challenge the reading proficiency of the average moviegoer. Anita's efforts brought her her first screen credit: "*Macbeth* by William Shakespeare and Anita Loos." "If I had asked, Daddy Woods would have given me top billing," she explained later.

Macbeth also provided Anita with her first opportunity to watch the production of a movie she had written. Though excited at the prospect of meeting Beerbohm Tree, she, like everyone else at Fine Arts, was perplexed about how to address him. "Sir Tree" was tried but didn't sound right. Someone asked the actor what he wanted to be called; "Why not Herb?" he answered affably. Since Griffith would never have approved, Herb became Sir Herbert.

The actor found the film medium not to his liking. "I prefer more space and less pace," he said; and to the horror of the director, John Emerson, he mouthed every word of Macbeth's speeches. Reels of film were wasted before Emerson found a solution to the problem. Every time Sir Herbert started to emote, Emerson turned off the camera, and he kept it off until the actor was winding down.

Macbeth is known as a bad-luck play. Over the centuries, so many productions have resulted in near-disaster for actors—not only brutal reviews but physical casualties as well—that a suspicion arose that Shakespeare had revealed more about the supernatural than the supernatural wanted known. And from that suspicion grew a superstition: never at any time was the play to be referred to as *Macbeth*. It was "the Scottish tragedy." Anita was warned never to mention the cursed name. She held her tongue, as did the other members of the crew, but nonetheless the production came close to fulfilling the prophecy.

The mishap started with the casting of the witches. Guided by Shakespearean tradition, Emerson used men in these roles; and the men selected were, in accordance with the text, sexually ambivalent. But too much ambivalence, Emerson decided, might confuse filmgoers, so he stuffed the bodices of the witches' gowns and discarded the beards mentioned by Shakespeare. Then he wired the witches' fingers so that each "Double, double, toil and trouble" would be accompanied by a streak of lightning. The fiery fingerwork went beautifully in rehearsal, but on the day of shooting one witch was set aflame. "My tits!" he screeched. "My tits are on fire!" Though physically unharmed, the poor witch refused to continue, and production was halted until a replacement was found.

No better fate awaited this *Macbeth* on its premiere. Shakespeare and Sir Herbert Beerbohm Tree got high marks, though a few critics felt the actor looked uneasy "in the realm of the photodrama." Emerson was slapped down for lacking "the imagination and dramatic sweep" Griffith would have brought to the tragedy. As for Anita's alterations, they were generously overlooked.

Macbeth was not really her kind of material; why Daddy Woods passed it on to her is a question only he could answer. Possibly it was because at seventy-five dollars a week, versatility was expected of her; or possibly Woods thought she might like trying her hand at heavier stuff.

Every day she appeared with a new book under her arm, each bearing a hefty philosophical title, and there was no question as to whether they were meant only as props. Whenever she had a spare moment, she removed her bookmark and started making notes as she read. These notes were edited and placed in a small, leather-bound notebook. The entries, arranged alphabetically from Aristotle through Voltaire, are brief and uncritical, some suggesting that she had read about the philosopher rather than reading the philosopher himself—a shortcut many students take when faced with Spinoza or Kant.

Her elevated reading made an impression around the studio. "I was positively in awe of her," remembers Lillian Gish. "We called her Mrs. Socrates." But not everyone was quite so intimidated. For the first time Anita had girlfriends her own age, among them Lillian's mischievous sister, Dorothy; Constance Talmadge, just about to have her first success in the Babylon segment of *Intolerance;* and Mae Marsh, the star of Anita's next picture, *Wild Girl of the Sierras.*

Mae Marsh is not as well remembered as Lillian Gish or Mary Pickford, though most film historians agree that she was their equal. It is her performance in *Birth of a Nation,* not Gish's, that lingers longest in the mind, and in *Intolerance* she has a simplicity and emotional depth that has led commentators to mention Duse. Her specialty was playing naughty tomboys who unexpectedly are confronted with the darker realities of life. A gifted comedienne, she had enough range to reach the outer limits of tragedy.

When they first met, Mae was twenty, eight years younger than Anita, and there was still something of the child about her. She was vivacious and full of pranks and practical jokes. She alone had the temerity to refer to Griffith as "Griff" and to Lillian Gish as "Teacher's Pet" or "Goody Two Shoes." With Anita as an accomplice, she substituted flour for Lillian's talcum powder, and together they wrote a note to Robert Harron (Marsh's husband in *Intolerance*), then smitten with unrequited love for Dorothy Gish, suggesting a rendezvous and signing it "D.G." The next morning, Harron looked so doleful that the two culprits were swamped with remorse and swore to act their age. The oath lasted, Anita remembered, for the better part of two weeks.

Beyond high spirits, Mae held another attraction for Anita: the actress had captured the attention of poet Vachel Lindsay. The first of the

Mae Marsh, Anita's close friend who acted in several films Anita wrote

literati to fall under the spell of the movies, Lindsay wrote a column for *The New Republic* that was part film theory, part mash note to his favorite stars, Mary Pickford, Lillian Gish, and Mae Marsh. Lindsay's hymns to Mae were so lyrical that Mae felt that common courtesy alone demanded an acknowledgment. But, she told Anita, "I wouldn't know what to say to such an intelligent gentleman."

Anita volunteered her help. A joint composition was mailed off, and lively correspondence ensued. Vachel Lindsay expressed the hope that one day he might meet Miss Marsh, if not in his native Illinois, then perhaps in New York, which he visited frequently. Mae promised Anita could be chaperone at the meeting, if it ever occurred, which seemed unlikely since Fine Arts–Triangle rarely shot in the East. Still, it was something to dream about.

As it turned out, that meeting was only a few months away. Anita and Mae were soon to be in New York because of *Intolerance*.

Anita's involvement with the picture began when one morning Daddy Woods told her Mr. Griffith wanted to see her immediately. "Don't be frightened, Nita," he said reassuringly. "He isn't going to eat you." Griffith came straight to the point. At long last a rough cut of *Intolerance* had been assembled, and perhaps Miss Looze would look at it: he would like her help with the dialogue and explanatory titles.

Anita didn't know what to expect. She had asked Mae about the plot. "Gosh if I know," Mae replied. "My scenes were done months ago and they had nothing to do with that Babylonian temple."

Anita was both excited and baffled by the cascade of images she saw — scenes of modern life, vistas of Babylonia, a few glimpses of Judea and of Huguenot France, all intercut, and occasionally interrupted by a portrait shot of Lillian Gish rocking a cradle adorned with roses. This Anita recognized as a tribute to Walt Whitman, but otherwise she had no grasp of what was going on — a predicament shared by audiences when the film was released. And while she later expressed admiration for Griffith's achievement, she implied that she didn't much care for *Intolerance:* overwhelming, of course, but except for Connie and Mae's scenes rather remote and pretentious.

As to how much she contributed to *Intolerance,* this was a question she tended to evade. Today, it would be risky to assign credit or blame to either Anita or Griffith, though a good portion of the titles would appear to be his handiwork. Whatever it was she contributed, she didn't expect recognition. As God with the creation of the world, Griffith took full responsibility, and while the actors were acknowledged, the rest of the crew went unmentioned. Their recompense came in other ways.

Intolerance was to open in New York in September 1916. Griffith would attend the premiere with Miss Marsh, Miss Geesh, and Mr. and Mrs. Woods. Perhaps Miss Looze would join them?

Anita rushed off to tell Mae the news. "Write Vachel Lindsay we'll be in New York in September."

5

Excursion

A N I T A told her mother she would be going to New York alone. "There comes a time," she wrote, "when youth simply has to be served," and for her that time was past due: she was now twenty-eight.

With Mae and Daddy and Ella Woods, she boarded the Santa Fe in late August 1916. The train was scorching as it passed through the Mojave Desert; and even with icebags strapped to foreheads, everyone felt half-broiled. Anita's braid unraveled and fringed her face like strands of limp spaghetti.

The temperature became bearable once they transferred in Chicago for the Twentieth Century. Mae and Anita spent most of the day on the observation platform, where they caught the attention of several rube Casanovas. Fending off the crude passes made them feel very worldly.

They were dressed long before the train arrived at Grand Central at seven in the morning. Anita felt exhilarated as they pushed their way through the crowds and found a cab to take them to the Algonquin Hotel on West Forty-fourth Street. There were more fashionable hotels, but if Daddy Woods had chosen one of them, Anita would have been disappointed. Frank Case, manager (and later owner) of the Algonquin, catered to theater and literary people, and the hotel's restaurant was an unofficial clubhouse for the Broadway community.

Anita and Mae had little time to themselves until after the opening of *Intolerance* a few days later. That event came and went without leaving much of a lasting impression on Miss Loose. The reviews were mixed, and it was clear that Griffith's second masterpiece wasn't going to repeat the financial success of *Birth of a Nation*. But Anita was too preoccupied to give much thought to what this might mean to Griffith or to her own future. She was now free to explore New York City.

Though most of the *Intolerance* party returned to California immediately after the premiere, she and Mae stayed on for a few weeks. Mae found an apartment on Riverside Drive while Anita took furnished rooms in the theater district. Then, impulsively, she invited Minnie to join her. Ever since leaving California, she had felt twinges of remorse at not bringing Minnie along, and felt she would never be able to live with herself if she didn't offer Mom a holiday.

Minnie was so grateful for the invitation that she was on her best behavior in New York, never intruding on her daughter's privacy or complaining when Anita left her for business appointments.

Just before she left California, Anita had received a check for a short story submitted to *Vanity Fair;* and after she arrived in New York, editor Frank Crowninshield asked her to join him and a few friends for the evening. About a hundred other people were at the party, which was so noisy and crowded that, noticing Anita's discomfort, Crowninshield apologized and asked her to meet him the next day for a quiet lunch.

At Delmonico's, Anita formed an instant rapport with Crowninshield, who regaled her with "inside, but proper" stories about such international celebrities as Picasso, Jean Cocteau, and Colette. Though she might have preferred his stories to be a bit more improper, Anita was delighted when he promised they'd meet again soon.

Two days later Crowninshield sent her a gift she feared was inappropriate. It was a dress copied from the uniform worn by French schoolgirls and called a "Claudine" after Colette's teenaged heroine. During their lunch, Anita had spoken admiringly of the Claudine novels, but still the gift seemed too personal. Perhaps Mr. Crowninshield was a gentleman who preferred little girls.

No, she was mistaken about that. Crowninshield just liked giving thoughtful gifts to people he cared about. And both he and *Vanity Fair* liked Anita a lot. In the years ahead, not many months passed without a mention or a photograph of her in the magazine.

When she wasn't lunching uptown, Anita strolled around Greenwich Village with Mae. Everything was enchanting, especially the brightly colored and individual clothes. Having inherited Minnie's gift for needlework, Anita was able to turn out a Village costume overnight. Her original was cut from heavy olive drab linen, with tufts of brilliant yarn strewn over the bodice and sleeves.

With ribbons of matching shades intertwined in her braid, Anita
went off to meet Mae, who was too excited to notice the new finery. A
letter from Vachel Lindsay had been forwarded from the Algonquin. The
poet was coming to New York and could be reached at the Hotel Brevoort.

Mae was in a tizzy. A rendezvous at the Brevoort was out of the
question—visiting a man at his hotel was compromising—and yet she
couldn't invite him to the Riverside Drive apartment, where relatives were
staying with her. Anita suggested her apartment for a tryst. She would
send Minnie off to see Walter Hampden in *Cyrano de Bergerac*—that
would keep her occupied for over four hours—and while Anita would be
present as duenna, she would vanish once Mae gave her the sign.

They pooled their resources to create a poetic atmosphere. "We spent
hours on our decor," Anita recalled, " . . . which featured a number of
heavy cut vases with American Beauty roses; pink bulbs in the light
sockets to dim out the freckles of which Mae was painfully self-conscious;
and the air was perfumed with incense specially imported from Chinatown. . . . Mae [wore] a green-and-gold Fortuny robe which clung to her
graceful figure . . . and [made her look like] Mélisande."

Lindsay destroyed the artfully crafted magic. He strode in wearing a
baggy suit and muddy boots. "He resembled neither Byron nor Shelley;
from head to toe he failed to conform," Anita recalled. "His hair was full of
cowlicks without any attempt at control." Years later, when she first saw
Mortimer Snerd, she experienced a moment of déjà vu: the dummy was
the spitting image of Vachel Lindsay.

The poet had little to say, and when he did find his voice, it came
out in a roar. What he said might pass as poetry, Anita felt, if only it
weren't bellowed. His boisterousness was the camouflage of a sensitive
and insecure man, she realized; but it was too much for Mae, who bolted
from the apartment after fifteen minutes.

Lindsay then transferred his interest to Anita. His boots were muddy
from hiking in Central Park. He loved the outdoors, and the park was
about all the city had to offer in that direction. Maybe Miss Loos would
join him for a walk?

For the next two weeks, they spent their mornings tramping through
urban greenery and their evenings exploring what Lindsay called "the real
Bohemia." Anita enjoyed every moment of this companionship, except the
outcome. Lindsay proposed—not unpredictably, and yet Anita didn't
know quite what to say.

Even if she had been romantically inclined, she would have spurned
him when he starting speaking (quite poetically she had to admit) of the

joys of rural domesticity. She was evasive, but he knew she was only trying to let him down easily, and he had enough generosity of spirit to overlook the rejection and go on with their friendship. They saw each other occasionally and corresponded faithfully until Lindsay's death in 1931.

Anita was grateful for the fascinating people Lindsay helped her meet that fall. Most were radicals, and while there were notes on Marx in her philosophical handbook, she had never before encountered real-life socialists and Fabians. Her studio friends had no interest in world events, paid no attention to the war in Europe, never took sides in the raging debate about America's isolationist policy.

Her sole contribution to the war effort was a fifty-dollar check handed to a friend going off to France on a business trip. "Buy hats for the deprived mademoiselles," she suggested.

Listening attentively to the awesomely intricate debates of Lindsay's friends, and finding herself just a tiny bit bored, she began to suspect that she was apolitical. Certainly she wasn't much impressed by the impassioned rhetoric she heard. These anarchists and social utopians looked on people as cogs in a malfunctioning machine, while she kept an eye out for the odd individual.

Among the ranks of the left wing there were many strange birds, and the one Anita preferred was Max Eastman, editor of the radical monthly *The Masses*. Widely read and a dazzling conversationalist, Eastman was also a connoisseur of pretty women. In the midst of heated debate, he broke off to look Anita up and down. "You know," he said, "*The Masses* could use some bourgeois glamour. How about posing for one of our covers?"

Anita was delighted. What could be more Hegelian than a *Vanity Fair* contributor moonlighting as a cover girl for *The Masses?*

ANITA'S excursion ended with a telegram from Triangle, urging her to return immediately to California. On the train, she told Minnie she was planning to take her own apartment. Minnie accepted this calmly. A year earlier R. Beers had moved into the Hollywood Hotel, and he was doing well peddling gags to the studios. Clifford with his wife and baby daughter, named Mary Anita, had also settled in Los Angeles, so the whole family would be more or less together. Anita promised to find an apartment close to the Hollywood Hotel, and that pleased Minnie. It was nice that her children were prospering, but still wanted to stay close to her.

Returning to the studio, Anita learned that trouble was brewing.

Daddy Woods hurriedly filled her in on what had happened. Dashed by the failure of *Intolerance,* Griffith had gone off to England to make a picture urging America to enter the War. It didn't sound like a money winner; but worse, it wasn't for Triangle—this was another independent production. In two years Griffith had done little for the studio, but it was rumored he wanted out because his supervisory duties were sapping his energy!

As Daddy Woods was rarely so wrought up, Anita listened patiently till he got to the point. Even without Griffith, Fine Arts-Triangle could survive on the strength of its impressive list of actors. And here Anita was going to be important. The studio needed screenplays for Mae Marsh and especially Doug Fairbanks, who in popularity polls was running a close third behind Chaplin and Mary Pickford.

6

Fairbanks and Company

ANITA'S first encounter with Douglas Fairbanks predated her work on *Intolerance*. But it was not until late 1916 that, with John Emerson, they formed a team that made screen history.

Fairbanks had been a Broadway leading man for ten years when Fine Arts–Triangle brought him to Hollywood along with other stage stars expected to add luster to a status-seeking company. Doug was rushed into *The Lamb*, one of Fine Arts's three initial releases. It did well, but Griffith felt that Fairbanks wasn't suave enough to suit his unit. "Send him to Sennett," the director said. "He belongs with the slapstick cops."

Fairbanks's stage career had been built on his boyish charm and physical agility. Uncomfortable in romantic scenes, he got out of kissing the leading lady by interjecting "Aw, shucks!" or "Gee whiz!" and then executing a handstand to show how head over heels in love he really was.

Sennett didn't want Fairbanks, so Griffith handed John Emerson the task of dreaming up some way of keeping Doug occupied. Emerson looked through the files in Daddy Woods's office, hoping to find a suitable scenario. What he came up with were some unproduced scripts by Anita. "Look at these!" he exclaimed. "They're wonderful!"

"No, no!" Griffith protested. "Miss Looze is good, but she relies too heavily on verbal humor. Too many titles! People come to the movies to watch the action, not to read."

Emerson wasn't convinced, so Griffith told him to go ahead, use one

of the scripts, or get Miss Looze to write a new one; it didn't matter as long
as Fairbanks was kept before the cameras till his contract ran out.

Whether *His Picture in the Papers* was a script Emerson found in the
files or whether it was created specifically for Fairbanks isn't known—
Anita contradicted herself on this point. Usually she implied it was an
original, though it bears more than a fleeting resemblance to *The Man of
the Hour,* one of Fairbanks's earliest stage successes. Both deal with what
today is called instant celebrity. Pete, the hero of Anita's script, manufac-
tures vegetable products. He falls for a girl who wants a guy who gets his
picture in the papers. To prove he's not all vegetable, Pete gets involved in
a series of improbable adventures and winds up on the front pages of all
the dailies.

Griffith sat through the first screening without a smile. His disapproval
kept the picture on the shelf until a booking crisis forced Triangle to put it
in circulation. A huge critical and popular hit, it guaranteed the future of
Fairbanks and the printed caption as a legitimate form of screen humor.

Over the next two years Anita supplied scripts for nine additional
Fairbanks films, most directed by John Emerson. The toughest part of the
job, she recalled, "was finding a variety of spots from which Doug could
jump." All the pictures used pretty much the same formula: a not-so-
bright young man gets caught up in a series of crazy escapades, extricating
himself only through sheer physical ingenuity. The Fairbanks hero substituted bravado and muscle for brainpower. Born smart, he would never
have been lured into such dumb predicaments. Definitely he wasn't the
type of fellow to appeal to Anita; and through deft, guying touches, she
managed to suggest that Doug was a charming, all-American boob.

Nearly all her Fairbanks scripts poke fun at some fad or pretension.
In *Reaching for the Moon,* she kids Couéism, a then-popular self-help
program promoting autosuggestion as a way of achieving its slogan, "Every
day in every way I am getting better and better." The picture opens with a
caption describing the Fairbanks character as having "a vaulting ambition
which is likely to o'erleap itself and fall on the other side." After this comes
a shot of Doug straddling the headboard of his bed, riding it for a while,
then leaping down and bouncing on the mattress before finally disappearing
from view.

There were also parodies of the film medium itself, like *Wild and
Wooly,* a takeoff on Westerns and the best of the Fairbanks-Loos-Emerson
films. Doug plays Jeff Hillington, a well-to-do New Yorker who dreams of
testing his manhood in the Old West he's read about in dime novels.
Arriving in Bitter Creek, Arizona, Jeff finds a sleepy town, nothing at all

RIGHT: Anita and Douglas Fairbanks between takes of Anita's *Wild and Wooly* (1917)
BELOW: Douglas Fairbanks and crew shooting *Wild and Wooly* not far from the present-day site of the Beverly Hills Hotel

like the frontier of his imagination. Sensing his disappointment, the Bitter
Creek citizens stage a Wild West show, which becomes real when a
genuine holdup and Indian attack take place.

If you want something badly enough, you can will it to happen. This
message runs through works by Anita as diverse as *Wild and Wooly,*
Gentlemen Prefer Blondes, and *Happy Birthday.* It is, of course, highly
personal. Anita wanted to be a famous, respected writer; and without
much formal education, starting out in one of the lowliest of literary
forms, she was working steadily and purposefully to achieve her goal.

W H E N Fairbanks's contract with Triangle expired in 1917, his popularity was so enormous that he was offered superstar terms by Famous
Players-Lasky, the most prestigious film company in Hollywood. Fairbanks
was paid five thousand dollars a week and allowed to choose his own crew.
He asked Anita and John Emerson to come along. How much they earned
isn't known—perhaps five hundred dollars a week—but certainly it was
enough to quiet whatever qualms they had about leaving Triangle.

The Fairbanks unit worked out of a small studio on Santa Monica
Boulevard and spent several months of each year in New York. Whenever
possible Anita used Manhattan as the setting of her scripts, simply because
she enjoyed a working holiday at the Algonquin. So the Fairbanks team
not only worked together, they also traveled together and frequently lived
together under the same hotel roof. Thus Anita became a witness of, and a
not unwilling participant in, one of the great romantic dramas of Hollywood
history: Doug's affair with Mary Pickford.

Both were already married—that was the first difficulty. Doug's
wife, Beth, came from a socially prominent, though impoverished, New
York family. Mary's husband, Owen Moore, was an actor with both a
drinking and a career problem. Though they had been estranged for years,
there was no talk of divorce.

Divorce—the second obstacle—was unthinkable for Mary and Doug.
She was a Catholic and "America's Sweetheart." Vamps like Theda Bara or
Louise Glaum could get away with illicit romance, but America's sweet-
hearts didn't cheat on their husbands, not if they cared about public
opinion. And Mary *cared.*

So did Doug, who advocated clean living in articles he wrote for the
fan magazines, later collected in book form as *Laugh and Live.* In a
chapter called "Wedlock in Time," he warns the reader (the advice seems

aimed at a cub scout) not to rush into marriage but says to stick in there once the step is taken: "Given a good wife, after his own heart, no manly man has a righteous kick coming against the fates. Under such circumstances if things go wrong he will find the fault within himself."

Doug had set himself up for a hoist on his own petard. If he left Beth, he'd have to admit to a fault within himself. He would deserve a righteous kick—if not from the fates, then from his fans. It was a pretty kettle of fish, and Doug was to stew over it for the better part of two years before he hit on a justification. "Julius Caesar got a divorce! So did Napoleon!" he told Anita. "They weren't weak characters!"

Anita first realized something was amiss in the Fairbanks household when Beth started treating her with glacial politeness. Mrs. Fairbanks enjoyed lording it over Hollywood, but toward Anita she had always been genuinely warm. So why had she suddenly turned on the hauteur? Fairbanks admitted he was to blame. He was crazy about Mary Pickford, and to get out of the house some nights, he said he had script problems to discuss with Nita. Not unnaturally, Beth surmised that the two of them were plotting something other than their next movie.

Doug's confession amused Anita. She felt no strong loyalty to Beth, had no scruples about Doug using her as a shield as long as he kept her posted on his romance. Fairbanks told her all that propriety permitted, and her favorite tale concerned an incident that occurred after one of his clandestine trysts. To get out of the house unnoticed, he had taken to making his bed on an upstairs sleeping porch—the night air, he told Beth, was wonderful for the constitution. Once everyone was asleep, he'd climb down a pillar, release the hand brake of his car, coast it down the steep incline of his driveway, and start it up where no one would be awakened by the sound of the ignition. Then he'd speed off to meet Mary.

Returning home wasn't quite so easy—he had to push the car up the driveway, a tour de force that left him exhausted and hungry. So he asked his valet to leave a slice of cake on his bed table, and he always gulped it down in the dark, afraid he might rouse someone by turning on a lamp.

One night the cake had an odd, faintly Oriental tang, but Doug wolfed it down and went to sleep. The next morning he discovered the reason for the exotic taste—on the plate were a few crumbs and a creeping mass of red ants. He must have swallowed hundreds of the insects the night before. (Years later, Anita used this incident in her novel *No Mother to Guide Her.*)

Often Doug, Emerson, and Anita went riding through the tangled wildwood then covering most of Beverly Hills. By prearrangement, they met Mary. Emerson and Anita discreetly reined in their horses while Doug and Mary galloped away for a half hour of loving solitude.

Anita was acquainted with all the Pickfords: Mary; her mother, Charlotte; brother Jack and sister Lottie. Jack was her favorite. While still in his teens he was the bedmate of one of the most celebrated Ziegfeld girls, Lillian Lorraine, and he had been drinking hard long before he met her. He was reckless and irresponsible, but, said Anita, "you couldn't help loving Jack. He was the only lush I ever knew who was good company."

She was also fond of Ma Pickford, "as Irish as Mother Macree," with a sharp business sense and a healthy thirst. "She could match Jack drink for drink," Anita said. "Just before Prohibition, she bought out a liquor store, stashed the bottles in her basement, and padlocked the door so Jack wouldn't drink it all up."

Anita knew Lottie mainly through tales told by a maid who once worked for the younger Pickford sister. Lottie, it seems, was fond of all-night parties at which the guests got so tight they felt constricted in their clothes. But, reported the maid, "when they heard Miss Mary's car coming up the drive one morning, oh, boy! did they jump into their knickers!"

About Mary, Anita had mixed emotions. Since childhood Pickford had supported her family, toiling away while Jack and Lottie devoted themselves to having a good time. That was admirable, but Mary's dedication to being America's Sweetheart off-screen as well as on- was less appealing.

Pickford was, at best, a tattered valentine. John Emerson told Anita that while he was directing Mary in *The Foundling* in 1916, Ma Pickford gave him one piece of advice: "Mary gives her most when she's got a director on top of her." A wink told Emerson that Ma wasn't speaking metaphorically. (Apparently Emerson didn't act on Mrs. Pickford's advice: *The Foundling* was one of Mary's few box-office flops.)

Anita's feeling for Doug and Mary never ran very deep. They were entertaining to observe, but prolonged exposure revealed them as self-enchanted, shallow and sanctimonious about their obligations to their public. And yet working for Doug was quite pleasant, she had to admit. The schedule was heavy—nine scripts in eighteen months—but the atmosphere was casual, and Fairbanks was an easygoing boss.

Each film started with a conference at which Doug, Emerson and Anita thrashed out an idea for a script. Fairbanks then went off to his private gym; Emerson visited his masseuse; Anita returned to her apartment and started roughing out a screenplay. A few days later, with some scenes roughed out to her own satisfaction, there was a second conference, with Doug and Emerson suggesting improvements. Usually Anita accepted their ideas unhesitatingly. Doug had an instinct about what was right for him, and Emerson, Anita then believed, was far wiser than she was about dramatic construction.

She was more than a little fond of Emerson and was convinced he cared for her. They had reached a point where each had a pet name for the other: she was "Bug" or "Buggie"; he was "Mr. E."—affection mixed with condescension on the one hand, with respect on the other.

Mr. E. warned Bug that he wasn't the marrying kind, he was constitutionally incapable of being faithful to any woman. This confession was taken, perhaps as unconsciously intended, as a challenge. Anita resolved that she was going to be the exception to the rule.

Later, friends wondered why she married a man so much older than herself. Since he had the air of a worldly, slightly graying man of the theater and she still passed for a teenager, appearances were deceptive. Emerson was fourteen years older than Anita, not twenty or twenty-five, as many people suspected.

He was born Clifton Paden in Sandusky, Ohio, in 1874, the son of an Episcopalian minister who dabbled in politics and was mayor of Sandusky at the time of his son's birth. After high school, he entered a theological college in Ohio, where he married an assistant instructor.

Emerson soon realized he lacked religious fervor, that his ambition to be a minister was no more than an ambition to perform for an audience; so he left school to try for a career in the theater. His wife stayed behind and later sued for divorce on the grounds of desertion.

In New York he enrolled at the American Academy of Dramatic Arts, completing the course so brilliantly that he was invited to join the faculty. After teaching for a few semesters, he started practicing what he taught, first as an actor and stage manager with Minnie Maddern Fiske, the finest actress of the period; later as assistant to playwright Clyde Fitch, who wrote the first American comedies of manners. Then he graduated to directing for Charles Frohman, New York's foremost producer.

In 1912 he discovered a play called *The Conspiracy*, a promising, though not fully realized, melodrama by a stage-struck Harvard professor. Emerson added a few flourishes to the script, took sole credit for its authorship, directed it, and cast himself in the leading role. *The Conspiracy* was a huge success. It established Emerson as a Broadway star and led to his contract with Triangle.

Years later, when the marriage had gone sour, Anita was often asked by friends why she had stuck with it to the bitter end. There were two answers. Occasionally she'd quip, "Oh, it was never boring!" Alternatively she answered, "I don't know really. He always had some kind of magnetic hold on me."

What she never quite admitted was that she loved him deeply and unreasonably, and allowed that love to blind her to his many frailties for a considerable time. This seems the only explanation of why she went on with a relationship any clear-headed woman would have given up on long before Anita did.

Emerson was attractive, urbane, literate, and not ungifted. He wasn't in Griffith's league, but he could handle actors and bring out the best in a good script. An interpretative rather than a creative director, he was proficient within his limitations.

He received, Anita said, credit for screenplays to which he contributed virtually nothing. Emerson's friends have taken exception to this, but it's probably true. Those writings of Emerson's which have survived—mainly a portfolio of autobiographical sketches—are trite and sluggish, with none of the sparkle of the work he presumably co-authored with Anita.

Still, Emerson unquestionably assisted her in many ways. At the start of their relationship, he was far more sophisticated than she was, and by her own admission he "polished the rough edges." He taught her the value of self-promotion, a lesson she mastered very quickly. During her career with Fairbanks, she received as much coverage as Mary Pickford and Lillian Gish in the fan magazines. She was extremely photogenic and enjoyed posing for the camera, often choosing backdrops that emphasized her tininess. One of her favorite photographs shows her standing in front of a large Russian wolfhound: the dog comes up nearly to her waist.

Anita was one of the few film writers known to the public. She received ample credit and praise for her contribution to Fairbanks's pictures. In time, Doug started to feel she was getting too much attention. Justifiably, he considered himself the major attraction of his films. This had to be made clear to the critics and the public, and the swiftest way of getting it across was to get rid of Loos and Emerson.

Doug had another reason for dismissing his collaborators. He felt confined within the small comedies Anita tailored for him and was looking for a more expansive format to exhibit his athletic prowess. By the beginning of 1918 he was already thinking of those swashbuckling epics— *The Three Musketeers, Robin Hood, The Black Pirate*—for which he is best remembered. Since these pictures demanded Griffith-sized sets and technical wizardry, they lay outside the range of John Emerson's talents, and maybe Anita's too. One thing Fairbanks definitely wanted to banish was the boobish side of his personality.

Anita and Emerson demonstrate their method of collaboration for a magazine article on the art of screenwriting, published in 1918.

Emerson liked his picture to appear in the papers and magazines. Here he has captured a photographer's interest by spanking a stuffed crocodile, 1918.

The parting was amicable, Anita said. She and Emerson wanted to work in New York anyway, and Famous Players–Lasky offered them the chance. They were to make four pictures during the next year at the company's Manhattan facilities at a salary even better than what they earned with Fairbanks. How much better, Anita couldn't remember. "I always let Mr. E. make all the financial arrangements," Anita said. "He rarely consulted me."

Anita outside her brother's house in Santa Monica with a
wolfhound belonging to her sister-in-law, 1914–15

7

Getting Married

A DOLPH ZUKOR, head of Famous Players–Lasky, entered the film business after a career as a furrier by producing picture versions of stage dramas played by renowned actors. Unhappily, most of these illustrious stars looked foolish on the silent screen, and Zukor's enterprise would have gone under had he not managed to bring established screen favorites into his program, among them Mary Pickford.

By 1918, Famous Players–Lasky depended mainly on film personalities, but Zukor still wasn't ready to discard the past entirely. He kept looking for stage actors with talents that might translate to the screen, thereby salvaging his original concept. Since Anita had done wonders for Doug, and since Emerson came from the theater, Zukor assigned them to his most recent crop of Broadway imports—Billie Burke, George M. Cohan, Fred Stone, and Ernest Truex.

All four found success in the sound era, but in 1918 none knew much about screen acting. And as Anita freely admitted, she and Emerson gave them little help. "Part of the trouble was the material. For Billie Burke, I had to adapt an old Sardou clinker, *Let's Get a Divorce,* and Cohan for some reason chose one of his weaker stage vehicles, *Hit-the-Trail Holiday.* But the originals I wrote for Stone and Truex weren't much better. They were too crammed with titles."

In the Fairbanks films, the printed dialogue provided a pleasant respite between Doug's explosive bursts of energy, but the stage stars

Louise Huff and Ernest Truex in *Oh, You Women!* (1919). Anita wasn't happy with the film, but she and Louise became lifelong friends.

couldn't muster his kind of razzle-dazzle. Critics and the public found the pictures prolix. "While watching *Let's Get a Divorce*," wrote one trade reviewer, "I kept wondering if Miss Loos never suffered from writer's cramp."

Still, the pictures were fun to make. It was wonderful being in New York and living at the Algonquin, where she and Emerson kept suites on different floors. And Anita liked several of the Famous Players–Lasky actors, especially Louise Huff, a lifelong friend.

"At first Anita took a skeptical view of me," Huff recalled. "I was one of those actresses promoted as Mary Pickford rivals, and I suppose Anita thought I might actually be another Mary, whom she didn't really like very much. But I had made a couple of pictures with Jack Pickford, and one day Anita asked me about him. I said I absolutely adored Jack. So she kept asking me about his shenanigans, and that formed the basis of our friendship. I guess she decided that anyone fond of a scamp like Jack wasn't all vanilla ice cream."

Louise Huff wasn't making much progress as another Mary Pickford and confided to Anita that she wanted to test her individuality on Broadway. Anita wasn't especially encouraging. Broadway, she said, wasn't all that superior to Hollywood; Mr. E. took her to the theater nearly every night, and most of what they saw was no better than what was shown at the

New York picture palaces. She and Mr. E. exchanged words about this, but this was one time she wouldn't back down.

"There were two Anitas, really," recalled Huff. "When Emerson wasn't around, she was mischievous, giddy, very funny. But once he walked on the set, which usually wasn't until his assistant had solved the technical problems — lighting, camera movements, things which interested Emerson *not at all* — she became subdued, very ladylike. She deferred to him *completely*. It was obvious she worshiped him."

And how did Emerson treat Anita? "Affectionately, but with a patronizing edge. He could be very amusing, but he could be pretentious, too. He'd say, 'Now you see, Nita, we'll do this' or 'We'll do that,' and Anita would say, 'Oh yes, wonderful!' "

Anita's adoration led to some foolish errors in judgment. It was at this time that Emerson requested co-authorship credit, and Anita gave it to him willingly. He then demanded top billing — it was not fitting, he claimed, for a man of his prominence to play second fiddle — and this too was granted. Friends remonstrated, but Anita dismissed the issue as trivial. What was important was keeping Mr. E. happy.

This was not easy to manage. Emerson was constantly suffering from illnesses, some real, many imaginary. If seated in a draft, he changed places with Anita. If the hotel suite assigned to her was more luxurious than his, he found an excuse for a trade — the bed in his room was too hard for his back. Whatever the request, Anita granted it unprotestingly. Her subservience infuriated nearly everyone, but Anita turned a deaf ear to the protests.

When their Famous Players-Lasky contract wasn't renewed, Emerson put the blame on Anita: her scripts hadn't been up to scratch. She might have replied that he had been eager enough to see his name on those scripts, but she kept mum. And when she got a handsome offer for a new film, she brought Emerson in with her, though he hadn't figured in the original deal.

The producer was William Randolph Hearst, who had branched into film production to make Marion Davies a major picture star. So far that goal hadn't been reached: Davies's notoriety as a paramour didn't sit well with the American public, and her films were sneered at as vanity productions. To counteract this slur, Hearst hired one of Hollywood's best directors, Allan Dwan, for Marion's next two films, and Dwan suggested Anita as scriptwriter.

Anita liked Dwan — they had worked happily together on one of the early Fairbanks films — and she was intrigued by Marion. They had never met, but Anita had seen her on stage several times and was impressed by

Davies's ability to make herself noticed though she wasn't spectacularly talented and lacked the statuesque glamour of most Ziegfeld show girls.

Meeting Marion, Anita realized that fun was the key to her personality. It was Davies's impishness and irreverence that had to be spotlighted if she was ever going to make it big in pictures. One lesson she learned while working for Fairbanks was that when writing for an actor who was no actor, it was best to concentrate on personality and forgo the Barrymore dramatics. Hearst kept casting Marion in heavy, melodramatic roles that would have challenged a Maude Adams or an Ellen Terry. With Allan Dwan's help, she hoped to convince Hearst that Davies's exuberance had to be allowed to come across on screen.

She wrote a screenplay (to which Emerson contributed his name) called *Getting Mary Married*. The heroine is one of those girls with everything—beauty, personality, lots of money. But according to her father's will, if she marries, she loses her fortune, which then would pass to another branch of the family, the Bussards, who are naturally falling over each other trying to discover a beau interested in Mary, not money. The search, for all Mary's charms, proves more arduous than they anticipated.

Hearst didn't like the script: no man with blood in his veins would let a bankroll stand between him and Marion, he asserted. Anita argued that there had to be some conflict—if all the men were panting after Mary/Marion, there wouldn't be any plot. Finally Hearst agreed—with one provision: there must be a profusion of close-ups of Marion, emphasizing her beauty and desirability.

He then made another request: the film must have a scene with Marion in pants. Anita was startled but allowed that it wouldn't be difficult to include such a masquerade. Later, a Hearst assistant explained that the boss got a charge out of seeing women in men's clothing. It was a harmless quirk, Anita decided, and since Marion looked good in trousers, why not indulge it? She wrote a scene around a fox hunt, allowing the heroine to appear in jodhpurs and a riding jacket.

Davies's relationship with Hearst was not unlike Anita's with Emerson. When W.R. was present, Marion acted demurely: but when he was away, she indulged in monkeyshines. Knowing that Anita hated those close-ups Hearst insisted on, Marion set out to sabotage them. She would pose beatifically, then slyly part her lips to show a gap where her front teeth should have been: she had blacked them out with boot polish. Anita was an appreciative audience, though she realized that Marion's antics were delaying production and costing Hearst thousands of dollars in retakes.

Marion too felt remorse now and then, but, as Anita rationalized, "she needed some release from Hearst's pervasive self-importance. She needed time to be naughty."

Getting Mary Married got nice reviews, and while not a box-office smash, it was one of the few Davies films to end up in the black. Hearst loved it, which amused Anita, since the picture was her veiled comment on the Hearst-Davies situation: like Mary, Marion was a girl who had everything, but still she couldn't get W.R. to marry her. She had taken a calculated risk that Hearst wouldn't get the joke, the odds being in her favor, since W.R. didn't have much of a sense of humor.

Hearst encouraged Anita to write another script for Marion, but something better had come along. She and Emerson had accepted a long-term contract to create films for an old friend.

CONSTANCE TALMADGE —Dutch or Connie to friends—hadn't gone far after her success in *Intolerance,* and by 1919 she had been eclipsed by her older sister, Norma. Dutch didn't care; one star was enough for any family, and Norma had the better qualifications: she was an American

Constance Talmadge, 1916

Beauty rose while Dutch was, at best, a very leggy dandelion. "Leave the acting to Norma," Connie told her mother. "I'll get by all right."

But Peg Talmadge hadn't raised her daughter to drift with the wind. The women in the family had to pull their share or they'd wind up back in Brooklyn, where they had begun. Pop Talmadge, a carny roustabout, had disappeared years before, leaving Peg with three kids to raise. By the time

OPPOSITE: Constance Talmadge displaying a dress she would never have worn in real life. "Her reaction to this silly garment," Anita wrote, "would have been to get out of it as soon as possible." RIGHT: Norma was the beauty of the Talmadge family. Here she wears a chiffon frock from Mme. Frances, a New York couturier who (Anita wrote) "specialized in dressing gold diggers in an era when gentlemen clamored to pay their sweetheart's upkeep."

Joe Schenck and Norma Talmadge, 1919, at a beach near their home in Bayside, Long Island. Norma wasn't interested in building a family, so Joe worked out his paternal feelings by playing second father to his neighbors' children, one of whom appears in this snapshot.

the girls had reached their teens, Peg realized that their only marketable assets were their looks. Norma was patrician; Dutch, pert; and Natalie might get by in a chorus line, maybe find a rich husband. (Eventually she became Mrs. Buster Keaton.)

Peg pushed her daughters into show business, and for a while they went through the hoops as gamely as she had expected. So it was all the more aggravating that Dutch was ready to throw it all away just because of a lull in her career.

Norma had married Joe Schenck, an independent film producer who doubled as his wife's agent, and he agreed with Peg that Dutch just wanted an excuse for living it up as a playgirl. Give him the go-ahead and he'd have all three Talmadge sisters toeing the line.

Born in Russia, Schenck had come to the United States in the 1890s with his parents and his younger brother, Nick. While in school, the boys worked in a drugstore, slowly saving enough money to buy the store, then gradually acquiring others until they built a small empire of pharmacies, many located in New York's Chinatown. Next they invested in one of America's first amusement parks, and did so well that within a few years they were themselves the proprietors of Palisades Park, the prototype of this form of entertainment. Palisades presented movies, and soon the

Schencks met and became right-hand men to Marcus Loew, a vaudeville and movie impresario whose theater chain was the foundation for Metro-Goldwyn-Mayer.

Nick stayed on with Loew, eventually rising to the presidency of M–G–M, but Joe got restless. Without breaking ties with Loew, he dabbled in independent production, and after marrying Norma he took over the management of his wife's and his sisters-in-law's careers. Norma's progress was steady, but Connie, he felt, was dragging her heels.

It was Joe's idea to bring in Anita and Mr. E. They had written a nice little comedy for Norma in 1916, *The Social Secretary;* and in one of their Fairbanks films, *The Matrimaniac,* Dutch had her best post-*Intolerance* role, even though Doug never gave his leading ladies much of a chance to shine. If Anita and Emerson had been able to sneak in some nice bits for Connie, they might work wonders with Schenck in charge.

"When I first met Joe, I thought he was the ugliest man I had ever seen," Anita remembered. "Five minutes later I thought he was one of the most attractive." Schenck was magnetic, intelligent, clever, flamboyant—the kind of gentleman con artist that always appealed to Anita. To bring you to his office in New York, Joe sent his limousine, a custom-built model with mahogany paneling, doeskin upholstery, a bar, and crystal vases filled with white orchids. Anita complimented him on the car. "It was a Christmas present from a friend," Schenck said. "I like it so much that I'm having a duplicate made for California."

Writing for Schenck's sister-in-law struck Anita as an agreeable assignment. Dutch had a genuine flair for comedy, and in roles tailored to her personality she was beguiling, all razzmatazz and impudence, naughty but never vulgar or suggestive. Irving Berlin, one of Talmadge's many suitors, dubbed her a "virtuous vamp," and that, Anita felt, was the perfect description for the heroine Dutch ought to play: not a pre-Raphaelite lily like Miss Gish or a waif like Mae Marsh, nor a society clotheshorse like Gloria Swanson. Anita was after something more up-to-the-minute. The roles she created for Dutch were early flappers; and playing them, Talmadge was a John Held illustration come to life.

All Anita's screenplays for Talmadge were cut from similar cloth. Each is set against sophisticated surroundings, with Dutch cast as a young wife who teaches her husband a well-deserved lesson or, alternatively, as a flirt or a scatterbrain corrected by an adoring but much put-upon spouse. In *A Temperamental Wife,* the first of these comedies, Dutch is married to a congressman who she thinks is handing more than dictation to his secretary; eventually he convinces her that politics is all work and no playing

LEFT TO RIGHT: Unidentified, Emerson, Anita, Constance Talmadge, Sidney Franklin, and Oliver Marsh preparing a scene for *A Virtuous Vamp*. Emerson delegated directorial duties to his assistants—in this case Sidney Franklin. Oliver Marsh, the cameraman, was the brother of Anita's close friend, actress Mae Marsh.

Constance Talmadge and two extras in a scene from *A Virtuous Vamp* (1919)

18.

The boy then goes to ~~the~~ Crowninshield's office, smiling back at Gwen as he
goes *arranging his tie*

16. CROWNINSHIELD'S PRIVATE OFFICE. (Note. This
office and the ~~ante-room, particularly the~~
private office, must be very luxuriously fitted
~~up and made as attractive as possible.~~
Crowninshield is seated at his desk, Miss *Turner*
~~Ward~~ (his stenographer) ~~sitting opposite and~~
taking dictation. The boy comes in. Crowninshield finishes dictating the letter, sends
Miss ~~Ward~~ *Turner* away ~~(she leaving by another door)~~
and then ~~Crowninshield~~ asks the boy what ~~it~~
~~is~~ he wants. The boy says: "There are a
couple of people out there to see you."
He asks who they are and the boy ~~says:~~ *replies*

SP. "THERE'S A MAN WITH A LETTER OF INTRODUCTION AND A
GIRL."
Crowninshield, *interviewing them* bored at the idea, *in his office, and*
~~decides~~ to get rid of them ~~outside.~~ He ~~goes~~ goes out followed by the
boy.

17. ANTE ROOM, CROWNINSHIELD'S OFFICE. Crowninshield comes in followed by the boy, who looks
with his eyes still on her
admiringly at Gwen and sits down at his little
desk, ~~to the room very~~

19.

Gwen ~~who~~ gives ~~him~~ *the boy* a smile and then
devotes her attention to Crowninshield,
~~thinking what a grand man he is and~~ fishing
in her bag for her letter of introduction,
which she takes out so as to have ready ~~as soon~~
~~as she came in interviews her~~
Crowninshield goes to the ~~lounge lizard~~ *young society man* who
introduces himself and shakes Crowninshield's
in an extremely social manner.
hand ~~as if they were social equals.~~ He then
says to Crowninshield:

SP. "I HAVE A LETTER OF INTRODUCTION FROM MRS. REGGIE
VANDERPOEL."
Crowninshield frowns at this, ~~The lounge~~
~~lizard reaches in his pocket, takes out the~~
~~letter, hands it to Crowninshield.~~ Crowninshield gives him a disapproving glance and
then reads the letter, Gwen closely watching
all the time. Crowninshield finishes reading
young many
the letter, hands it back to the ~~lounge lizard~~
and says:

SP. *By using*
"YOUNG MAN, YOU ~~will~~ 'll NEVER GET ANYWHERE ~~by using~~ SOCIETY
LETTERS OF INTRODUCTION. WHEN I WENT INTO BUSINESS
I PUT FAMILY AND POSITION BEHIND ME AND MADE GOOD ON
MY OWN."
The boy bridles at this and says:

SP. "BUT ONE MUST BE A GENTLEMAN EVEN IN BUSINESS AND *after*
~~all~~ WHY SHOULD NOT ONE USE ONE'S CONNECTIONS FOR ONE'S
OWN ADVANCEMENT WHEN ONE CAN."
Vamp
(Crowninshield) ~~takes~~ *takes* thorough stock of him
~~and~~ looks him up and down, and then says:

From the script of *A Virtuous Vamp*

around. It was a great hit, as was Talmadge's next vehicle, *A Virtuous Vamp,* named after Berlin's epithet for Connie.

Both were made in spring 1919 at a New York warehouse Schenck had converted into a ramshackle studio. Norma's pictures were shot on the ground floor while Connie's crew worked on the second. Schenck and the Talmadges preferred New York to California, a matter Anita checked out before signing her contract.

She always stayed at the Algonquin, because she liked its clubby atmosphere and compatible clientele. H. L. Mencken, one of her idols, made it his New York home; and though Anita met him around this time, their friendship didn't start until a few years later. She did establish a nodding relationship with Ethel Barrymore, then appearing in *Déclassée,* a Pinero-esque exposé of fallen women. Anita hated the play—the shady ladies she observed around New York weren't draped for tragedy like Miss Barrymore.

Déclassée might be fraudulent, but Zoe Akins, its author, was genuine, purple-tinged in life as well as in prose. Akins was a resident of the Algonquin, sharing a suite with her devoted companion, Jobyna Howland, a statuesque actress and model for illustrators Dana Gibson and James Montgomery Flagg. Akins was constantly falling in love, nearly always unrequitedly. "Whenever Zoe set her sights on a beau, she pulled out this French lace dress that was her talisman for romance," Anita recalled. "It was a beautiful dress, but Zoe was several sizes larger than when she and the dress were virginal. To get into it, she had to diet."

Zoe favored a regimen of lean lamb chops and chilled blanc de blancs, but the amount of wine she consumed more than balanced the calories she otherwise saved, and the pounds refused to melt. Desperate measures were needed: "I had read that Austrian Empress Elisabeth wrapped herself in hot linen to stay slim," Anita remembered, "so why not try this with Zoe?" Anita and two girl friends ripped up linen sheets, boiled them, and bound Zoe up like an Egyptian mummy. "Zoe didn't die from lack of circulation," Anita said. "She got into the dress. But she didn't get her man."

Another of Anita's Algonquin companions was Tallulah Bankhead, newly arrived from Alabama. The young Tallulah wanted to be a serious actress like her idol Ethel Barrymore; whenever Tallulah encountered Ethel in the Algonquin lobby, she would half-curtsy deferentially. "It wasn't an act," said Anita, who persuaded Emerson to give Bankhead a small role in *A Virtuous Vamp.* "Tallulah had the manners of a true southern aristocrat. Even later when she became an exhibitionist, you'd still catch glimpses of her sweetness and generosity. When she arrived in Hollywood, she stayed at the Hollywood Hotel, and she often chatted with the elderly ladies on the front veranda. They adored her, my mother most of all. If I had told them she was known to hold court while sitting naked on her commode, they would have thought I had a foul mind."

One bond between Anita and Tallulah was a mutual distaste for the Algonquin Round Table, then in existence for only a few months but already making an impact on American humor. Appraising a witticism from one of its founding members, Bankhead commented, "Mr. Woollcott, there's a lot less here than meets the eye."

Anita, later to write a devastating putdown of the Round Table in *But Gentlemen Marry Brunettes,* emphatically agreed. Some members of the clique she liked individually, but en masse they were too much. Their quips were anything but spontaneous, and their conduct was fawning and exhibitionistic. In *Brunettes,* Anita describes a typical Round Table get-together:

> Well finally all the geniuses were present at last and the way the conversation worked out was really remarkable. Because first one genius said to another "What was that screamingly funny remark you made last Tuesday?" So then he told it and they all laughed. And then it was *his* turn to ask, "And what was that terribly clever thing *you* said on Friday?" So then the other genius got *his* chance, and it was all give-and-take, so that everybody had an opportunity to talk about himself.

In spring 1919 Anita and Mr. E. left the Algonquin for the Ambassador Hotel on Park Avenue, home for the Talmadges and the Schencks. Anita had more or less adopted them as her family, with Connie (like Mae Marsh before her) replacing the sister she had lost many years before.

When they weren't working, she and Dutch met for lunch, then went shopping at Elizabeth Arden, at Lucile or Madame Francis, always ending up at the shop of Nathan Gibson Clark, New York's premier milliner. No hat left Gibbie's without seventy-five dollars changing hands. But it was the milliner, not his wares, that was the chief attraction for Anita. When frazzled, which was most of the time, Gibbie treated his social-register clientele with high-handed, colorful abuse. "Get out, you cow!" he'd shriek. "You're too grotesque for my hats!" His customers were titillated by the abuse, so different from the deference doled out at Bendel's. Anita was an appreciative audience for these outbursts; and as a

Nathan Gibson Clark, New York's most expensive milliner,
vacationing in Venice. Anita thought his quips were funnier
than his hats and appropriated several for *Gentlemen Prefer
Blondes*.

token of their secret sisterhood, Gibbie gave her a discount on his hats as
well as an even more precious gift: many of Dorothy Shaw's snazziest
wisecracks in *Blondes* and *Brunettes* came straight from Gibbie's mouth.

Every so often Anita persuaded Dutch to pursue the higher things in
life. They'd visit the Metropolitan Museum or take in a concert at Carnegie
Hall. Once, along with Norma, they enrolled in a ballet class taught by
Adolph Bolm, a former star of Diaghilev's Ballets Russes. "We were all
pretty bad," Anita recalled, "but I was the worst of all." One day Bolm
blew up. "Mother of heaven, will you never stop thinking?" he shouted. If

one of the prerequisites for a prima ballerina was an empty head, a *cérébrale* like Anita was never going to make it on her toes.

Nearly every afternoon ended with a good gossip in Ma Talmadge's suite at the Ambassador. Tea was served, Peg lacing her cup with a shot of Irish whiskey. There was no pretense about this, just as there was no pretension in Peg's conversation. "She was the best of company," Anita said, even though Ma's opinions weren't always the ones Anita wanted to hear. About Mr. E., Peg had particularly harsh words. He was a good director for Dutch, she admitted, but he took credit when none was deserved, a bad trait in a man. "Watch out, Nita," Peg warned, "or that bum will be living off your dollar bills!"

To put space between Mr. E. and his infatuated partner, Peg insisted that Anita join the Talmadges for a Paris holiday that summer. Anita didn't need much persuasion; but as the liner slipped out of New York Harbor, she regretted leaving Emerson behind. "Put out that torch or you'll blind Miss Liberty!" Peg said.

The Talmadge-Schenck party stayed at the Crillon in Paris. Anita let Peg and her girls take charge of the visit, and since these ladies had limited enthusiasm for museums and monuments, most of their sight-seeing was restricted to restaurants, night spots, and fashion ateliers. Every day they shopped for dresses for Norma's and Dutch's forthcoming films. After a massage and a nap, the women dressed for dinner at Maxim's or an evening at the Lido or the Folies-Bergère.

The Crillon manicurist told the Talmadges that her younger sister was a Folies star, and on the night they attended the revue, they checked their programs and managed to single out *la petite soeur* among the many unclad mademoiselles. "How old is she?" Dutch asked. "Eighteen," Anita whispered. "Blarney!" Peg scoffed. "No girl gets her knees that dirty in eighteen years!"—a quip Anita later appropriated for *Gentlemen Prefer Blondes.*

On returning to New York, Anita and Dutch plunged into a heavy work schedule. In the next sixteen months, five Constance Talmadge films were released, all written by Loos and Emerson, though none was directed by Mr. E. Emerson had been feeling poorly that summer, and his doctor forbade him to carry on except in a supervisory capacity. Dutch's films didn't really need him on the set every day, he explained: cameraman Oliver Marsh (Mae's brother) was clever about the technical stuff, and Sidney Franklin, Emerson's assistant, could handle the routine directorial duties, though of course Mr. E. would be around now and then to guide him. For this service, Emerson would naturally receive his regular salary.

Things didn't work out as smoothly as he had planned. Franklin objected to doing all the work while Mr. E. took the credit and received a fatter paycheck. Franklin was replaced by David Kirkland. This was an even greater mistake, since Kirkland had the bad grace to take a shine to Anita, who showed signs of responding. Perhaps she was acting guilefully — trifling with David to capture John. If so, the ruse succeeded. Forgetting that he was not the marrying kind, Mr. E. proposed. Later Anita came to believe that there were ulterior motives behind his capitulation. If she married Kirkland, Emerson may have reasoned, she might dissolve their partnership, leaving him without a meal ticket. But at the time she was too happy to be suspicious.

Earlier, as a precautionary measure, she had filed for divorce and already had an interlocutory decree, though she wouldn't be free to remarry for a few months. Emerson's health would have prevented them marrying before then, anyway. His physician had suggested surgery for removal of the spleen, a serious procedure at the time but one the doctor felt Emerson should risk, provided adequate blood was on hand for on-the-spot transfusions. Anita volunteered to be the donor; so while Emerson was on the operating table, she lay in a nearby cubicle, giving up her blood. When he woke in his hospital room, she was sitting beside him, looking lots worse than the patient.

While Mr. E. recuperated, Anita worked on arrangements for the wedding. Emerson felt that a pastor's son ought to have a marriage blessed by the church, but Anita soon discovered that most clergymen balked at the idea of two divorced people crass enough to expect their new union to be sanctified by holy rites. Only through perseverance did she find a minister liberal enough to agree, reluctantly, to marry them on secular ground.

Joe Schenck offered his Long Island estate for the wedding on June 21, 1920. He was best man; Norma, Dutch, and Natalie, bridesmaids. It rained early that morning, traditionally a bad luck omen; but the skies soon cleared, and the marriage was held outdoors in the Schenck garden as scheduled.

Emerson was on the verge of nervous collapse as he took his place next to the bride. His voice couldn't be heard in the responses, so Schenck resorted to ventriloquism. John opened his mouth, but Joe spoke the words. When it was over, Anita wondered whether technically she hadn't actually married Joseph Schenck.

Of all the many wedding gifts she received, the one she valued most was a note from Vachel Lindsay: "May Santy Claus come to see you every

Anita and Emerson on their wedding day, June 21, 1920

Christmas and George Washington every Fourth of July. May St. Valentine appear ever and anon through the whole year, and may all the other saints bless you and keep you."

For a year or so it actually looked as though the Emerson marriage might be as blessed as Lindsay hoped.

PART
Two

MARRIAGE
À LA MODE

8

Mrs. E.

JOE SCHENCK'S wedding present was a European honeymoon, which was, Anita recalled, all too brief. After three days in Paris, they received a cable ordering them back to New York. There was trouble with Dutch's new picture, *The Perfect Woman.*

Emerson blamed David Kirkland for the problems and used this as an excuse for firing Anita's former suitor. Kirkland was replaced by Victor Fleming, who had directed a couple of Fairbanks pictures. Anita liked him, but Emerson didn't see him as a potential rival. Fleming was a ladies' man, but he was all bedroom, booze, and bravado—not Anita's kind of guy.

Later Fleming was to earn a reputation as a man's director—Gable swore by him—but he did well by Anita and Dutch, possibly because Anita's scripts, while occasionally concerned with feminist issues, ended by confirming male supremacy. In *A Woman's Place,* for example, Anita tackled female enfranchisement. Dutch played Josephine Gerson, selected by her women's club as a mayoral candidate because she's such a snazzy dresser. When the men get behind her, Josephine loses her women backers— they decide she's a flirt. She loses the election but wins the heart of the new mayor. Josephine has learned that a woman's place is behind the throne of power.

By no means was Anita guilty of playing to an all-male gallery. She believed what she was joking about. Intellectual voluptuaries like Aspasia or Mesdames de Pompadour and de Staël were smarter and ended up happier than a Joan of Arc, who got burned for doing a man's job. Let men keep their illusions about being the stronger sex! Years later, Anita was to say of Gloria Steinem and her followers, "The dumbest thing they could have done was let men in on the secret that women are smarter than they are."

Anita could, of course, be accused of limited perspective. She wasn't the typical American woman; hers wasn't the typical American marriage. She was free to be creative, free from household drudgery. There were maids, a secretary to type and look after the social calendar, and Mr. E. to sign checks and worry about investments.

There were no children. Nothing Anita ever said or wrote suggests she wanted them, and everything known about Mr. E. implies that he would have viewed them as inconveniences. He required undivided attention and never could have accepted a rival, not even one of his own flesh and blood. On several occasions Anita took on the role of surrogate mother, but evidence suggests she was miscast.

Viewed from the outside, the Emersons' marriage looked very modish. Here was a couple unencumbered by offspring, clever, productive, each contributing to a joint bank account, devoted to each other and yet modern enough to allow one another lots of freedom. All of which was true—up to a point. As before, Anita carried more than her load in maintaining the balance of their relationship. She was up by four and at work by six, often writing on a chaise longue in her bedroom. Around noon she dressed and went out for lunch or an afternoon of shopping with friends. Then there was dinner with Mr. E., after which they went to the theater, the worst way of killing three hours Anita could imagine. The Scandals and Vanities and Follies were diverting, but purgatory was preferable to an evening with O'Neill or Ibsen as interpreted by Blanche Yurka.

She went to the theater to please her husband, she told an interviewer from *Vanity Fair;* she would rather stay home with a good book. Anita was a heavy reader, especially at night. Frequently she woke after a few hours of sleep and picked up a book, hoping it would induce drowsiness. Schopenhauer or *La Nouvelle Héloïse* seemed the perfect soporific, but often she was still turning the pages at dawn. She figured she was probably the only nonacademic in New York to have read all of *Héloïse.*

After their marriage, the Emersons left the Ambassador and moved to a relatively modest apartment in Murray Hill—two bedrooms, living and dining rooms, servants' quarters—but Mr. E. felt their station in life demanded something grander. Dutifully Anita went out on a search, but when she found a palatial flat on Riverside Drive, Emerson told her to forget it. The Murray Hill pied-à-terre was fine. They'd been working too hard; and from now on, as he had just told Joe Schenck, they'd be making just one or two films a year. The rest of the time they'd be traveling.

They started out modestly with visits to friends living on Long Island. Emerson bought a huge and very expensive car which he insisted on driving himself, though he was notoriously inept behind the wheel. Fearing for her life, Anita urged him to hire a chauffeur, but he wouldn't hear of such an extravagance. Fortunately, he wasn't overconfident about his skills, always driving at the lowest possible speed. "A snail just passed us," Anita would remark. Other drivers cursed as they passed Emerson, who got so rattled he occasionally swerved into a ditch or veered off into a side road. "I thought we'd take a more scenic route," he'd explain.

Often they headed for the Oyster Bay home of film director George Fitzmaurice, whose specialty was adaptations of Broadway plays starring Broadway actors. His weekend guests always included a sprinkling of the best the New York theater offered, and the conversation invariably struck Anita as insular and self-promoting. But Fitzmaurice was a true gentleman, and she participated enthusiastically in his favorite weekend sport, photography. There were many camera buffs among Fitz's guests, and Anita was an obliging model. The results were pasted in albums and captioned in white ink, a practice Anita kept up sporadically for several years.

The snapshots for 1921 reveal that the Emersons' travels extended far beyond Long Island. They visited Florida for the first time and then possibly went on to Cuba. (The background looks like Havana, though there are no identifying captions attached to these photographs.) And there was a trip to Europe that summer with the Schencks and the Talmadges.

The crossing was stormy, though the sea was calm. Norma and Joe had a terrible row, leaving Norma so bruised she didn't leave her cabin until the ship docked in Le Havre. Anita had heard that Joe was cursed with a violent temper, but this was the first time she had seen evidence of his brutality. She had other girl friends who were battered regularly—one was musical-comedy star Marilyn Miller during her marriage to Jack Pickford—so she pushed aside the incident philosophically. It was an ugly side of male bravado that some women were too infatuated or frightened to resist. That there were subtle, equally insidious forms of male brutality Anita had yet to learn.

On their first day in Paris, Anita and the Talmadge sisters went shopping at Lanvin. As soon as they entered, the manager rushed forward and asked Anita to his office. Was she unworthy of such a refined setting?

Anita and Emerson often
visited the Long Island estate
of director George Fitzmaurice
in the early 1920s. Fitzmaurice
liked to photograph his guests
in playful tableaux.

On the contrary, the manager wanted a favor of Madame. Would she
permit her hairdo, a boyish bob, to be copied for his mannequins?

Anita told some very tall tales about her short hair, claiming that she
first was shorn about the time of *Intolerance*. This seems highly unlikely:
in none of the many photographs taken of her prior to her marriage is she
without her diadem plait, and probably she didn't part with it until 1921.
By then, all the smart magazines were featuring clipped hair; Irene Castle
was bobbed as early as 1914.

Still, it is possible that Anita was singled out at Lanvin for bringing a
new twist to what was already a conventional look: not severe or lacquered
like other bobs, hers was artfully disarranged—she called it "windswept."
If the bob was intended as a proclamation of female emancipation, Anita
sweetened the message—she looked like a pert and provocative schoolgirl.

The Emersons made their first visit to Palm Beach in 1920 with the Talmadges. Norma, Constance, and Anita were cycling enthusiasts.

Anita went on to say that the Lanvin manager was equally bowled over by her knee-length skirt. Seizing scissors, he snipped wildly at every hem in sight. Here again, fact is being shaped to personal advantage: no couturier promoted, and therefore no woman wore, short skirts until 1925, and the new look didn't catch on until a year later.

Her short hair and skirts wouldn't be worth mentioning except that, like her age, which she also abbreviated, they were part of the image she was then beginning to forge for herself. She wanted to be known as a trend-setter and early achiever, an independent, wised-up young woman who marched to her own drummer. Presenting herself in this way made for better reading than the drab truth that, underneath the smart exterior, she was shy, cautious, and conservative. Anita was what Max Beerbohm once called "an amusable person," and tit for tat, she felt obliged to amuse other people, whether they were friends or fans.

BEFORE leaving for Europe, Emerson hired a press agent to publicize their travels. Anita arched an eyebrow over such affectation, but Mr. E. insisted. James Ashmore Creeland, the young man who took the job, was affable and came highly recommended by a distant relative of his, novelist Sherwood Anderson, one of Anita's new friends. She liked Ash and Ash adored her, but he was no threat to Emerson. Creeland was homosexual.

Once in Paris, Anita realized that Mr. E. had hidden motives in bringing Ash along. One morning Emerson announced that he had hired a

Emerson and Anita at Malmaison during one of their first European holidays, early 1920s

chauffeur and a touring car for the day; he had business to attend to, and Anita should enjoy herself with Creeland during his absence. This routine continued for most of the vacation. Sometimes Mr. E. was gone all day. The Talmadges told Anita flat out that Emerson was prowling around, and she couldn't honestly disagree. She suspected he was picking up girls, taking them to lunch or a matinee, expecting at most a kiss in return. He was merely puffing up a menopausal ego: sad, perhaps, but innocent overall.

If Mr. E. wasn't back by lunch, Anita asked Ash to take her sight-seeing. And if her husband failed to show up for dinner, she took him to meet the celebrities she had been invited to visit. At Frank Crowninshield's parties in New York, she had encountered a number of Paris-based writers and artists, and now she began taking them up on earlier invitations, starting with Miguel Covarrubias, the Mexican-born caricaturist, and his wife, Rosa. The next day they took her to meet their good friend Gertrude Stein.

Earlier Anita had tried to read Stein's *Tender Buttons* and found it tough going. Sherwood Anderson explained that "one should look at the book as one looks at the palette of a painter, appreciate the words merely as words, and pay no attention to the context in which they are placed." Anita tried it Anderson's way, but still her concentration flagged.

Nonetheless she was delighted at the prospect of visiting the Stein apartment at 27, rue de Fleurus. Anita and Ash were given a half hour to examine the art collection before their hostess made an appearance. At first Anita found the paintings "too radical," but after Stein's entrance the distortions of Picasso and Cézanne looked less outré.

Dressed in a shirtwaist and skirt of drab color and coarse material, Stein settled herself in a thronelike chair specially built to accommodate her considerable girth. She looked, Anita thought, "like a monumental, sexless Buddha." Wanting to say something complimentary to her hostess, Anita mentioned how much Sherwood Anderson had appreciated *Tender Buttons.* Stein was not fooled by this subterfuge: "*He,* of course, understands," she replied.

When Alice B. Toklas came into the room, Anita felt more at ease. They were scaled to the same dimension, and Anita found Miss Toklas "cute." No one else has ever described Stein's devoted companion quite that way, and certainly no one besides Anita felt Toklas's femininity enhanced by the wispy mustache she fingered caressingly whenever she spoke. Perhaps Anita said this with tongue in cheek; more likely, though not particularly sympathetic to Stein, she was able to see Toklas through Stein's eyes.

Anita was asked back several times, but on each occasion Stein's greeting was less warm, until Anita couldn't fail to recognize she wasn't welcome on the rue de Fleurus. Not until years later did she understand why. Stein had discovered a letter from Toklas to Anita filled with too many endearments for her liking. The letter was never posted, and it wasn't until Stein's death that Toklas revealed why her friend took such a sudden aversion to Miss Loos.

While in Paris, Anita visited another expatriate ménage, not as celebrated as the rue de Fleurus apartment but fascinating all the same. One of the hostesses was the massively built Elisabeth Marbury, a highly regarded theatrical agent. Having entered the business when European authors were customarily robbed of their American royalties, she managed single-handedly to bring order and honor into a previously chaotic and corrupt system. In time she became American representative for Europe's leading dramatists and then European representative for their American counterparts. Basically a colorless and conventional woman, Marbury nonetheless earned the respect and affection of all her writers, among whom the Emersons were eventually included.

Elsie de Wolfe, Marbury's birdlike friend, had a history out of an Edith Wharton novel. Born to a New York family with more social standing than wealth, she was educated abroad and presented at the Court of St. James's; and then, when the money ran out and the invitations for Newport weekends diminished, she went on the stage. Untalented and not outstandingly beautiful, she got by on presence and sheer determination.

Elsie and Bessie set up their first home in the Washington Irving house on East Seventeenth Street, which de Wolfe refurbished with such éclat that visitors begged her to brighten up their living rooms. Soon she left the stage to establish herself as one of the world's first interior decorators. Almost single-handedly, she banished Victorian gloom in favor of light, colorful fabrics and an atmosphere she called "primavernal."

Moving to France in 1901, she and Bessie bought a moldering house in Versailles for a modest price. Furnished with eighteenth-century antiques, the Villa Trianon was de Wolfe's grand obsession and masterpiece. Until the outbreak of World War II, the rich, talented, and notorious flocked to Elsie's intimate dinner parties and elaborate masked balls.

"Elsie wasn't admirable," Anita once said. "She was irresistible!" Well, maybe, but nothing written about de Wolfe has ever made her seem other than an egocentric harpy with a passion for chintz. The list of writers who failed to capture the quintessential Elsie includes Anita, who later wasted too much energy on a play about de Wolfe and the Villa Trianon.

W H A T E V E R Paris had to offer that summer, Anita tried to experience. For a dedicated observer like herself, everyone—whether as titanic as Miss Stein or as ineffable as Miss de Wolfe—was of interest; everything—whether the Louvre or the swank boutiques on the rue de Rivoli—was a source of fascination. Nothing was overlooked, certainly not the city's glittering nightlife.

Paris was invaded by South American playboys that particular year. Around midnight, they glided arrogantly into the Montmartre clubs, teeth glistening like Valentino's in *The Four Horsemen of the Apocalypse*, redolent of sex and expensive scent. Overhearing that Anita worked for the movies, they asked if she knew Rudy. Yes, they had met. Had she tangoed with him? No, she sighed, she didn't know the tango. Would she care to learn? ¡*Por favor!* The gauchos also let her in on the secret of their alluring fragrance: they were all fond of a cologne called Carnaval de Venise. Anita went out and bought two bottles the next day.

When the *boîtes* closed, Anita and her crowd went on partying at Le Jardin de ma soeur, an after-hours club owned by the Irish-born couturier Edward Molyneux. Entertainment was provided by Elsa Maxwell, one of those buffoonish gadabouts who gave the international highlife of the twenties and thirties much of its distinctive flavor. It didn't take Elsa long to insinuate herself into a position of favor with Anita's entourage.

Short, stout, and as jowly as an English bulldog, Maxwell was blessed with little except a small talent for music. She had started her career in her native San Francisco playing piano in bars and movie houses, graduated to vaudeville, and came to Europe as accompanist to Marie Doro, a popular entertainer of the period. When the tour ended, Elsa decided to remain abroad. By then she had discovered a second knack: the rich were in constant search of diversion, and if they supplied the cash, she had the imagination to make things happen. Even while performing at Le Jardin de ma soeur, she was well on her way to becoming the mistress of the revels for the then-emerging café society.

Maxwell was often catty and opportunistic, as Anita knew from the start. But Anita always had a soft spot for hustlers clever enough to overcome their limitations: she gave Elsa credit for refusing to fade into a wallflower at the lavish party going on in Europe between the wars.

Toward the end of her Paris vacation, Anita was seeing Elsa in the afternoons as well as at the nightclub. Often they went for long walks, a form of exercise favored by Elsa's companion, an intelligent and very seductive Englishwoman, Dorothy Gordon Fellows, known to everyone as Dickie. Though devoted to each other, Elsa and Dickie squabbled constantly. Elsa disapproved of Dickie's flirtations with titled bachelors; Dickie disapproved of Elsa's opportunistic stunts. When on the outs with Elsa, Dickie plotted activities to make Maxwell appear foolish, and she found a willing collaborator in Anita.

One prank evolved out of the three women's promenades about Paris. Because of her weight and tiny feet, Elsa found walking a trial, and her companions had to snail along if she was to keep up with them. So when irritated by Elsa, Dickie started picking up the pace, Anita following her lead, while Maxwell, huffing and puffing, lagged far behind. Elsa imagined Dickie saying the most horrid things about her, but she couldn't catch up, and finally there was nothing to do but quit the race, hail a cab, and go home.

Elsa didn't hold these humiliations against Anita, and when it came time for the Emersons to leave Paris, she insisted that Molyneux host a farewell party at Le Jardin de ma soeur. By the close of the evening, everyone was sentimental and tipsy on champagne. Dickie said she'd miss their walks: when would Anita be returning to Paris?

Well, she and Mr. E. talked of returning every summer, but she couldn't be sure. Mr. E. made a habit of changing his mind.

9

Broadway
Transfer

O N   T H E I R   return from Europe, the Emersons wrote another screen-play for Dutch. Called *Polly of the Follies,* it had the wispiest of plots—something about a show girl so overwhelmed by stage fright that she realizes it's love, not stardom, she's really after—but it pleased Dutch's fans.

And Schenck liked it enough to offer Emerson and Loos a new five-year contract. Mr. E. declined: while they'd always be interested in working on an occasional Talmadge film, they didn't want any long-term commitments. He was kind of disenchanted with the picture business.

Off and on he had been feeling that way ever since he and Anita left California and settled in New York. Mr. E. then began developing strong political convictions. He was dismayed by the capitalistic complacency spreading through America and felt obligated to awaken the country to its duties. His father had been a mayor; maybe he too should run for public office. Anita tried to squelch that idea; the public life of a politician's wife wasn't for her. And while she was quick to point out that she "always respected John's opinions," her own political stance, if it can be said she had one, was skeptical. She voted Republican, but it was all "a crooked setup."

Emerson found an opportunity to act on his beliefs, although in an arena smaller than he had envisioned. In August 1919 Actors Equity went on strike and managed to close nearly all New York's legitimate theaters. Emerson volunteered his services and was placed in charge of public relations. He organized a huge rally at Columbus Circle and persuaded Pickford and Fairbanks to put in an appearance. They locked arms with their stage brethren and sang a parody of George Cohan's "Over There":

> So beware, have a care
>> Just be fair, on the square, everywhere
>>> For we are striking, yes, we are striking
>>>> And we won't be back till the managers are fair!

Cohan was enraged. A producer as well as a performer, on this occasion he was on the side of management.

Emerson's greatest effort was staging an all-star benefit at Madison Square Garden to raise funds for actors with no savings to tide them over the strike. As it was virtually the only show in town, the benefit was a huge success. After four weeks the producers surrendered unconditionally. Emerson's role in the victory was, Anita later said, "his finest hour"; and in gratitude for his contribution, the members of Equity chose him as their president a few years later.

Emerson's work in support of the foundation of Actors Equity was his greatest contribution to the American theater. Here he is shown with soprano Dorothy Jordan in a still publicizing the formation of Equity.

The strike left Mr. E. believing that the theater was where he belonged; so after finishing *Polly of the Follies,* he told Anita that they were going to transfer to Broadway. That she wasn't exactly thrilled about this idea or its results is implicit in her memoirs. None of the six plays she and Emerson wrote during the next nine years is given more than cursory attention; some aren't mentioned at all. But at the time, typically, she bowed to Mr. E.'s wishes.

In switching from movies to the stage, Emerson may have been unconsciously maneuvering himself into a position of power over Anita. Her efforts at playwriting were few and far in the past, while he considered himself "a man of the theater," much more knowledgeable about stage technique than she was. Anita thoroughly agreed—it wasn't a contest she cared much about winning. It was tacitly understood that while she would do most of the actual writing, Emerson would be at hand to provide guidance and editorial assistance. He would also, of course, receive co-authorship credit.

"I'm a storyteller," Anita once said. "That's my only gift as a writer. And I'm sure that's why I was successful in the early days of the movies, when plot was all that mattered. I didn't know how to do anything else, so when I started writing for the stage I just did what I had always done. Except I wrote a lot more dialogue and kept the action confined to one or two settings."

This was the heyday of the frivolous, lighthearted comedy, and Anita's maiden effort was very much in that vein. *The Whole Town's Talking* is the story of Chester Binney, an affable, boobish salesman in Toledo, Ohio. He wants to marry Ethel Simmons, his business partner's daughter; but Ethel, who's grown up at the movies, dreams about Valentino. To impress her, Chester invents a past for himself, inscribing the back of a movie queen's photograph with suggestive references to "happy, hectic Hollywood hours." Ethel is enraptured until the movie queen, Letty Lythe, arrives in Toledo on a personal appearance tour, accompanied by her brawny fiancé. The play ends with Chester winning a bare-fisted duel with the fiancé, thereby retaining Ethel's admiration.

In some ways Anita seems to be gazing over her past: the plot is reminiscent of *His Picture in the Papers,* her first film for Fairbanks, and the fisticuffs between Chester and Lythe's boy friend are perhaps drawn from memories of Coronado. Silent-film buffs will recognize that in name, Letty Lythe resembles Betty Blythe, a popular silent-screen siren, and *The Whole Town's Talking* is one of Anita's first satiric swipes at Hollywood.

With Grant Mitchell playing Chester and Emerson directing, the comedy opened at the Bijou Theatre on August 29, 1923. It got nice reviews and ran for 170 performances, at a time when 100 performances guaranteed box-office success.

S H O R T L Y after the opening, the Emersons moved to a small house on Gramercy Park, then as now one of the city's most civilized residential districts. All occupants received a key to the little fenced-in park at the center. On their first visit, Anita and Mr. E. were stared at so rudely that they never returned. Other theater people lived on the square, so their professional status wasn't the reason for the hostility. Perhaps, Anita decided, the neighbors thought Mr. E. was a cradle snatcher, maybe a white slaver. Bobbing her hair had taken years off her appearance, and though she had recently celebrated her thirty-fifth birthday, with a bow perched on her head she could still pass for sixteen. Mr. E., on the other hand, was—and looked—forty-nine.

Once settled in their new home, Emerson approached Anita with a revised schedule for their life together. Every Tuesday evening they were to go their separate ways, a weekly respite from marriage observed in the better households. This way they'd keep the bloom on their romance.

Anita was distressed at first, but Emerson's assurance that he would return with renewed vigor was comforting. So she let Mr. E. have his way, though gossips reported that each Tuesday he was in the front row at a Broadway show with a young lady as his companion, usually a different girl each week. Once again, Anita chose to dismiss this as nothing more than innocent flirtation. Possibly she had come to suspect that husbands always fooled around, and that there was nothing a wife could do but accept the inevitable with as little fuss as possible. That was the way Minnie had handled R. Beers's indiscretions; it was the way Beth Fairbanks had treated Doug. These were perhaps not the happiest examples she might have chosen, but she knew lots of women who kept the situation in hand by looking the other way.

Left to her own devices every Tuesday, Anita started entertaining her girl friends, a clique that included the Talmadge sisters and Mama Peg, Marion Davies, Marilyn Miller, Adele Astaire, and an assortment of chorus girls kept by prominent gentlemen. The faces changed according to which of the Broadway and Park Avenue recruits happened to be free that particular evening, and in time "the Tuesday Widows" rotated their "cat parties" among their various homes and love nests. "Toujours gai" was the motto; the atmosphere was heightened, Anita wrote, "only by youthful high spirits, giggling, gossip, soft drinks, or, at most, the type of sweet concoctions that are mildly flavored with gin."

Anita heard and learned much at these soirées that would influence her later writing. "Unconsciously I was taking the measure of all these delectable ladies," she wrote, "and I found them contrary to my expectations." Beautiful women were supposed to be bitches, but these Aphrodites "had an unusual kindness towards each other."

They shared the common bond of "being mauled by practically every man they [met]." Men made "absolutely appalling declarations in words of four letters," especially to "the more opulent type of show girl," who consequently developed "an almost apologetic sense of being a freak of nature." Their biggest gripe was that their protectors regarded a mistress only as a means of calling attention to themselves. Bedding one of these beauties bolstered their status with their peers. It was, Anita concluded, "the ultimate form of male vanity."

But sometimes a girl needed an escort, particularly if she was going to Harlem, one of the Tuesday Widows' favorite hangouts. "It was the gayest place this country ever produced," Anita once said. "Every window had a gramophone in it, blaring out on the street. People were dancing in alleys, hanging out of windows, singing."

It was here she learned to dance the Charleston the way it should be done, not the watered-down version performed on Broadway. Going to Harlem deepened her admiration for blacks and their culture. They were more in step with the realities of life and had a natural talent for enjoying themselves which had been withheld from whites. Over the years Anita tried to come up with a project for Josephine Baker or Lena Horne or Diana Ross; and near the end of her life, she talked of a black version of *Blondes* to be called *Gentlemen Prefer Bronze,* with Flip Wilson as Dorothy Shaw.

S O M E Tuesdays she forsook both Harlem and her girl friends to spend the evening with H. L. Mencken. Ever since reading his articles in *The Smart Set,* she had been a confirmed Menckenite. His diatribes against American philistinism struck a responsive chord and very possibly sharpened her own attitude toward "the booboisie." When they finally met, she was delighted that he was everything she hoped he'd be: "a gifted monologuist" ready to improvise on themes ranging from Emily Post to Emily Dickinson,

Abie's Irish Rose to Rosa Luxemburg; and yet, unlike so many monologuists, he was also "a receptive listener."

One thing she couldn't understand was why he chose to live in Baltimore instead of Manhattan. Mencken's answer was a polemic against "the glittering swinishness of New York," which forced "its people . . . to rid themselves of the oldest and most powerful instinct, the love of home." Baltimore, he added on a more practical note, kept him in touch with the foibles and inanities of the American booboisie, supplying him with material for his articles. Anita thought this was perhaps too great a sacrifice for art.

Faithful to his love of all things Teutonic, from sauerbraten to Schumann, Mencken sought out German hangouts when in New York. His favorites were Lüchow's on Fourteenth Street and a rathskeller in Union City where, he claimed, the beer was piped in direct from Munich.

They were rarely alone. Mencken had an entourage that included theater critic George Jean Nathan, essayist Ernest Boyd, popular novelist Joseph Hergesheimer, Theodore Dreiser, Sherwood Anderson, Sinclair Lewis: book-review stars, every one of them, yet there was nothing Round Table-ish about these gatherings. Writing about Mencken's Union City hideaway in *But Gentlemen Marry Brunettes*, Anita said: "They [the authors] did not even mention their literary work. And nobody could have heard them if they had, because they kept putting nickels in an electric piano and breaking into [risqué] songs."

Yet beneath the all-male harmony, there was enough quiet for Anita and Menck to touch each other in some way that Anita never described as love. In her memoirs, she speaks of her "depth of feeling for Menck" and quotes from his letters to show he was not unresponsive: "I can imagine nothing more lovely than seeing you again and kissing your hands"; "Are you in New York? I crave the boon of witnessing you." There's a mocking Galahadism in Mencken's mash notes, but the mockery doesn't necessarily imply that this knight was insincere. Perhaps Mencken was secretly too conventional to cross the boundary between chivalry and adultery.

If he had, would Anita have welcomed him? Probably not—she was, she claimed, still very much in love with Emerson. And yet Mencken must have provided something Emerson wasn't supplying. Anita was gradually growing aware of Emerson's shortcomings: he wasn't as smart as she was; he was restricted in his range of intellectual curiosity. And for a *cérébrale* like Anita, who thought the sexiest part of a man was his brain, he must have shriveled in comparison with Mencken.

High-IQ gentlemen didn't fall for bright women, she realized. Just the opposite—Mencken, among others she could mention, fell for girls with lots downstairs but nothing in the attic but cobwebs. Kierkegaard, Lamarckian evolution, Madame Blavatsky and the Theosophists—all these the gentlemen could analyze or annihilate in a single paragraph; so why did they search for mysteries in their mistresses, waste hours evaluating their allure? As far as Anita could see, what they had to offer was conspicuous.

That it wasn't that simple she realized when she got around to investigating the mystique of these jazz-age Circes. Probably she wouldn't have put her mind to it if in the spring of 1924 Emerson hadn't sent her to California for another Dutch Talmadge picture. Anita didn't want to leave New York and Mencken, but Emerson explained that Wall Street was sluggish and soon they might be strapped for money.

O N   T H E train to the West Coast in March 1924, Anita began to write *Gentlemen Prefer Blondes.* Over the years she gave several accounts of its genesis, each differing as to specific detail, though the gist was always the same. In one version, she is traveling by herself; in a second, she runs into Douglas Fairbanks and a party of friends. Alone or with Doug, she meets a blond cutie who is either the lady friend of a Supreme Court justice or one of Mencken's playmates. If she belongs to Mencken, as she does in most accounts, her name is either Mae Davis or Mae Clarke, always identified as an actress. Miss Clarke, best remembered for getting a grapefruit squashed in her face in *Public Enemy,* insists that she was not Anita's model. She did meet Anita on a train, but not until several years later; in 1924, she was only fourteen and had never heard of Mencken. As for Mae Davis, no actress by that name is mentioned in any film or stage encyclopedia.

Whoever she may have been, the blonde inspired Anita to write the history of the kind of girl protected by Mencken and his fraternity, as that girl herself might describe it in her diary, grammatical errors and all. With nothing to occupy her mind, Anita got out her pad and started jotting down notes. It might amuse Mencken—if she decided to show it to him. Long before reaching Los Angeles, she had finished her sketch and shoved it into her luggage, forgetting about it once she started her script for Dutch Talmadge.

• • •

IN CALIFORNIA, she was happy to find her mother and father living in close harmony. R. Beers's behavior was still occasionally erratic, but his escapades were no longer of a romantic nature; and toward Minnie, growing absentminded with age, he was touchingly solicitous.

Anita felt that Hollywood too had grown and changed, though not for the better. There was an aura of pretension wafting about, much of it emanating from Pickfair, the Beverly Hills mansion Doug had bought for Mary after their marriage in 1920.

The Fairbankses invited her for dinner, and she accepted, mainly to find out if the gossip she had been hearing was true. Supposedly, Mary and especially Doug were so puffed up with prestige that they actually believed they were what a press agent had dubbed them, "America's ambassadors to the world." The turning point was the king of Siam's visit to Pickfair. Since then, Anita was told, Doug's favorite bedtime reading was *Burke's Peerage*.

Sure enough, the other Pickfair dinner guests included a maharajah and two British gentlemen with minor titles. The table glittered with gold dishes, and there were so many knives and forks that even Emily Post might have lost her bearings. But the conversation was tin plate, and Anita withdrew into herself, wishing she was in Union City with a stein of beer.

Mae Clarke (here with James Cagney in a still from *Public Enemy,* 1931) was one of Anita's models for Lorelei Lee in *Gentlemen Prefer Blondes.*

Minnie Loos, Anita's mother, in the late 1920s

• • •

BACK in New York, Anita quickly finished *The Fall of Eve,* a stage comedy about a suspicious wife who in turn is suspected of infidelity. With Emerson as producer and director, the show opened in Washington in the spring of 1925. Ruth Gordon, then on the verge of stardom, played Eve.

Gordon had a lot of offers that season; and to get her, Emerson offered a lavish contract: $500 a week for the first year, escalating to $2,000 when the play celebrated its third anniversary. The four-figure salary was so dazzling that she forgot that few plays had ever run that long. Emerson had pulled a fast one, Gordon later realized. She would have been smarter to ask for more at the start and let the future take care of itself.

The out-of-town response to *Eve* was favorable, but Anita and Mr. E. decided to delay the Broadway opening until the fall. They weren't happy with the actor who played Eve's husband, and both felt the script needed reworking.

That summer the Emersons spent a few weeks in London and Paris, where they met Ruth Gordon, also on a European holiday. Mr. E. turned her presence to his advantage, urging the two women to spend the day shopping while he prowled the boulevards. They should look for gowns for *Eve*—Gordon's costumes in the tryout lacked essential chic.

They went to all the smart shops, Gordon recalled, and Anita unerringly spotted the "swellest" dress on display. Best of the lot was a *robe de soirée,* black chiffon studded with tiny diamanté spangles. Anita ordered two: one for the play, one for herself, provided it came in dark blue. Black was more dramatic, Gordon advised. "Yes," Anita said, "but Mr. E. doesn't like me in black."

How much Anita deferred to John was not fully evident to Gordon until she saw the revisions for *Eve.* "What had been pretty good was now not so good," Gordon recalled. The revisions were made by Emerson, and Gordon gently requested that Anita revise the revisions. "Oh, no!" Anita gasped. "I couldn't! Mr. E. is the expert on the theater."

Just before *Eve* went back into rehearsal, the Emersons took Gordon to Asbury Park, New Jersey. One of the stars of the local stock company had been recommended as the leading man for the show, and they wanted her opinion about his abilities. After the afternoon performance, they started back to New York, Mr. E. driving so slowly that it was pitch dark before they were halfway home. Suddenly there was a fork in the road, but Emerson went straight ahead, ending up in a corn field. For a moment no one spoke. Then Anita sighed. "Oh, Mr. E.! You never think of anyone but yourself!"

Ruth Gordon in 1925, in a snapshot taken by Anita on an outing to Rye, New York. During this time Ruth Gordon was appearing in Anita's play, *The Fall of Eve.*

Ruth Gordon was startled. "Anita's comment wasn't very appropriate," she remembered thinking, "but it sure covered a *lot* of ground!"

T H E "not so good" version of *Eve* opened on August 31, 1925, and got terrible reviews. "They hated the show, they hated me, I think they even hated the theater we were playing in," Gordon recalled.

The next morning she dropped by the Gramercy Park house to console and be consoled and, to her surprise, found that Anita was chipper and taking it all in stride—as was her secretary, who brought in a new batch of reviews. "Look at these," she said. "They're wonderful!"

"Is the girl crazy?" Gordon asked. "I've read them and they're worse than the earlier ones."

"Well," Anita replied, "she thinks it's wonderful that Mr. E. and I get our names in all the papers."

Anita never allowed adverse criticism to get her down, just as she never let adulation go to her head. It was all part of the game, and whichever side of the coin came up, it served to keep your name and picture in the papers. The important thing was to get on with your work.

When *Eve* closed after forty-eight performances, Anita was already close to finishing another stage project and looking forward to publication of her first book, *Gentlemen Prefer Blondes*, the novel that had grown out of her sketch about Mencken and his vacant lady friends. Printed earlier in *Harper's Bazaar*, it had attracted the attention of a prominent publisher who was now issuing it in a hardcover edition.

The first printing was small, and Anita didn't expect it to make much of a stir, but here she miscalculated. To paraphrase Lorelei Lee, her heroine, fate was just about to start happening.

10

Diary of a
Professional Lady

*T*HE STORY behind the publication of *Blondes* begins with Anita
unpacking her bags on returning from California in early 1925. In
the flap of a suitcase she discovered the sketch she had written on the train
and since forgotten; reading it over, she decided that Mencken might get a
laugh out of it, put it in an envelope, and mailed it to Baltimore.

What Anita had written was a short story in diary form. In the first
entry, dated March 16 (no year), the heroine (who has no name) explains
that the diary was a present from a United States senator so impressed by
her mind that he wants to see her thoughts on paper. Thinking is her
"favorite recreation"; often she sits for hours "doing nothing but think."

In later entries, the diarist delves into personal history. She worked in
Hollywood, appearing in *Intolerance* "as one of the girls that fainted at the
battle when all of the gentlemen fell off the tower." Then she encountered
Gus Eisman, "the Button King of Chicago," who has established her in a
love nest and encourages her to "improve her mind." Improving her mind
and collecting expensive baubles are the girl's favorite hobbies. At times
she regrets abandoning her movie career, but Mr. Eisman is an indulgent
protector, preferring to live in his hometown; and he doesn't mind his
friend seeing other gentlemen during his absences, as long as they encourage her pursuit of higher knowledge.

She meets unhappily married British novelist Gerald Lamson, who
is so dazzled by such philosophical aperçus as "Bird life is the highest

form of civilization" that he proposes marriage. Gus Eisman advises her against becoming a co-respondent and promises her a trip to Europe if she rejects Lamson's proposal. As travel is known to broaden the mind, and as Mr. Eisman won't be accompanying her, she agrees. The story ends as she and a companion, a Ziegfeld girl named Dorothy Shaw, board the *Majestic* for England.

Mencken's reaction was more than Anita anticipated: not only did he laugh, he insisted the piece be published. Placing it might be tricky, though, he warned, since no previous American author had poked fun at sex, and few magazines dared print anything controversial. *Vanity Fair* seemed out; Frank Crowninshield's Boston heritage made him shy of anything risqué. The best bet was *Harper's Bazaar,* a glossy fashion magazine which sometimes published good fiction.

Henry Sell, *Bazaar*'s editor, not only accepted Anita's story but urged her to go on with her heroine's adventures. So she wrote a second installment in which her heroine gets a name and a birthplace. She calls herself Lorelei Lee "after the girl who became famous for sitting on a rock in Germany" and was born in Little Rock, Arkansas, the capital of Mencken's "Sahara of the Bozarts."

In her own semiliterate brand of stream of consciousness, Lorelei goes on to divulge a little more personal history. While bettering herself at a Little Rock business school, she formed an attachment with a gentleman who turned out to be a cad. Catching him with another woman, she shot him. An all-male jury absolved her of guilt, and the judge became her first protector.

Chapter 3 opens in London—"nothing much" compared with New York. British gentlemen offer their lady friends "bangles" instead of jewels, but Lorelei manages to wheedle a diamond tiara out of Sir Francis Beekman. Then she flees London and the wrath of Lady Beekman, a Gorgonian dowager who might intimidate Oscar Wilde's Lady Bracknell.

"Paris is devine": so begins chapter 4. Lorelei has crossed the Channel but hasn't escaped the clutches of Lady Beekman, who hires lawyers to retrieve the tiara. Lorelei escapes to Vienna, where she visits Sigmund Freud (who advises her to cultivate a few neuroses) and embarks on a romance with Henry Spoffard, a Philadelphia millionaire she met on the train to Austria.

The final chapter brings Lorelei back to America. Spoffard has proposed, but she wavers. He's overly devoted to his senile and randy father, his gaga mother, and a sister who reeks of stables and gasoline. Only when Spoffard agrees to sponsor her career in films does she resign herself to marriage.

Long before this final episode appeared in *Bazaar* in August 1925, it was clear that the Lorelei stories were a huge success. The magazine's circulation jumped month by month, and ads for masculine products poured in as advertisers learned men were reading a publication aimed at their wives and mistresses.

From the outset Anita was urged to publish the Lorelei stories as a book, but she dismissed the idea as presumptuous until Mencken told her to go ahead. She talked to a few publishers, finally signing with Liveright, partly because a close friend, Tommy Smith, was editor in chief and partly because of Liveright's reputation. In 1925, the year of *Gentlemen Prefer Blondes*, the company also published Dreiser's *An American Tragedy;* Hemingway's *In Our Time;* Faulkner's *Soldier's Pay;* Scott-Moncrieff's translations of Stendhal; poetry by Eliot, Pound, and Robinson Jeffers; and nonfiction by Lewis Mumford, Hendrik van Loon, and Sigmund Spaeth. It was, wrote one critic at the time, "the most notable list ever released by an American publishing house."

Tommy Smith had definite ideas about presenting *Blondes.* Since the material had already been widely read in *Bazaar,* there might be only a small audience for a book edition, though a second printing could be brought out quickly "by popular demand." It would be handsomely bound, printed on quality paper, and would include the original *Bazaar* illustrations by Ralph Barton. Designed as a deluxe gift item, it was priced at $1.75, about twenty-five to fifty cents more than the average book of that size (217 pages). "You can always hand them out as Christmas presents," he joked. Anita laughed and always referred to the original *Blondes* as a "vanity edition."

Blondes first appeared in bookshops in early November 1925 and sold out overnight. Two weeks later a second printing of 20,000 went so quickly that two more printings were released before the end of the year. By March of 1926 a ninth edition came out, followed by ten more during the next three years.

The first edition sold out without the benefits of reviews, which when they appeared (about the time of the second edition) were surprisingly bland in their praise: "side-splittingly funny"; "droll and merry"; "sly and sophisticated." One of the more perceptive reviews appeared in *The New York Times* and was written by Herman J. Mankiewicz, the paper's second-string theater critic. (Today he is best remembered as co-author of the *Citizen Kane* screenplay.) "Miss Loos's book," he wrote, "is civilized, human, ironic and never crude in its effect."

There was some minor carping. The critic for the *Boston Transcript*

"Kissing your hand may make you feel very good but a diamond bracelet lasts forever."

"Gentlemen Prefer Blondes"

The Illuminating Diary of a
Professional Lady

By

Anita Loos

Intimately Illustrated by
RALPH BARTON

NEW YORK
BONI & LIVERIGHT
1925

ABOVE AND OPPOSITE: Ralph Barton illustration and title
page from an original edition of *Gents,* first published in 1925

apparently felt that *Blondes* was not for all female readers when he
qualified his praise by saying "this is a book that will make any man and
most women roar with laughter not once but fifty times." And Ruth
Goodman in the *New York Tribune* resented "Miss Loos's straining for
misspelled words for comedy."

Blondes didn't need critical praise to become the surprise best-seller
of 1925. It was one of those books that sold itself through word of mouth,
and the word was good along every avenue of American life. Lorelei's
diary made a hit with those who read nothing but light fiction as well as
with James Joyce, whose failing eyesight made him highly selective about
what he read. Anita was told that her book was one of the few he chose
from the list of current fiction.

Blondes was enthusiastically endorsed by the literati. Anita received
notes of appreciation from William Faulkner and Aldous Huxley; novelist,
photographer, and music critic Carl Van Vechten proclaimed the book
"a work of art." And George Santayana (dismissed by Anita in her book on
philosophers as an archpessimist) praised *Blondes* only half-jestingly as
"a great work of philosophy."

What part of the collective international consciousness had Anita
tickled to arouse such a response? Mencken was on the right track when he
said that she was the first American to make fun of sex, though it wasn't so
dangerous a sport as he imagined. After the First World War, America
started casting off its puritan shackles, and by 1925 the country was
disposed to laugh at institutions and moral virtues once held sacrosanct.
And while many of the pieties Anita touches on in her book had been
questioned and condemned by earlier American writers, she was among
the first to make light of them.

In her view sex had almost nothing to do with romantic love ("love"
is a word rarely, if ever, mentioned in the text) and practically everything
to do with acquisition. This is a reflection of what she had learned at the
parties held by the Tuesday Widows. Lorelei's gentlemen want to possess
her for much the same reason she wants to possess diamonds: she bolsters
their egos just as the jewels enhance her self-esteem. The jewels are not—as
some commentators have suggested—an insurance policy against old age:
mentally, Lorelei is too myopic to see beyond the day after tomorrow.

She is also perhaps the first courtesan in the history of literature who
is not aware of being *déclassée,* who genuinely believes herself the equal,
if not the superior, of any woman who crosses her path. (This is, of course,
the reason for Freud's failure with Lorelei—she is so well adjusted that she
invalidates his theories about the discontents of modern society.)

Men offer marriage, and Lorelei leads them on, though she's not eager to legitimize herself. Experience has taught her that men shower gifts on women other than their wives. Henry Spoffard may be richer than the Biddles and the Warburtons, but when Lorelei realizes she could be trapped in Philadelphia with only loony in-laws for company, she tries to maneuver him into a breach-of-promise situation and changes her mind only after he promises to take her to Hollywood.

Families never fared well in Anita's writings, and the Spoffards are possibly the worst of the lot. They are a double target representing both the family unit and also the top echelon of American society (just as Lord and Lady Beekman are emblematic of British nobility). Money, Anita seems to be saying, is in the hands of those too simple-minded (the Spoffards) or too rigid (the Beekmans) to enjoy it. Wealth should be bestowed on people like Lorelei, who know how to spend it.

Much of *Blondes*'s humor stems from a simple, time-honored comic inversion. Lorelei is a kept woman and a murderess, but she is also more dignified and far shrewder than any of the well-born or gainfully employed characters who surround her. Her sense of propriety forbids her from uttering or writing a profanity, and her diary is free of allusions to sexual intimacy. Though *Blondes* quickly gained a reputation for being suggestive, it is perhaps the cleanest exposé of illicit romance ever written.

If Lorelei has any literary ancestor, it is that other famous connoisseur of diamonds, Cunegonde in Voltaire's *Candide,* who is gang-raped by Bulgarian soldiers, has her belly slit, and loses half of her buttocks and yet manages to retain an aura of innocence. "A lady of honor may be raped once," she explains, "but it strengthens her virtue." Lorelei, like Cunegonde, manages to maintain her illusion of purity against all odds—it is both her shield and her sword, protecting her and disarming others.

Anita isn't moralistic about Lorelei. She doesn't punish her for her venality, as Balzac punished Esther Gosbeck and Mme Marneffe. And she isn't sentimental, either. Clearly Lorelei doesn't belong to that romantic tradition which presents the courtesan as a languorous lost soul like Marguerite Gautier or Manon Lescaut. Nor does she belong to the later, naturalistic school in which the fallen woman is a victim of society and environment. Some commentators have spoken of her as though she were a cousin of Zola's Nana or Dreiser's Sister Carrie, women brought low by male lust who turn that lust to their own advantage (at least temporarily). Though this analysis is not entirely invalid, it is too doctrinaire to fit a work so slyly subversive. Not only does it rob the book of its gaiety, it also misrepresents the way Lorelei sees herself. In her own eyes, she is not a victim but one of the elect in whom Fate takes a special interest.

Much of what is elegant and endearing about *Blondes* stems from the modesty of its design and the perfection with which that design is executed. As Edith Hamilton would write nearly forty years after its publication, "[*Blondes* is a] book of balance and proportion . . . Anita Loos does not bring an indictment against the universe in the person of Lorelei. She knows how to laugh, and that knowledge is the very best preservative there is against losing the true perspective . . . Without a sense of humor one must keep hands off the universe unless one is prepared to be oneself an unconscious addition to the sum of the ridiculous."

S H O R T L Y after the publication of *Blondes,* Anita was asked a question she was to hear too many times over five decades: Who were the models for Lorelei and her circle of friends? Tactfully and not untruthfully, Anita said that the characters were composite portraits, though occasionally in private conversation, she would be more expansive.

Sir Francis Beekman was based on both novelist Joseph Hergesheimer and movie mogul Jesse Lasky, "shameless flirts . . . big pussycats who purred but never pounced." Henry Spoffard and his family resembled a prominent Philadelphia family who vacationed on Coronado Island, though Anita took some liberties in drawing Henry: "I advanced his mental status," she said, "by making him a halfwit."

As for Dorothy Shaw, she was, Anita said time and again, pretty much a self-portrait. They were both girls who liked laughter more than jewels. Beyond that, though, the resemblance was faint; Dorothy owed a lot to Connie Talmadge and other members of the Tuesday Widow sorority.

Lorelei Lee was also a mosaic pieced together from remembrances of the many soiled lilies Anita had met in Hollywood and on Broadway. Heading the list was Lillian Lorraine, the most celebrated of Ziegfeld showgirls. Lillian was fond of all things sterling, forty-carat, or unflawed, and she collected so many trinkets that when forced to sell the lot at the height of the Depression, she pocketed over two hundred thousand dollars. Like her monogram twin, Lillian Lorraine was thrilled to discover new places to display diamonds: Lorelei is enchanted when she discovers the tiara, while Lorraine introduced the diamond ankle bracelet to New York.

Like Lorelei, Lillian had no sympathy for skinflint millionaires. As a lesson to one suitor who gave less than he received, she sent orchids to herself, specifying that they be delivered a few minutes after his carefully established arrival time. "How sweet!" she exclaimed. "Only you could send something so *evanescent!*" Lorraine's benefactor got the point, as does Sir Francis Beekman when Lorelei uses much the same ruse in *Blondes*.

Among the other women who contributed to the portrait of Lorelei are two who would seem to have little in common with the Little Rock siren. Lorelei's dippiest comments—"Bird life is the highest form of civilization," for instance—were, Anita said, direct transcriptions of sentiments uttered by Lillian Gish. And Lorelei's allegiance to Christian Science is certainly a dig at Mary Pickford, who embraced that faith after abandoning Catholicism to marry Doug Fairbanks.

Readers thought that the key to Lorelei's identity could be found in Ralph Barton's illustrations. Barton said that he really had had no one

Anita, Aileen Pringle, and H. L. Mencken (far right) greet Joseph Hergesheimer on his arrival in Los Angeles in 1925. Hergesheimer was one of the models for the character of Sir Francis Beekman in *Gentlemen Prefer Blondes*. Actress Aileen Pringle was proof that Mencken didn't always prefer blondes.

specific in mind, though occasionally as he worked he thought of his friend, film star Aileen Pringle. Miss Pringle was aghast at being identified with Lorelei. They had nothing in common—she was a brunette and had never set eyes on Miss Loos. But that changed when Mencken, belying the title of the book his sexual preferences had inspired, started squiring the raven-tressed Pringle. The ladies then met, but they were not destined to be bosom buddies.

M R. E. was ambivalent about *Blondes*. Though pleased when the stories appeared in *Bazaar,* he was against their publication in book format. And Frank Crowninshield agreed that a hardcover edition could damage Anita's reputation. "Darling Nita," Crowninshield told a mutual friend, "I do love her, but I wish she hadn't written that naughty book!" Tommy Smith dismissed Crowninshield's and Emerson's objections with what seemed to be irrefutable logic: as the Liveright edition of *Blondes* was to be small, it could hardly dent Anita's reputation in a big way. He then added that only a Boston Brahmin like Crowninshield could find *Blondes* salacious.

Having lost that round, Emerson shifted ground for the next. Since Anita had received solo credit in *Bazaar,* he couldn't request his usual co-authorship acknowledgment at this late date; instead he asked for a dedication that implied Anita hadn't done it all on her own. Lest she forget the phrasing, he typed out the sentiment in uppercase letters: "TO JOHN EMERSON, EXCEPT FOR WHOSE ENCOURAGEMENT AND GUIDANCE THIS BOOK WOULD NEVER HAVE BEEN WRITTEN." Tommy Smith looked it over and decided some blue-penciling was needed. His version read: "TO JOHN EMERSON." Emerson accepted the emendation without fuss, surprising since his actions—first trying to suppress publication, then attempting to edge his way into a place of prominence—suggest he realized *Blondes* might be a threat to his control of the Loos-Emerson teamship. What he could not have foreseen was how great a triumph *Blondes* was to be, how much acclaim was about to be heaped on his wife, who he probably sincerely believed owed everything to him.

11

Stage Whispers

GENTLEMEN PREFER BLONDES was quickly picked up by European publishers, and its success abroad was as great as at home. It made its author an international celebrity and a rich woman — by her own calculation, she earned over a million dollars by the end of the decade. She was now in the agreeable position of being able to live off royalties, and in her memoirs she claimed that this is precisely what she did. "In 1926," she wrote, "I'd given up writing to live a private life with the husband I adored."

This is misleading on several counts. Her period of semiretirement did not start until close to the end of 1926, and it was forced on her, not freely chosen. For most of the year after *Blondes* she worked continuously and often overlappingly on three lengthy projects as well as on several shorter pieces for magazines and newspapers. Part of this activity was due to commitments made prior to the book publication of *Blondes*. She had agreed to write another novella for *Harper's Bazaar,* and the first of three installments appeared in the January 1926 issue. Called *Why Girls Go South,* and written almost entirely in dialogue, it is the story of a not-too-bright society girl who has to find either a career or a rich husband to bolster her family's dwindling income. It was popular with *Bazaar* readers, and while broad and unfocused, its depiction of the underside of jazz-age frivolity makes it one of the more fascinating of Anita's occasional pieces. There is more acid here than Anita usually permitted herself—more, in fact, than the framework of the story can stand.

Simultaneously she was working on what never was intended as more than a potboiler, a musical version of *The Whole Town's Talking* called *Pair o' Fools.* This was commissioned by C. William Kolb and Max W. Dill, a team of German-dialect comics with a big following in the Midwest and on the Pacific coast. The musical opened in San Francisco in January 1926 and had a long and profitable run on the road, but it never opened in New York: Kolb and Dill knew their limitations.

Even before the Liveright publication of *Blondes,* producers started bidding for the stage rights, and Anita recklessly accepted the most attractive of the early offers. This she regretted when she learned that Ziegfeld wanted the book for a musical, possibly with a Jerome Kern score. There was some consolation in knowing that her producer, Edgar Selwyn, was sensitive and professionally astute. Though he had written several successful plays, he asked Anita to prepare the adaptation, which she completed by spring of 1926. The play went into rehearsal almost immediately and opened a few weeks later in Chicago for a lengthy engagement.

Originally Emerson wanted to stage *Blondes,* but he withdrew because of poor health. It started with a case of severe laryngitis. Anita ordered him to bed, supplied pencil and pad, and told him to rest quietly. When his whispering got worse, she consulted a specialist and followed his instructions faithfully, but nothing helped. Each day Mr. E.'s voice got fainter, and Anita began to fear he might have cancer.

Finally Emerson went to see America's foremost throat specialist in Philadelphia. After a thorough examination, the doctor gave Anita his diagnosis. "There's nothing wrong with your husband's throat," he said. "His problem is some sort of neurosis that can be brought to light through psychotherapy." He recommended that they see New York's leading psychiatrist, Alfred Jelliffe.

Jelliffe confirmed the earlier diagnosis. He prefaced his remarks by quoting one of Anita's favorite authors: "H. L. Mencken once wrote," Jelliffe said, "that a husband may survive the fact that his wife has more money than he, but if she *earns* more, it can destroy his very essence." Suffering from the success of *Blondes,* Mr. E. had invented a disease as a means of attracting attention. "The only cure for your husband," Jelliffe concluded, "is for you to give up your career."

Surely a less drastic treatment might have been tried, but Anita sought no second opinion: she accepted Jelliffe's evaluation as final. She was responsible, and therefore obligated to undo the terrible wrong she had unwittingly done Mr. E.

Over forty years later, in a chapter of her second memoir, *Kiss Hollywood Good-by,* titled "Sex Can Make a Dunce of You," Anita wrote: "My own experience in sex turned a strong-willed character I had adored into a sick man. If only we'd remained sympathetic co-workers without the complication of marriage, no stranger would ever have addressed Mr. E. as 'Mr. Loos.' . . . " While the tone is bantering, it's clear that nearly half a century after the event, Anita still accepted responsibility for Emerson's decline into mental instability. And guilt was largely the source of the hold he maintained over her until his death.

She resolved to retire after her next book. A sequel to *Blondes,* it had been promised to both *Bazaar* and Liveright, and sections had already been written. She figured she could plug away at it when Mr. E. was out of the house, lunching at the Lambs Club or visiting the throat specialist he had chosen for himself, a wizard whose magic infusion had worked miracles for the great Caruso.

The Emersons were planning a lengthy European holiday, which Dr. Jelliffe felt would provide diversion for Mr. E. Anita went ahead with preparations, but at the last minute Emerson announced that business would detain him in New York for a few weeks. Bug was to go alone; he'd join her later. Anita knew that this was a fabrication, but she couldn't change his mind. On May 16, 1926, accompanied only by Yvette, her French maid, she boarded a Cunard liner for Southampton.

She reached London as the General Strike and its threat of Bolshevism had ended, and after all the anxiety and inconvenience the city was in need of fun and laughter. And what greater diversion could society hostesses offer guests than the author of *Blondes?* As her English publisher had informed the press of her visit, Anita found a packet of invitations waiting for her at the Savoy Hotel.

She was taken up by Sybil, Lady Colefax, one of the foremost hostesses of the day. Neither wealthy nor nobly born, and certainly not beautiful, Sybil was considered an *arriviste* by her more established rivals. Even close friends made fun of her celebrity hunting, but it was widely acknowledged that she was kindhearted, with a quick mind and a flair for spotting talent in the young. As well as being on a first-name basis with Max Beerbohm, Bernard Shaw, and Bernard Berenson, she was entertaining Noel Coward, John Gielgud, and Harold Nicolson before other hostesses were aware of their existence. Her drawing room was a favorite meeting place for those titled or moneyed pleasure seekers known as "the bright young things."

A frequent visitor to the Colefax drawing room was the Prince of Wales, later the duke of Windsor, who asked to meet Anita. She was apprehensive, as she had poked fun at his mother's bonnets in *Blondes*, but Sybil said not to worry—the prince adored the book. At their first meeting he complimented her on her "entrancing story" but found nothing else to say. As Anita was equally shy, his lack of conversation put an impasse to whatever friendship they might have had. Nor did she care much for the crown prince of the English theater, Noël Coward, "so bloated with conceit."

But in the Colefax den there were lions worth pursuing. One was novelist and playwright Arnold Bennett, more highly esteemed in 1926 than today. Anita met him shortly before she was to address a literary luncheon, an engagement she dreaded, as she knew little about public speaking. Bennett went to hear her and noted approvingly in his diary that she was "all right. As regards literature, she has given up imitating others (such as Flaubert) because she found she couldn't get her effects with a large vocabulary, but only with a small and very simple one. . . . She had read philosophy, but had given it up because she had found it didn't get her anywhere."

There were fleeting encounters with H. G. Wells, Somerset Maugham, and John Galsworthy and the start of a lasting friendship with Margot Asquith, the wife of a former prime minister, and her youngest son, Anthony, straddled with the Milne-esque nickname "Puffin." An aspiring film director, Puffin was planning a trip to Hollywood, and Anita gave him letters of introduction. She was constantly amazed by the British fascination with American filmmaking. At home, it counted for little, but abroad her experience with Griffith and Doug and Mary opened as many doors as *Blondes*.

Photographs of Anita in Europe started appearing in all the New York rotogravure sections, and several papers carried squibs about her hobnobbing with the London elite. Mr. E. looked and read and clutched his throat. Anita and he spoke two or three times a week, but his whispering was hard to catch over the transatlantic connection, so conversation was brief and, on her side, guarded as to how much she was enjoying herself.

Suddenly Emerson stopped phoning. She put through a call to New York and learned from the housekeeper that her husband was out of town. Two nights later, as she was dressing for the theater, the phone rang and there, just barely audible beneath the interference, was Mr. E. asking, "Well, Buggie, how does it feel to be world famous?" Without answering, Anita broke into sobs and slammed down the receiver. The rest of the evening she spent lying on a chaise longue in despair. She feared, she later wrote, that Mr. E. was "slipping away."

But two weeks later, when he at last arrived in London, he was in such high spirits that occasionally he forgot about his throat and spoke in natural tones. He made no allusions to his wife's success in London, though he seemed eager to push on to Paris. Before they could leave, however, there was one piece of pressing business. The London producer of *The Whole Town's Talking* was about to start rehearsals and had asked the Emersons to check out the actors' American accents.

To keep Mr. E. happy, Anita took him to the theater every night: Bankhead miscast in *They Knew What They Wanted,* Beatrice Lillie and Gertrude Lawrence in *Charlot's Revue,* Fred and Adele Astaire in *Lady, Be Good!* The last was the best occasion of all. Anita was not especially fond of Fred, but "Dellie" had been a pal for years. "Fred was always *so* proper, *so* correct," Anita once said, "while Dellie was irrepressible, buoyant, spontaneous. The difference between them was that Fred privately tried to teach the Prince of Wales to tap-dance while Dellie gave demonstrations of the Charleston in the London streets."

The Charleston was just beginning to alter the dance patterns of Europe, and every night outside the Leicester Square Empire stage door,

Adele Astaire and her husband Charles, Lord Cavendish during a holiday in the south of France, 1930s

crowds gathered, begging Adele to show them how it was done in Harlem. She obliged but seldom got far, since Fred quickly pushed her into a cab. But on the night the Emersons attended the show, she went through the whole routine, teasing Anita into joining in at the end. Anita feared that Emerson would disapprove, but instead he sang with the other bystanders. Instead of drifting further away, he appeared to be taking a new lease on life.

I N P A R I S, Anita had lunch with Edith Wharton who, a year earlier, after getting halfway through *Blondes,* had sent a postcard to Frank Crowninshield: "[I am] now reading the great American novel (at last!) and I want to know if there are—or will be—others and if you know the young woman, who must be a genius." Crowninshield sent the card to Anita with a covering note: "[Wharton] is getting very fussy and peculiar as she grows older, but still has a streak of humanity, kindness, humor, and love left in her." A great fan of *The House of Mirth,* Anita treasured Wharton's postcard.

She sent a thank-you note and Mrs. Wharton wrote back, asking her to promise to let her know whenever she was planning to visit France. While in London, Anita had announced her imminent arrival, and Wharton immediately replied, suggesting lunch at the Ritz. Their meeting was pleasant but quite formal, and no lasting friendship was to grow from it.

With this courtesy call out of the way, Anita settled down to enjoying Paris. There was a reunion with Elsa Maxwell and Dickie Gordon Fellows, who introduced her to Cole Porter, his wife, Linda, and their traveling companion, Howard Sturges. A nephew of George Santayana, Sturges had come to Paris to study the piano and stayed on to make a career of having fun, managing to go through "several fortunes" (his words) before Linda Porter helped him lick a drug and alcohol problem. Anita liked Porter and admired the regal and reserved Mrs. Porter; and as for Sturgie— well, he was as good company as anybody she'd had the pleasure of meeting.

F O R new friendships, 1926 was a vintage year for Anita. Sybil Colefax and the Asquiths, the Porters, Howard Sturges. . . . And then one day as she was walking on the place Vendôme, she was stopped by a lady who asked, "Hey! Aren't you Anita Loos? Didn't you write *Gentlemen Prefer Blondes?*"

Anita smiled affirmatively and was ready to pass on when she realized that this woman wasn't the average, oppressive fan; besides boldness, she also possessed chic and glamour—she was as languorous and lithe as the ladies jumping through hoops or walking borzois on art deco powder boxes. This was the kind of creature, Anita thought, that the French call an *animale de luxe*.

Fascinated, Anita invited the woman to tea at the Ritz. There they launched a lifelong friendship, though until the late 1940s they saw each other only sporadically. Anita's companion had been born Ruth Obré in Dutchess County, New York, shortly after the turn of the century. She moved to New York City when she was seventeen and there met and married a much older artist, Walter Goldbeck, who took her to Paris. When he died early in 1926, she decided to go on living in France, since she felt her talents could best be applied there. Not that she was enormously gifted, as she was the first to admit; but she did have a knack for spotting and nurturing talent in others. Clothes were her specialty, and even before her husband's death she had had a hand in several dressmaking establishments, including the fashionable Irène-Dana.

The lady had another specialty—*l'amour*. Her husband had been dead only a few months, but already she was being courted by a European aristocrat. Ruth Goldbeck was, Anita immediately realized, a sister of Lorelei Lee, though Ruth's mind was a lot quicker and her tongue far sharper. She never minced words in English or French or German; and once her mind was set on something, nothing short of being drawn and quartered made her back down.

She took one look at Anita and decided help was needed. "She went to the best couturiers—Worth, Cheruit, Lanvin—but she bought the wrong things. She was fashionably but unflatteringly dressed. I helped her find her own style." After Ruth, there were no more rotogravure shots of Anita wearing the latest "at-home ensemble"—velvet trousers, a tartan jacket with a matching plaid tam-o-shanter. (She looks about as chic as one of James Barrie's lost boys.) Soon she was posing for the camera in Irène-Dana and Mainbocher originals, though Ruth was never to wean her from middy blouses and straw boaters.

A L S O in Paris that summer was Anita's chum Marjorie Oelrichs (who bears more than a faint resemblance to the heroine of *Why Girls Go South*). Anita once described Marjorie as "a society-register drop-out,"

Marjorie Oelrichs, Ruth Dubonnet, and Anita in Paris in 1925. As a lark, the three friends decided to have a group portrait taken by Manuel, a photographer whose specialty was aesthetic portraits of the great stars of the Comédie Française.

which was putting things the wrong way round. Born to a poor branch of a patrician New York family, Marjorie was one of the first socialites to lend her name and face to advertising endorsements, leading to her banishment from the better New York drawing rooms. Marjorie didn't mind in the least. She preferred people who made things happen to those who sat at home blue-penciling *The Social Register*.

Anita, Ruth, and Marjorie were inseparable that summer. "Anita was really a terribly shy person," says Ruth. "She could be hilariously funny when with two or three people; then she felt relaxed. And the three of us complemented each other. We shared a common sense of humor."

Other people, men especially, thought them irreverent, even brazen. "My future brother-in-law, the duc de Vallambrosa, was scandalized at the things we said and did," Ruth recalls. "We were amusing, he said, but he would never want to be married to any one of us." Mr. E., who *was* married to one, may have shared the duke's attitude. He never approved of Ruth's influence on Anita, and Ruth felt Anita was "a patsy" to put up with a parasitic hypochondriac like Emerson.

THE EMERSONS cut their vacation short when Edgar Selwyn wired that he was moving *Blondes* to Broadway in September and needed Anita for revisions. The show had been running in Chicago for several months; but seeing it after a long interval, Anita recognized that it fizzled before it really got started, that on stage, Lorelei's adventures played like a libretto in need of several catchy tunes.

Part of the problem was Lorelei. Nearly every actress in New York had auditioned, and with Anita's approval Selwyn had chosen June Walker, a promising comedienne. Tallulah Bankhead had hooted at "this perfect casting." Just after her marriage, Walker told Bankhead she wasn't prepared for children and asked what she could do to postpone a blessed event. Tallulah stared at Walker, who was known to have played house before getting to the altar, in disbelief. "Honeychile," Bankhead drawled, "just keep on doing what you done before!"

As Lorelei, Walker was too cozy and sweet, and she broadcast her funniest lines as though trying to reach Antarctica by radio. The script could be tinkered with, but Selwyn wouldn't replace Walker at such a late date. Anita tried to be optimistic; maybe *Blondes* would get by in New York if the audience's warm feeling about the book carried over to the stage.

And that happened to an extent. Business was strong for a month or so, then started easing off. Anita did what she could to keep the show alive, interviews and that sort of thing, but when it closed in April 1927, she held no wake. She was too busy looking over page proofs for her second novel, already serialized in *Bazaar* and about to be issued by Liveright.

June Walker and Frank Morgan in the 1925 stage version of *Gentlemen Prefer Blondes*

Ruth Taylor and Alice White in the 1928 film version of *Blondes,* directed by Mal St. Clair. Anita felt her film adaptation of *Blondes* was an improvement on her stage version. Ruth Taylor scored a great success as Lorelei, but soon gave up acting for the security of marriage to a New York stock financier. This was one of those instances, Anita noted, when an actress keeps on playing a role after the show is finished. Ruth Taylor's son is screenwriter and sometime-actor Buck Henry.

TIMES SQUARE THEATRE

SELWYN & CO.
LESSEES' AND MANAGERS.

Times Square Theatre

42nd Street, West of Broadway

The SELWYNS........................Owners and Managers

FIRE NOTICE: Look around NOW and choose the nearest
Exit to your seat. In case of fire, walk (not run) to THAT Exit.
Do not try to beat your neighbor to the street.
JOHN J. DORMAN, Fire Commissioner.

WEEK BEGINNING MONDAY EVENING, FEBRUARY 7, 1927
Matinees Thursday and Saturday

EDGAR SELWYN   *Anita Loos*
Presents

"Gentlemen Prefer Blondes"

By Anita Loos and John Emerson
An Adaptation of Anita Loos' Book of the Same Name
Staged by Edgar Selwyn

Cast
(In the order of their appearance)

DOROTHY SHAW ....EDNA HIBBARD
HARRY, a steward......................HAROLD THOMAS
GLORIA ATWELL ....RUTH RAYMONDE
LORELEI LEE ....JUNE WALKER
HENRY SPOFFARD ....GEOFFREY KERR
LADY BEEKMAN ....GRACE HAMPTON
SIR FRANCIS BEEKMAN...................G. F. HUNTLEY
MRS. SPOFFARD........................MRS. JACQUES MARTIN
MISS CHAPMAN ....MAUD SINCLAIR

PROGRAM CONTINUED ON SECOND PAGE FOLLOWING

Content*mint!*

after a
heavy meal ~

*"Always
Good Taste"*

12

A Cure
for Mr. E.

*T*HOUGH usually described as a sequel, *But Gentlemen Marry Brunettes* is actually more of a companion piece to *Blondes*. Starting where the earlier book ends and continuing with Lorelei's adventures for a few chapters, it then goes into flashback to recount the story of Lorelei's best friend, Dorothy Shaw.

The diary format of *Blondes* is discarded, but Lorelei is the narrator throughout—it is she who tells Dorothy's history. This intricate narrative device is a mistake. While it is understandable that neither Anita nor her editors wanted to abandon Lorelei, it might have been wiser to introduce a new voice, an alternative point of view, since Dorothy's biography is not so different from Lorelei's.

The best part of *Brunettes* is the early chapters about Dorothy, possibly because Anita is here drawing on childhood memories. Like Loos, Dorothy is a California girl, raised by an alcoholic father employed by the Grand Pacific Street Fair and Carnival Company, a fly-by-night operation that puts on benefits for church and social clubs. Mr. Shaw resembles R. Beers, who worked the carny circuit for a time, possibly with Anita in tow. Once Dorothy leaves the carnival, most of the fun goes out of the novel, which proceeds along conventional lines. Dorothy escapes to New York, gets into the *Follies,* and marries a violent-tempered and, it is delicately suggested, homosexual saxophonist. Could Dorothy's husband be modeled after Frank Pallma? If so, perhaps Anita did have reason to fear for her life when Pallma stalked the Triangle studio.

Like Anita, Dorothy regrets her marriage before the ceremony is over. She soon divorces the saxophonist to marry a polo-crazed playboy with a serious case of the DTs. Naturally Lorelei sees this as a happy ending for her friend, now the wife of a millionaire, but the joke doesn't have the zest it should. Something's very askew in the final chapters of the book, an unsavory lump of sourness that chokes laughter.

Mencken assured Anita that *Brunettes* was superior to *Blondes*, but few critics shared his enthusiasm. The reviews were mixed, a sizable portion being downright unfriendly. Still, it did relatively well for both Liveright and its author, and there has always been a small party of readers who, like Mencken, prefer the darker, more astringent *Brunettes* to *Blondes*.

For *Brunettes* Anita composed an obsequious dedication: "TO JOHN EMERSON who discovered, developed, fostered and trained whatever I may have if I have anything that is worth while." Mr. E. couldn't have said it better himself! If Anita composed this nonsense to forestall an aggravation of Emerson's imaginary illness, it was a ploy that failed. Just before publication, his voice started getting fainter and he came down with hives, then with boils. Thinking a change of scenery would do him good, he said he was going to Europe; maybe Anita would join him once *Brunettes* was launched.

"Mr. E. leaves me alone!!!" Anita wrote in her journal on April 21. Grass widowhood did not agree with her. She came down with bronchitis and was still feeling poorly when she sailed for Europe on May 7. When she arrived at the Crillon in Paris, Mr. E. wasn't there, just a note asking her to join him in Rome at once. But she came down with the flu and couldn't leave for Italy until three days later.

Emerson had to carry her off the train. After getting her to bed, he explained that he had come to Rome because he had been promised an audience with Mussolini, one of his idols, and as it happened, the meeting was scheduled for the next morning. He hoped Anita would feel well enough to go along, but she didn't. Emerson returned with glowing praise for Il Duce, who had just read *I signori preferiscone le bionde* and was eager to meet "La Loos."

That didn't seem likely, since Mr. E. had earlier made appointments with throat specialists in Berlin, and to meet them, he had to leave Rome the next morning. But Anita was still too sick to travel, so Mr. E. went alone. For two weeks Anita depended on the kindness of room service and

This photograph was taken in 1927 when Anita was close to forty.

the hotel doctor. Nearly every day she received communiqués from Mussolini, promising an audience, but it wasn't until she was feeling well enough to join Mr. E. in Berlin that she was ordered to report to the Palazzo Chigi at ten the following morning.

In *But Gentlemen Marry Brunettes,* Dorothy gives up red satin when informed that gentlemen really prefer dotted swiss. So perhaps not entirely by accident did Anita choose to wear gingham for her meeting with Mussolini, who was astonished that such an innocent could write a book as worldly as *Blondes.*

In her 1927 journal, Anita describes Mussolini as *simpatia* [*sic*].

Directly after the meeting, she told a reporter for the Paris *Herald Tribune* that when the prime minister asked her to autograph her book, she had written, "To Benito Mussolini who has given to our age its one flame of grandeur." He was, she went on to say, a great fan of the movies because they had "dynamism, and do not make use of the human voice, which is generally ugly." When would he come to America? she asked. "I cannot come," was the reply. "I stay here at this table. It is my duty."

Mussolini was, Anita concluded, "the most forceful, the most earnest, and the most heroic personality I have ever met." Later, of course, she changed her mind, and the account of her meeting with Mussolini given in the memoirs is less complimentary than the one printed in the *Herald Tribune.*

Two days later she met Emerson in Berlin and they went on to Carlsbad, where Mr. E. was to take a cure. It didn't help him, but Anita put back some of the weight lost during her illness. They spent a few days

Benito Mussolini, from Anita's photo album of her trip to Italy in 1927

in Nice and then returned briefly to Paris before sailing for America on the
Homeric.

But their travels were not over. Four days after arriving in America,
they were on their way to the West Coast to work on the screenplay for
Blondes. Then in October they sailed again for Europe on the *Ile de
France* with a maid, seventeen pieces of luggage, and an AC/DC transformer,
which nearly electrocuted Mr. E. the first time he used it.

This trip was for health, not pleasure. Mr. E. had got wind of a new
batch of doctors who might ease his throat; so after docking in Le Havre,
the Emersons left for Vienna, where the recommended specialists were
located. His first appointment had to be canceled: on the train to Austria,
Mr. E. ate a bowl of cabbage soup and awoke the next morning with
ptomaine poisoning. He was rushed to a hospital and later moved to a
sanatorium for a stomach cure.

Meanwhile, Anita came down with a sinus attack. She was in such
agony that a Viennese friend, actress Grete Mosheim, urged her to consult
Professor Emil Glas, an eminent nose-and-throat specialist. Glas recommended a simple surgical procedure that could be performed in the office,
provided the patient held a basin to catch the drippings. Anita nearly
fainted from the pain, but she managed to keep a grip on the basin, only to
be told that more work was necessary: a very minor operation to be
performed in a hospital. As she was pulling herself together, Anita mentioned
her husband and his throat trouble. Glas was intrigued: no promises, but
perhaps he could help.

Once Mr. E. was out of the sanatorium, Anita persuaded him to see
Glas, whose diagnosis was precisely the same as Jelliffe's: Emerson's
condition was psychosomatic. Nonetheless, he felt he could help. His plan
was to stage an operation during which Emerson's throat would be scratched
so badly that he would be unable to speak for a few days. While he was
recuperating Glas would present Emerson with a vial of alcohol containing
flecks of membrane, explaining that these were nodes removed from his
vocal cords. Emerson would then be guaranteed that once his throat had
healed, he would be able to speak normally. Glas warned Anita that there
was an element of risk: if Mr. E. preferred to remain an invalid, this piece
of psycho-surgery would not succeed. But if he was tired of whispering,
the removal of the "nodes" would provide a logical basis for a cure.

A week later the Emersons entered the Auersbach Sanatorium, where
on the same day Dr. Glas performed minor surgery on Anita's sinuses and a
sham operation on Mr. E. Anita was up and about the next day, while her
husband, unable to talk because of his bruised throat, looked and felt

miserable. She was released from the sanatorium before Emerson, and as she left, Dr. Glas told her not to worry—Mr. E.'s "operation" was certain to prove a success.

Anita stayed in Vienna for a few days but then decided to take the Orient Express to Paris. She was edgy and apprehensive; and whatever the outcome of Emerson's surgery, she felt she could face it best amid the comforts of the Crillon. Two weeks later he arrived, talking like his old self and bearing a vial of what looked like egg-drop soup. Those white specks, Mr. E. explained, had been the source of all his woes. He brought out the vial for visitors to inspect; and thanks to his endorsements, Dr. Glas suddenly found himself so celebrated that he was later sought out by Hitler, whose throat was frequently raw from so much speechifying. (Glas, who was not pleased at having Hitler for a patient, emigrated to New York long before World War II.) Anita told only a few discreet friends that Glas's cure was all showmanship.

Back in New York, Anita found herself in an unusual position. For virtually the first time in her life, she had no commitments or assignments. And while Mr. E. seemed to be in a good frame of mind, she resolved not to upset the delicate balance of their relationship. From now on her only career would be that of devoted wife. She was officially a lady in retirement.

13

Palm Beach
Story

D u r i n g the winter of 1927-28, Anita had a series of colds and rarely felt fit for more than a day or two at a time. As a last resort, her doctor suggested she head south, a proposal that appealed to Mr. E. Palm Beach was the ideal spot for a winter vacation, he advised. She should leave immediately and he'd catch up with her as soon as he had finished some business for Actors Equity.

Anita wasn't enthusiastic. The Emersons had visited Palm Beach before, and she never had cared for it as much as her husband did. The sun and surf were nice, and she enjoyed the costume parties that were staged there, but to her mind, Palm Beach was "the silliest of all pleasure resorts, inhabited mainly by phonies." Mr. E., on the other hand, liked brushing shoulders with the hibernating East Coast socialites. He was a bit of a climber, not an admirable trait but one that Anita saw no way of correcting. And as long as he didn't force her to climb along with him, it was a fault she was prepared to overlook.

While he was hobnobbing, she would not lack for companionship. Irving Berlin and his wife, Ellin, had a house in Palm Beach; Marjorie Oelrichs and her mother, "Big Marge," spent part of the season at the Royal Poinciana Hotel; Joe Hergesheimer was often there visiting rich friends.

Anita stayed at the Royal Poinciana, on the same floor with the Oelrichses, who insisted she join them for dinner to celebrate her arrival.

But first they would have drinks at the home of designer and architect Addison Mizner, the man chiefly responsible for making Palm Beach look the way it did. Anita tried to beg off, but Marjorie insisted she'd have fun.

And after one look at her host, Anita knew Marjorie was right—this *was* going to be fun. Sprawled on an oversized divan, corpulent, fair-haired, and balding, the fiftyish Addison Mizner was a dead ringer for the Oscar Wilde drawn by Toulouse-Lautrec. And while not so epigrammatically polished as Wilde, Mizner could have held his own in any gathering of celebrated wits.

Mizner was a *Blondes* fan, and he knew something about Anita's background. He too had had the bad luck of being born in California, and in his youth he had spent many pleasant hours with that gentleman and scholar R. Beers Loos. Then he winked, telling Anita what she had already guessed: this Palm Beach sultan was a graduate of the Barbary Coast academy of con artistry.

Mizner and his younger brother, Wilson, were the black sheep of a prominent California family whose European ancestry included Sir Joshua Reynolds. The brothers had spent part of their childhood in Guatemala, where their father was the U.S. ambassador; had attended and been kicked out of several California military schools; had gone prospecting in the Yukon.

Then Addison became convinced he had inherited his great-grand-uncle Reynolds's talent; but, unable to draw a straight line, he settled for interior decoration—all the rage then, thanks to Elsie de Wolfe. He figured that what Elsie had done, he could also do: his social connections were as good as hers.

He did collect some good clients, and when New York society discovered Florida around 1914, he went with them; as they bought up acres of beachfront, he told them what kind of houses to build. Backed by a wealthy patron, Addison formed his own corporation, which flourished despite its chief architect's lack of technical knowledge. On one job, Mizner omitted a staircase and was forced to pretend that the oversight was intentional: a stairway running up the outside of a hacienda was more dramatic, he improvised.

Addison brought brother Wilson to Florida as secretary-treasurer of the Mizner Corporation. They shared a house, but Anita visited there many times before she met Wilson, who never left his bed while the sun was shining. She was eager to meet him: he was a legendary character of Broadway anecdotage.

There are those who contend that not everything told about Wilson

is true, not even the tales he told on himself. He enjoyed being a bad, bad boy and was capable of inventing escapades to bolster his image. But once the possibly apocryphal has been subtracted, there's still lots of color. And for a girl like Anita, with her weakness for scamps, Wilson was bound to be a knockout.

After parting company with his brother in the Yukon, Wilson headed for San Francisco, where he gambled and managed a crew of punch-happy boxers. Moving to New York, he married Mrs. Myra Yerkes, the widow of a public-transit mogul. Six months later Wilson was ordered out of the Yerkeses' Fifth Avenue mansion for spending too much money on dope and doxies. Wilson felt that he was the aggrieved party—the widow had treated him like "a licensed gigolo"—and he swore never again to hand out his heart on a long-term basis.

Wilson then started earning a living as a card shark on Atlantic luxury liners. It was a pleasant occupation, as most Americans, he discovered, belonged to the "genus sucker." But the suckers had a way of coming out on top, as Wilson ruefully admitted to Anita. None of the many con games he played ever brought him much money.

At Jack Dunstan's Cafe, a hangout for big-time gangsters and slum-

Palm Beach, 1927

ming theater stars, he met Paul Armstrong, a playwright with a bad case of writer's block. Mizner said he was full of plots, even some dialogue, but needed an experienced collaborator to get it all down on paper. Together they wrote *The Deep Purple*, "a realistic drama of the underworld," built around "the badger game," which Mizner himself had played: a floozy lures a dude into her bed, then her supposed husband breaks in with a gun and threatens to shoot unless conscience money is handed over. This was rough stuff for 1911, and while critics deplored its depravity, audiences lapped it up. *The Deep Purple* was followed by two other stage collaborations before Mizner switched to screen writing, staying with it pretty steadily until his brother brought him to Palm Beach.

In his Florida period, Wilson was in his early forties, tall, as slender as Addison was fat, with sparse hair, a scrawny neck, and an oversized head. In photographs he looks a lot like Sterling Holloway, the goon-faced

Wilson Mizner, Addison's brother, and Anita,
Palm Beach, 1927

comedian of 1930s movies; but on first sight Anita was captivated. Wilson
dressed flawlessly, and his manners might have cast a shadow on Galahad.
"Always treat a lady like a whore and a whore like a lady"—this, perhaps
Mizner's most quoted epigram, was a misrepresentation of the way he
really operated, Anita insisted. Whether well-born or blowzy, all women
were treated with ecumenical deference.

Wilson was born with the gift of spontaneous wit. He said precisely
what came into his mind, and his mind apparently thought in the vernacular.
Specialists in the fields of slang and humor have paid tribute to Mizner;
Dorothy Parker, Gene Fowler, Mencken tried to analyze why he made
them laugh, only to give up the job as hopeless. Out of context and on
paper, Mizner's quips look off the mark, crude, often cruel. It was his
quiet manner, Anita decided, his manner of voicing ribaldries in cultured
yet natural tones, that gave him his peculiar elegance. His voice was "sexy
to the ear."

Even after Mr. E.'s arrival in Palm Beach, Anita went on seeing
Mizner every day. While Emerson was dining and dancing with the elite,
they spent the evening at Mizner's favorite retreat, a seedy oceanfront café

called Guss'es Baths. There was a deep bond between them, too passionate to be simple friendship and yet too chaste to be compromising. "Well, Nita, what are we going to do about this?" he asked. "Nothing!" she replied. And he left it at that.

Anita's confidante during this period was Ruth Goldbeck, who had recently married Count Paul de Vallambrosa at St. Paul's Cathedral in London and was now spending her honeymoon in Palm Beach. When she learned about Wilson, Ruth was pleased. Never fond of Emerson, she felt it was high time he was paid back in kind. "John was clever and amusing, but he treated Anita abominably. All that throat business—whenever Anita left the room he spoke quite naturally. And of course he was an

The Count and Countess Paul de Vallambrosa on their honeymoon, Palm Beach, 1927

incorrigible bottom pincher, many of the bottoms belonging to Anita's best friends."

Ruth was all for Mizner—until she met him. Then she decided Anita was deluding herself. "He didn't care for her *at all.* I don't think he cared about any woman, except for momentary pleasure. On the night we met, when I got back to the hotel, he called up and said, 'How about it, Babe?'—or something equally crude. Imagine—I was on my honeymoon!" Always one to speak her mind, Ruth told Anita what she thought. Anita wasn't perturbed. What Ruth wanted in a man wasn't what she wanted; anyway, no man was perfect, not even the Count de Vallambrosa, always a little sloshed before the cocktail gong was struck.

She listened to Ruth with a deaf ear and went on meeting Mizner until the Emersons returned to New York. They'd be back the next year, Anita promised. Wilson said he might be in New York before then. As it turned out, they were to meet only fleetingly during the next two years.

P A L M   B E A C H didn't help Anita's health. Back in New York, she was continually plagued by colds and the flu, as well as by cases of ptomaine and bursitis. Perhaps retirement didn't agree with her, or perhaps she was physically as well as emotionally depressed at being separated from Mizner.

Mizner might also have been responsible for a sudden recurrence of Mr. E.'s throat problems. Unable to face another siege of speechlessness, Anita insisted that they leave immediately for Vienna. Dr. Glas obligingly staged a repeat performance of the mock operation, and again the results were beneficial.

Afterwards they went to Paris for a week with the Vallambrosas, then to Berlin, Nice, and London, finally returning home in early December. The crossing was smooth, but Anita was sick most of the time. On her first night in New York, though, she felt well enough to attend the premiere of Ethel Barrymore's new play, and the next morning she was packing bags for the West Coast.

"TOO MUCH TRAVELING!," she scrawled across her diary. Definitely there were moments when she found retirement exhausting, but on the whole both Emersons enjoyed the pattern that their lives had taken, one that they continued to follow for the next two years: fall and

Anita in costume for another Palm Beach ball. This time she is impersonating Gertrude Lawrence singing "Limehouse Blues" in *Andre Charlot's London Revue* of 1924.

Anita and Mr. E. on their way to another Palm Beach party. They are dressed as
Mr. and Mrs. Stolesbury, an English couple noted for the disparity in their heights.
Anita played the tiny husband, Emerson the Junoesque wife.

early winter in New York, January and February in Palm Beach, spring and summer in Europe.

Much later Anita referred to this period as her "wasted years"—all the gallivanting was to please Mr. E. But while it was going on, she took pleasure in it too. It wasn't until after it ended that she realized that during this term of enforced indolence part of herself had been absent.

14

Altered States

O N OCTOBER 24, 1929, the day of the New York stock market crash, the Emersons were at the Savoy Hotel in London. They had tickets that evening to see Yvette Guilbert, the renowned French diseuse, but Anita was overweight and in a foul mood: Emerson would have to go by himself—she was going to spend the whole day in bed, reading Proust and drinking milk. A fashionable Mayfair doctor, recommended by Sybil Colefax, had promised that a milk diet would get rid of the unwanted pounds.

The next morning she discovered that she somehow had managed to gain another quarter-pound(!!!). Weary of both milk and Proust, she decided to go out to lunch with Sybil and photographer Cecil Beaton. They went to a Chinese place in Soho—chosen by Cecil because he knew Nita loved "to show off with chopsticks"—where they bumped into a friend of Sybil's who casually mentioned the American financial crisis. The London papers were full of it, but Anita hadn't seen them that morning.

When she got back to the hotel, she questioned Mr. E. about what she had heard. Bug was not to worry, he replied. He had checked into the rumors and had been assured they were alarmist: not only would Wall Street weather the storm, it would spring back stronger than ever.

Two weeks later in New York, Anita decided that Mr. E. must be right. No one she met seemed financially embarrassed; everyone was confident the worst was over. The parties that autumn were possibly more lavish than the year before, including her own. Lots of the Emersons' international friends were in town just then—Elsa Maxwell and Dickie Gordon Fellows, the Vallambrosas, Beaton—and all were repaid for earlier hospitalities.

From the moment she met him until the day he died, Anita adored Beaton. "It was one of those instant things," she remembered. "We clicked immediately"—so much so that Emerson got edgy. But Anita laughed off his sneers about "that snotty peacock." Yes, Cecil was a social butterfly; yes, he was narcissistic and foolish at times and touchy at others. But she'd forgive him anything, do anything for him.

"Is there anything special you want to see in America?" she asked. "Hollywood," he replied.

Well, why not? She and John could give Cecil a Cook's tour of the movie colony and then take the train from Los Angeles to Miami, arriving in Palm Beach only a week or so late for their annual visit. Mr. E. didn't like the idea of traveling with Beaton, but this time Anita insisted on having her own way, and Emerson agreed to go.

Almost certainly there was an ulterior motive behind her determination. Some months before, Wilson Mizner had again taken up screen writing and was presently residing in a suite at the Ambassador Hotel in Los Angeles.

Beaton and the Emersons left New York in mid-December and spent a full day in Chicago before boarding the Southern Pacific for California. Instead of going all the way into Los Angeles, the Emerson party left the train at Santa Barbara, where by prearrangement Joe Schenck's limousine was waiting to drive them to Los Angeles. As Anita had hoped, Beaton was dazzled by the ostentation of the car and delighted by the beauty of the California landscape.

They stayed at the Roosevelt Hotel on Hollywood Boulevard, described by Beaton in his diary as "a mock Moorish conceit with patios, fountains, and shawl-draped balconies." Wherever he looked there were "blondes in black satin, osprey, and furs," though the temperature was in the high eighties. Outside, the streets were decorated for Christmas, and Hollywood Boulevard had temporarily been renamed Santa Claus Lane. Hollywood was living up to all of Cecil's gaudiest expectations.

That first evening the Emersons had dinner with R. Beers and Minnie, Clifford (now separated from his wife) and his daughter, Mary, a tall and beautiful teenager with a strong resemblance to Dolores Del Rio. Besides Beaton there was one other outsider included in this family reunion—Wilson Mizner. Anita had told Beaton most of Wilson's life story, and whatever details she had omitted Mizner supplied himself. He was an inventor, he said. What had he invented? Cecil asked. A rubber pocket for waiters who wanted to steal the soup, Mizner replied. Cecil thought this a capital joke.

In the weeks ahead, while Anita showed Beaton around Hollywood, Mr. E. often went his own way; but there was frequently a third member to the party—as long as the partying didn't start too early in the day. Anita and Cecil took to having a late lunch at Mizner's favorite haunt, the Brown Derby restaurant on Wilshire Boulevard. From the Brown Derby, they often went to Wilson's second-favorite hangout, El Cholo, which he claimed served the finest mole poblano this side of the border. It also allowed the patrons to bring their own bottles, and Mizner always arrived with a couple of quarts of Napoleon brandy.

Anita, Beaton, and Irving Berlin (then in Hollywood writing songs for a Jolson musical) were with him one evening when Wilson got chatty with two burly Mexicans at an adjoining table. Relations turned unfriendly when Mizner, high on French brandy, made too much of a mispronunciation, and the Mexicans, high on *cerveza,* started throwing bottles. Soon the room was bombarded with flying glass. Berlin told Beaton to get Anita out of the place, but there was no escape: El Cholo had no back or side entrances, and the battlefield was along the front door. But then a huge mirror crashed to the floor, creating a momentary diversion which allowed Anita and Beaton to flee to safety. Outside, Cecil was still very shaken, but Anita had taken it in stride. "I haven't felt so invigorated," she said, "since I saw Isadora Duncan dance *The Internationale.*"

CHRISTMAS EVE was spent with Anita's family at Clifford's house and Christmas day at a party given by Ina Claire and John Gilbert. It was a dull affair until somebody knocked an aquarium into Gloria Swanson's lap. Beaton was thrilled: there was something almost surreal about a devilfish flapping about in Swanson's crotch.

For the New Year holiday, Anita had arranged a special treat for Beaton—an invitation to San Simeon. To reach San Luis Obispo, the town nearest the Hearst castle, took five hours by train, and then another hour by car to arrive at the outskirts of the grounds. The Emersons were assigned a three-room suite in one of the guest villas. Their sitting room had brocade walls, and the ceiling was carved with life-sized gilt angels. Beaton's quarters were not so grand, and his knowledgeable eye detected that everywhere genuine masterpieces were indiscriminately mixed with kitsch.

Cecil's wicked appraisal reinforced Anita's own feelings about the place. San Simeon, she once said, was a series of colossal movie sets, a theatrical fantasy you enjoyed visiting but didn't miss once the curtain came down. You were always on stage, always making entrances and exits. At nine every morning, a servant knocked and announced, "Mr. Hearst is now awake." Lunch and dinner were also at set hours, and snacking was frowned on. Because of Marion's drinking problem, liquor was rationed: a glass of wine at dinner and a cocktail before.

Marion had her own stash, which she shared with friends; and some guests smuggled in their own supply, but it took skill, since the San Simeon staff was expert at sniffing out the gin inside a mouthwash bottle. These domestic rum raiders were vigilant, but rowdy incidents did occur at San Simeon; one happened during Anita and Beaton's visit.

Charlie Lederer, Marion's eighteen-year-old nephew, arrived at the cocktail hour on New Year's Eve already well fortified. He wrested a scimitar from a wall and chased actress Eileen Percy around the room—he was a sheik and she the Christian damsel about to be ravished. Percy and the onlookers whooped with laughter until Hearst's frozen face quieted them. But Charlie wasn't intimidated. At dinner, he rose unsteadily and, with tongue-in-cheek, berated himself as unworthy of such noble sur- roundings and asked forgiveness for putting his foot through a priceless Goya. Hearst was not amused. After a prolonged, dramatic silence, he ordered everyone out to the veranda. And there they remained for a full hour, sobering up in the chill night air.

Hearst had his good points, Anita remarked to Beaton as they were standing in the chill, but the ideal host he would never be. All his rules and regulations made spirited people like Marion and Charlie pull foolish, rebellious stunts just to thwart him. She didn't care about the ban on liquor, but the food rationing was annoying. The meals at San Simeon weren't in kilter with her appetite, so she always brought along dried fruits and nuts to nibble when the kitchen was off limits to guests.

During the day Hearst's guests were free to pursue their own amuse- ment. Mr. E. worked up two or three flirtations, which Anita observed with amused detachment when she wasn't reading or assisting Beaton with his camera.

Eileen Percy woke with a bad headache on New Year's Day but gamely agreed to pose on the back of a white marble unicorn. Then Charlie Lederer, also feeling a bit liverish, got into cowboy regalia and tried to lasso the fabulous beast. Equestrianism being the theme of the day, someone came up with the idea of horsing around on real horses. Eileen Percy begged off but agreed to take a picture of Anita and Cecil before they cantered off. The photograph shows Anita with riding crop and derby astride Beaton's back, a pose that led one wag to comment, "Anita is probably the only woman ever to straddle Cecil Beaton."

Neither Beaton nor Anita rode well, and Lederer had swallowed so many hairs of the dog that he listed in the saddle. Along the way signs warned: DANGER! THIS ROAD DANGEROUS ON ACCOUNT OF WILD ANIMALS. Meeting a stray ostrich, they turned back, fearing they'd be trampled to death.

Lederer appeared for dinner that night looking fit after a long nap, almost as bright-eyed and ready for fun as Eileen Percy and Davies. They encouraged the other guests to pep up the cocktail hour with some dancing. Beaton and Eileen shimmied lewdly while Charlie and his aunt showed Valentino what the tango was all about. Then Hearst appeared and announced dinner as though it were the Last Supper. But to cheer them up, he promised a Clara Bow talkie before bed. Watching Clara having fun wasn't as good as having it yourself, Anita whispered to Cecil, but it beat another half hour on a freezing *terrazzo*.

B E A T O N and the Emersons left Los Angeles for Palm Beach later that week. Mr. E. was depressed and irritable, and Anita worried that another siege of voicelessness was at hand. Instead, he clearly articulated what was on his mind, and the next day Anita wrote in her journal: "Make resolution: *never to go out to lunch*—except alone—or with Mr. E!!!!!!!!!!" In a footnote, added many years later, she explains that this was "Mr. E.'s propaganda to break me down—it succeeded for years."

Emerson had accused her of ignoring him to be with Beaton and Mizner, though if anyone was guilty of neglect, it was really he. It had been his idea to spend one night apart each week; for years he had lunched and dined with whomever he pleased, and she had asked no questions, raised no objections. And she raised none now. For the next year the word that appears most frequently in her diary is "alone." She lunches alone, she has dinner alone; she spends the evening alone in bed; she is alone in New York, Paris, London, and Vienna.

A far more dramatic change was to occur after their 1930 summer holiday in Europe. Emerson then told Anita that he had been guilty of some unwise investments and one impetuous piece of speculation. A year earlier he had bought German marks on the assumption that they were sure to increase in value in the near future. And they might have done so, he explained, except for the worldwide depression. By no means were they destitute, but changes were in order. Perhaps she would like to pick up her writing again?

Anita didn't blame Emerson. After all, she had gratefully assigned all financial matters to his care. And the idea of returning to work wasn't distressing; at this moment, she realized how much she had missed writing during her retirement.

Not long after this, she sent a letter to Cecil Beaton, warning him of the pitfalls of "drawing-room fame" and advising him against drifting into "a scrambled, footloose life." She then goes on to say: "I know that the only real artistic satisfaction comes from a regime of honest work. To be 'professional,' to win the respect of 'workers' in the arts and cut out the 'players' at art—is the only way to make a career that will last and get more and more important, as time goes on, to yourself and others." That the letter is addressed as much to herself as to Beaton is clear when she adds, "Cecil, dear, do not feel I could lecture you like this if I had not had exactly your problems."

The old regime agreed with her. In less than five months, she managed to complete two full-length plays. The first was a dramatization of *But Gentlemen Marry Brunettes,* which was titled *The Social Register* and in which the heroine's name is changed from Dorothy to Patsy. After working all morning on *The Social Register,* in the afternoon Anita turned to *Cherries Are Ripe,* an adaptation of a Hungarian comedy about a neglected wife toying with infidelity. Thanks to Ferenc Molnár, there was then a vogue for Middle European plays on Broadway, and Mr. E. thought that despite its tired plot this one stood a chance. Anita had doubts but convinced herself that Mr. E. knew best.

Both plays were scheduled for production in fall of 1931; *Cherries* was due to open on Broadway only three weeks prior to *Register.* They were to go into rehearsal simultaneously, with Emerson directing both, assisted by Anita. While he was working on *Cherries,* she would supervise the *Social Register* cast; while he was editing her work on *Register,* she would take over on *Cherries Are Ripe.*

That the Emersons took on this heavy load indicates that their financial situation was becoming dire. Their Palm Beach holiday was greatly abbreviated, and there was no European jaunt in 1931. They decided to give up the Gramercy Park house and take quarters in a residential hotel while looking for an apartment that suited their reduced budget.

While packing for this relocation, Anita discovered in a wardrobe drawer, behind some socks, a love letter to her husband. The writer (unknown to Anita) spoke of the joy she felt at compensating for his "unfulfilling marriage." When confronted with the evidence, Mr. E. burst into tears. Between sobs he repeated what he had said ten years earlier—he just wasn't the marrying kind. He deeply regretted it, but his nerves couldn't stand up to that kind of restriction.

Disarmed at making a grown man cry, Anita started placing some of the blame on herself. Perhaps the reason Mr. E. strayed was that, like Minnie with R. Beers, she had been too much the forgiving angel; or perhaps, as the letter suggested, she hadn't satisfied her husband's sexual needs.

Did he want a divorce? she asked meekly. Oh, no, he replied. Left to her own devices, his Bug might fall prey to a crook who would take all her money. The irony of his comment was not lost on Anita, but she said nothing.

What Emerson had in mind was an amicable separation. They would live apart but go on seeing each other nearly every day and would, of course, go on working together. He would find her an apartment and give her a weekly allowance. "You've given me so much and now I can give you something back," he said. Anita knew that the allowance was going to come out of whatever remained of her earnings from *Blondes* and *Brunettes*, but again she made no comment.

A few days later she moved into a small apartment at 170 East Seventy-ninth Street while Mr. E. took a room at the Lambs Club. Later, he subleased a friend's flat at Coney Island—not exactly Palm Beach, he admitted, but he enjoyed the sea air and the raffish atmosphere, as did Anita, who visited him frequently.

Though initially "chagrined" at her "failure as a wife," she discovered that Mr. E.'s design for living had its compensations. First and foremost, she was free to spend her allowance as she liked. Over the years there had been squabbles with Emerson over jewelry and furs. She bought them, he made her take them back, insisting they couldn't afford such luxuries. Now, when she really couldn't afford it, she went out and bought a mink coat. It made her look and feel just wonderful.

Which was a lot better than she felt when she saw the first rehearsals for *Cherries Are Ripe*. The script wasn't right, and she didn't know how to improve it. She was actually relieved when, after two weeks on the road, it closed in Trenton.

Social Register, on the other hand, was well received during its tryouts and opened on Broadway in November 1931 to generally favorable reviews. Two or three years earlier it might have managed to last out the season, but by then Broadway was feeling the full impact of the Depression, and it closed after ninety performances. Still, it returned a small profit, thanks to a movie sale. (Three years later it was filmed with Colleen Moore in the leading role.)

Whatever other money Anita earned in 1931 came from a magazine serial, *The Better Things in Life,* published in *Cosmopolitan,* and from *The Struggle,* D. W. Griffith's second talkie. Though she and Emerson received sole screen credit for the script, it goes unmentioned in her diary and her autobiographical writings. Probably she preferred to forget this unhappy film which ended Griffith's career; possibly she contributed little to it except some polishing of someone else's dialogue.

Hollywood had never stopped courting Anita. Joe Schenck was always trying to lure her back to write for Dutch and Norma; and with the coming of sound, the offers had become more persistent and financially attractive. But she turned them down for fear of upsetting Mr. E.

When she got an offer from Metro-Goldwyn-Mayer, the most glamorous and prestigious of the major studios, Emerson urged her to accept. Her salary was $1,000 a week, and she would be working for Irving Thalberg, perhaps the only studio executive ever widely admired by his subordinates.

The M–G–M contract was for the Emerson-Loos team, but Mr. E. surprised Anita by refusing to participate. "They want you," he explained. "I'm just an afterthought." If this was meant to make Anita feel contrite, it succeeded. She pleaded with him to come along, but he wouldn't hear of it. She was to go alone, and if she discovered she needed him, he would follow.

PART
Three

WESTWARD,
WOE!

15

Hello
and Goodbye

A N I T A was close to forty-three when she arrived in Hollywood to start a new career, or to resume an old one—she wasn't sure which. Writing sound pictures was, she had been warned, a different craft than writing for the silents, and she was nervous about whether she had the knack. But the studio welcomed her, booking her into a suite at the Roosevelt Hotel, where another recent addition to the M–G–M stable of writers was also lodged, F. Scott Fitzgerald.

As she was going up to her room, Fitzgerald got off the elevator. He recognized her, though they hadn't seen each other in years. "Beware Thalberg," he warned. "He's worse news than the ides of March."

The next day she reported early for her first meeting with Thalberg and sat in an antechamber for two hours before he received her. Keeping people waiting was his one flourish of self-importance, and Anita quickly learned to deal with it: whenever she reported for a conference, she took along a bag of knitting. "What's that you're working on?" he asked. "Your Christmas present," she answered. "And since I'm knitting it on M–G–M's time, it's going to be the most expensive scarf you've ever worn!"

A small assembly of co-workers (Fitzgerald included) saw the physically fragile Thalberg—he had had a bad heart since childhood—as cold and exploitative, but Anita adored him from the start. Thirty years later in her novel *A Mouse Is Born,* Anita paid tribute to Thalberg, who appears there as Leo Montaigne. Discussing Thalberg/Montaigne's

Irving Thalberg and his wife, Norma Shearer. Anita was a Thalberg partisan, but when asked about Mrs. Thalberg, she replied, "Well, Norma was a wonderful tennis player."

philosophy of filmmaking, the heroine (a semi-illiterate like Lorelei) comments:

> . . . In the heart of Leo Montaigne, there was a great Compassion for Human Beens. So he felt that, when they paid their hard-earned money to get into Moving Picture Theatres, he wanted them to be entertained. And he never thought it was excombrint to exploit anybody's opinion, or to prove something or other. (Such as the case where our Government caught Script Writers trying to prove that "Left" is "Right.") So a Montaigne picture was inveritably as Success, but it was a terrible cost to Leo.

After her first visit to Thalberg, Anita went off to meet Wilson Mizner at the Brown Derby. She was shocked by his appearance, though she knew he hadn't been well. Mizner had spent much of the previous year in a hospital undergoing drug withdrawal, and he had kept the Emersons posted on his progress. One letter, signed "The Faculty," reported, "The patient [has] acquired a habit entirely unknown to this institution, i.e., rubbing Patagonian rhubarb under his arms which he flaps up and down the while, to an accompaniment of a terrified guinea hen." For some reason the Emersons thought this an indication that Willy was coming along fine.

But the man Anita met at the Derby looked wasted and ashen. He knew what she saw but tried to reassure her. He was weak but doing fine, working steadily at Warners, making big contributions to *Little Caesar* and *20,000 Years in Sing Sing.* No screen credit for those, but Jack Warner was a drinking buddy, and he was sure to get recognition for *One Way Passage,* almost entirely his creation.

It was all bravura. Physically he was a wreck, and whatever Anita may have wanted from Willy was nothing he could supply for very long. Leaving one invalid in New York, she found herself in Los Angeles with another: the only difference was that Mr. E. played at being sick while Mizner feigned good health. Anita sat by while he drank himself into a stupor, ate a Brown Derby lunch with him every day, took him to the movies, arranged picnics in Santa Monica or Malibu every Sunday afternoon.

When she wasn't looking after Willy, she was working on her first M–G–M assignment, *Redheaded Woman,* an adaptation of a novel by Katharine Brush. Honing a script from Brush's saga of a trollop's progress from secretary to wife of a French aristocrat had originally been Scott Fitzgerald's job, but he had botched it, according to M–G–M's story editor, Sam Marx. "I couldn't get him to grasp the idea that Thalberg and I wanted the audience to laugh with Lil Andrews [the heroine] instead of at her." So Thalberg ordered Fitzgerald taken off the script.

Lil Andrews was a juicy part, and practically every actress on the M–G–M lot tried to get it—especially Joan Crawford—but the role went to Jean Harlow, who needed, more than Crawford did, the right vehicle to make herself a star. Sam Marx says it was Harlow's mentor and soon-to-be husband, Paul Bern, who suggested that Anita take over the script. Anita, on the other hand, says the assignment was thanks to Marcel De Santo, then set as director of *Redheaded Woman.* A Rumanian, De Santo was, according to Marx, "a very flaky kind of a guy," but Anita found him amusing, and she saw a lot of him during her first months back in Hollywood. He made a pass at her, which she tactfully deflected. "I'm flypaper for pimps," she wrote in her diary.

She talked to Thalberg about the script and agreed to his view of how it should be developed, and went to work without knowing that Fitzgerald had not yet been informed that his script was being discarded. "The problem was to get rid of Scott without sending him over the brink," recalls Sam Marx. "I was debating how to handle it when one day Scott ran into Marcel De Santo, who said 'Hey, you know, they don't like your stuff and they're bringing in Anita Loos.' "

A few days later De Santo was also removed from *Redheaded Woman*, possibly because of this indiscretion; but this was no balm for Anita, who knew that sooner or later she'd have to face Fitzgerald, still on the M–G–M payroll. And from past experience she knew he could be very ugly when he was angry. Shortly after the book publication of *Blondes* (which Fitzgerald disliked, arguing that too many tricks had been stolen from Ring Lardner's hand), Anita was walking on Fifth Avenue when Scott pulled up in a roadster, stopped, and urged her to get in: he was driving back to the house he and Zelda had rented on Long Island, and insisted she come for dinner. On a whim, Anita accepted, and almost immediately regretted it. Scott started swigging champagne from a bottle between his knees, and in the backseat there were several others waiting to be opened.

Martinis were served before dinner, and Scott and Zelda were both well oiled when they sat down at the table. Zelda made an innocent remark that provoked Scott to thoughts of murder. He went in search of a knife, locking the dining room door behind him. Anita and Zelda tried to escape through French windows into the garden, but these were bolted from the outside. A butler, hearing the commotion, ran outdoors and freed them. They rushed across the lawn to Ring Lardner's house and stayed there until Fitzgerald passed out.

When Fitzgerald inevitably wandered into Anita's office at M–G–M, he was sipping a soft drink, looking meek and apologetic: No bitterness, just good wishes for *Redheaded Woman*. He had recently gone on the wagon, which hadn't made for much of an improvement, Anita felt. Giving up spirits had literally made him spiritless: he was "a burned-out case."

Within a month Anita completed a screenplay which Thalberg approved. But Jack Conway, De Santo's replacement as director, didn't like it. "You can't make jokes about a girl who deliberately sets out to break up a family," he said. "Why not?" Anita countered. "Look at the family! It deserves to be broken up!"

Redheaded Woman was completed by May 1932. Much to everyone's surprise, it was coolly received at its first sneak preview. Thalberg summoned Anita to his office. "People don't know whether they're supposed to laugh or not," he said. "We need an opening scene to set the mood."

So Anita wrote a prologue showing Lil Andrews looking at her new hairdo in a hand mirror. Turning to the camera, she winks and says,

Ironically, the picture that made platinum blond Jean Harlow a major star was Anita's *Redheaded Woman* (1932), Anita's favorite of the five pictures she wrote for Harlow. ABOVE: This publicity still of Anita, Chester Morris, and Harlow was M–G–M's way of preparing the public for a titian-tressed Harlow.

"Gentlemen prefer blondes?? Sez who?!!" Then she is seen leaving a department-store fitting room. "Is this dress too tight?" she asks a salesgirl. "It certainly is!" clucks the clerk disapprovingly. "Good!" says Lil as she shimmies out the door.

The new sequence did the trick—at the next preview, audience reaction was enthusiastic. The picture became a smash success, established Harlow as a star, and placed Anita again in the front rank of screenwriters.

Unlike Fitzgerald and other New York and European authors who kept striving to raise the material assigned them to their own level of self-importance, Anita didn't think screenwriting beneath her. Unlike Fitzgerald, who despaired of tailoring a role to suit Joan Crawford, she enjoyed writing for star personalities, including Crawford. She worked happily within set limitations, polishing and perfecting, but not struggling to expand or break the boundaries of the conventional M–G–M screenplay. She prided herself on her professionalism.

"She was a very valuable asset for M–G–M," recalls Sam Marx. "Because the studio had so many femmes fatales—Garbo, Crawford, Shearer, and Harlow—we were always on the lookout for 'shady lady' stories. But they were problematic because of the censorship code. Anita, however, could be counted on to supply the delicate double entendre, the telling innuendo. Whenever we had a Jean Harlow picture on the agenda, we always thought of Anita first."

Anita moved to a small apartment in West Hollywood, working there every morning and reporting to the studio in the afternoon. After dinner with Mizner or Clifford or her parents, she, like everybody else in the film community, went to movies. Nearly every evening she saw a picture, sometimes a double feature. She developed a passion for James Cagney, "the best actor in Hollywood," later naming a pet Pomeranian after him. Her favorite actress was Bette Davis, and she regretted that she never had the chance to write for either. They were both under contract to Warners.

Anita was surprised that life in California was so agreeable. She liked her work, and she didn't miss New York or think at all about Emerson. He, however, was thinking of her. One day in February 1932, as she jotted in her diary, "Mr. E. arrives out of the blue, moves in on me because I'm making money and making good." In a parenthetical comment written at a later date, she added, "This marked the beginning of a real period of pimping for Mr. E." (Any man who lived off a woman was a pimp to Anita.)

On her return to Hollywood, Clifford and R. Beers had questioned her about Emerson, urging her to get rid of him forever. Before she could respond, Minnie spoke up: "I don't know. I feel sort of sorry for him." Tacitly Anita agreed. Men like Mr. E. — or her father, for that matter — not knowing what they wanted and hurting others in their confusion, were indeed to be pitied . . . and protected.

Predictably she took him back; predictably she came down with the flu the next morning. This was the first time in months she had been ill. When she was feeling better, they moved to a larger apartment so Mr. E. could have his own bedroom.

"I was under the impression that she adored him," says Sam Marx. "And he was very charming. My recollection is that he always had her by the hand, and she was constantly gazing into his eyes. They were like father and daughter, he very dignified and she wearing a straw hat with streamers. At M-G-M everybody knew everybody else's business, but there was no gossip about them. They always seemed so devoted."

More even than before, Mr. E. was contrite about his past misconduct, though his remorse was expressed in peculiar, even perverse, ways. Once Anita mentioned that a man had never sent her flowers, and Emerson took this as a cue. But as it was a Sunday, and all florists were closed, he was

Anita and her Pomeranian, Cagney, in the 1930s. Cagney was supposed to have been "as nasty and mean-spirited as any of the gangsters Cagney played on screen."

Anita and her brother Clifford in the early 1930s

forced to steal a bouquet from Forest Lawn Cemetery—a funeral spray for a dying marriage.

Another time he presented her with a list of his lady friends during their marriage. Anita didn't want to look at it, but in shoving it aside she spotted one name: Tilly Losch. She was infuriated: not long before, she had persuaded the Astaires to give Losch a part in their Broadway musical revue *The Band Wagon,* perhaps at the very time Losch was carrying on with Mr. E. In a day or so she calmed down. What else could be expected from people like Losch and Mr. E., who thought the only thing a man and a woman could do together was to jump into bed? Anita always showed generosity toward the shortcomings of her friends, and when Tilly arrived in Hollywood, she greeted her husband's former mistress as her own friend.

Emerson's contrition did not include a reformation of his bad-boy behavior. He talked about getting down to work, and did receive co-authorship credit on a script of Anita's to which, as usual, he had contributed nothing. At Anita's request, Thalberg invited him to join the M–G–M staff of producers, an offer Emerson promised to accept once he came up with something to produce. He didn't want to be assigned to just any

M–G–M project—it had to be a picture worthy of his talents. But Mary Loos, Anita's niece, remembers that most of his energies were spent "promising screen tests to young girls in exchange for a couple of nights with him at the Coronado." Anita knew about this and tried to make a joke of it. Any girl dumb enough to believe Mr. E. could get her a screen test deserved what she got.

Only in one way did Emerson alter his former ways: he no longer placed restrictions on where Anita went or who she saw. This arrangement occasionally led to awkward situations. At Charlie Chaplin's house one night, she encountered a very drunk and lecherous John Barrymore. "Anita, honey, I've had my eye on you for years," he said. "Now our moment has come!" "John, I'm a married woman," she protested. "So is Marie of Rumania," he shot back. Switching ground, she whispered, "Keep my secret. I've got a lover; he's very jealous, and he's waiting outside right now." She rushed to the door, Barrymore running after her and shouting, "I'll kill the bastard!" Outside, she jumped into the car waiting for her and ordered the chauffeur to pull out fast.

But the advantages outweighed the inconveniences. Anita went right on seeing Mizner, and not only did Mr. E. accept the situation, he went out of his way to be cordial to Wilson. Mizner became so close to both Emersons that he started referring to them as his "parents," and sometimes

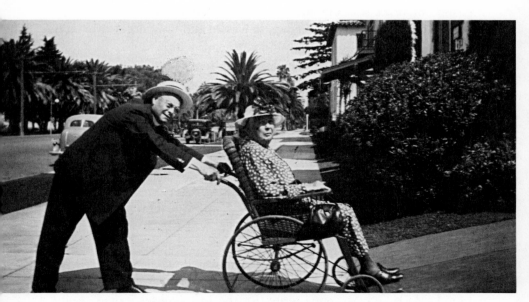

Minnie and R. Beers Loos in the early 1930s. As his wife's health declined, R. Beers became increasingly thoughtful and attentive.

RIGHT: Tilly Losch in California, 1937. Anita first met the Austrian dancer and actress in Vienna in the 1920s and entertained her when she arrived at M–G–M to play Lotus in *The Good Earth*.

OPPOSITE: Anita, Emerson, artist Kees Van Dongen, and Tilly Losch at a Beverly Hills party, 1937. Van Dongen later painted a portrait of Anita.

he called Anita, perhaps not entirely to her liking, "Mama." Mr. E.'s change of heart was undoubtedly partly attributable to Wilson's poor health. By the end of 1932, he was so wasted and wan, his eyes so febrile, that even old friends sometimes didn't recognize him.

Since childhood Mizner had suffered from a weak heart, a condition aggravated by drug and alcohol abuse. Anita and others urged him to take it easy, but he pushed the advice aside: he had walked "a wide mile" in his time and he wasn't going to slow down now. But his pace did slacken—he didn't have the capacity for drinking and brawling as in the past.

In late January 1933 he learned that his brother, Addison, was terminally ill in Florida. "Stop dying," he wired Addie. "I'm trying to write a comedy." But Addie couldn't stop—he was gone a few weeks later. Wilson was hard hit: his brother's death seemed to sap his own will to live. In mid-March, he suffered a heart attack in the Warners writers' building. Efforts were made to get him to a hospital, but he insisted on being taken to his suite at the Ambassador, where he was immediately placed in an oxygen tent. Anita visited every day, sometimes accompanied by a mutual friend, Mark Kelly, a sports writer for the Los Angeles *Times*. Kelly, a devout Catholic, always brought along a crucifix. "Do you think you can postpone the main event with that thing?" Mizner asked. "I *know* I can," Kelly answered. "But look at the fix that poor guy got himself into!" Wilson retorted.

He died two weeks later, on April 3. Anita attended the funeral services at Forest Lawn and then held her own private rite. In her journal, she circled the day of Wilson's death in black and marked the date similarly for years to come.

16

Studio Politics

M ONTHS before Mizner's death, in the summer of 1932, Thalberg told Anita that M–G–M was renewing her contract for the coming year. She and Harlow made a good team, he continued; he'd like her to think up an original story for the actress. The suggestion pleased Anita. She enjoyed writing for a specific personality, especially one as sharply contoured as Harlow's.

She roughed out a hard-boiled comedy, *Hold Your Man,* about a girl who throws over her respectable fiancé for a con man and eventually takes a rap for him. The boy friend's specialty is the badger game, and there's little question that Eddie Hall is the first of several roles Anita based on Mizner (a number of them—including Hall—were played by Clark Gable). She was finishing the script when events occurred that forced her to revise extensively, and not necessarily for the better.

Over the Labor Day weekend, Paul Bern, Harlow's husband, shot himself. The press started printing innuendos about Harlow's private life; and though M–G–M did its best to suppress the rumors, Harlow's flagrant screen image made them all too believable. Public moralists were already campaigning against Mae West, and now Harlow looked like an easier target. Lest her career be destroyed, the studio resolved that Harlow must henceforth be presented in a more favorable light. Anita was ordered to present her *Hold Your Man* heroine in a more sympathetic light.

She kept the first part of the script pretty much intact. But once

Harlow takes the blame for a murder committed by Gable and winds up in a girls' reformatory (which Anita depicts as a sort of strictly disciplined Seven Sisters sorority), the picture gets sticky with sentiment and uplift. Learning Harlow is pregnant, Gable confesses to his crime and goes to jail after first marrying Harlow in the reformatory chapel. When he gets out, she is waiting for him with a bouncing baby. (Penal sentences for murder were apparently brief in the early thirties.)

Hold Your Man is so deficient in anything resembling logic or reality that today it seems almost quaint, quite charmingly so. And at the time of its release, it was a hit; neither critics nor audiences minded that Harlow was now watered down, not so potent as before.

Production started at the end of 1932. Shooting stopped early on December 24 for M–G–M's annual Christmas party, which Anita felt obliged to attend. She nursed a weak drink, exchanged greetings with

Harlow and Gable in Anita's *Hold Your Man* (1933)

Thalberg, then went on to Santa Monica to help Clifford trim his tree. The next morning a studio friend called with terrible news: Thalberg had had a heart attack the previous evening.

A few weeks later, Louis B. Mayer relieved Thalberg of his studio duties, though he might remain at M-G-M in a lesser capacity. Mayer insisted that he was acting for Thalberg's own good; but Thalberg partisans, Anita among them, believed L.B. was seizing an opportunity to get rid of a protégé who had grown into a rival. Gloom settled over the studio. The people Thalberg favored were especially apprehensive, since it was rumored that Mayer was setting up a pogrom.

There were days when Anita regretted signing on at M-G-M for another year. In Thalberg's absence, she was assigned to an Abdullah-abducts-gentlewoman epic, *The Barbarian;* and it was torture trying to think up dialogue Ramon Novarro could mutter while baring his torso, the chief attraction of any Novarro film.

She became more optimistic when she learned that Thalberg would return to M-G-M to head his own production unit. He had first call on all M-G-M talent—actors, writers, directors, cameramen—and two of the first people he wanted to see were the Emersons.

He asked Mr. E. to read scripts for him, an unworthy position for a man of his achievements, but one which must be entrusted to someone with taste and judgment. Thalberg didn't need Emerson, Anita realized, and was only trying to keep him out of her hair. To her relief, Mr. E. accepted.

Thalberg then assigned Anita to *Biography,* an Ina Claire stage vehicle written by S. N. Behrman. Anita said it would never work without Ina, and she was right. At a party some months later, Behrman joshingly accused her of ruining his play. "Not *me,* Sam," she replied. "Ann Harding!"

Then she worked for another producer on a Harlow picture, *The Girl from Missouri.* Emerson received unwarranted co-authorship credit on this, though he was helpful in other ways. Anita was pleased with her script, and appalled when it was handed to Jack Conway to direct. M-G-M had Thalberg and wonderful stars, but with the exception of Ernst Lubitsch, George Cukor, and King Vidor, most of its directors were hacks, Anita was starting to realize. And the hack of hacks was Conway, who hadn't understood that *Redheaded Woman* was supposed to be funny. Rather than hassle with him every step of the way, she asked Emerson to keep an eye on the shooting. If Conway started stepping on her jokes, he was to call her and she'd talk to the producer. She figured that

Conway didn't like being bossed by a woman and would accept "suggestions" better from a man, even the scriptwriter's husband. She was correct about this: Conway accepted Emerson as a peer. So she was often to use Mr. E. as ventriloquist's dummy; in the years just ahead, she frequently spoke through him—an illusion that bolstered Mr. E.'s vanity and created the aura of a happy partnership for Sam Marx and other M–G–M executives.

A N I T A committed herself to Hollywood—and maybe to some kind of ongoing married life with Mr. E., too—when she bought a house in Beverly Hills in 1934. It was suburban Tudor, nothing grand, but with lots of rooms and a garden where she wrote when the weather was clement. As a bonus there was nightly entertainment provided by the next-door neighbors, Humphrey Bogart and Mayo Methot. First came curses, then crashing glass, screams, and eventually moans of passionate reconciliation. Anita rather regretted that she didn't get to know the Bogarts more intimately; but they worked at Warners, and between people employed at different studios, there existed an all-but-impassable social barrier.

"Everything revolved around the studio. The people you worked with were the people you played with," Anita told an interviewer. "Nobody knew what was going on in the outside world—we were too busy working or too busy worrying about our work. It was movies every waking hour of the day."

She went to the parties given by the Thalbergs and the Goldwyns and the Selznicks—drinks and dinner and then a screening of a new movie. As she wrote Ruth de Vallambrosa, "the movie people are all so overpowered with work, preoccupation, and worry that there isn't even time for a good scandal. The countess di Frasso gives big 'social' parties, but dull as hell. Aside from that, not even a ladies' lunch of any interest."

There were exceptions. She enjoyed the Sunday brunches given by George Cukor. Cukor was then very overweight (later he would slim down) and enjoyed making his presence felt; he prided himself on his no-nonsense attitude toward his profession and co-workers. He could turn on you without warning, and yet he was the loyalest of friends. "Anita and I hit it off instantly," he recalled.

On her first visit to Cukor's glamorous home, Anita found Tallulah Bankhead floating nude in the pool while Constance Collier (the Lady Macbeth of Anita's 1916 film) sat under a huge Japanese parasol, sipping

Edwin Hubble and Aldous
Huxley in Santa Monica, 1938

tea with Hugh Walpole, then writing the script for Selznick's *David Copperfield*. Anita asked Cukor, who was to direct *Copperfield*, if the stories she'd been hearing were really true—did Walpole write with a quill pen? Cukor rolled his eyes to heaven in reply.

Katharine Hepburn and Greta Garbo were regulars at Cukor's Sunday parties. And there were bound to be one or another of the fabled first ladies of Broadway, a Gish or two, a fashionable photographer or artist, maybe a titled European. Cukor adored the rich, beautiful, and talented, but guests weren't invited a second time unless they held up their end of the conversation. "George kept the closest thing to a salon that Hollywood ever knew," Anita said.

His only rival was Salka Viertel, a Polish-born screenwriter at M-G-M. Mrs. Viertel's home in Santa Monica was a haven for the more intellectual foreign visitors in Hollywood, and it was here that Anita would meet Sergei Eisenstein, Lion Feuchtwanger, Thomas Mann, and Bertolt Brecht. The atmosphere was *"echt Deutsch,"* she wrote without much enthusiasm.

The only close friendship she established at Salka's was with the renowned astronomer Edwin Hubble, whose work at the Mount Wilson Observatory at the California Institute of Technology enthralled Anita.

She was outraged that Hubble often had to beg for money to get the equipment he needed. "Just imagine," she complained, "one lousy M-G-M picture costs more than a telescope!"

IN 1935 Anita completed another Harlow picture, *Riffraff,* co-starring Spencer Tracy. It's a Steinbeckian, *Cannery Row*-type tale about tuna

Jean Harlow and Spencer Tracy in *Riffraff* (1935). "Tracy was a fine actor," Anita said, "but his black Irish temperament made him difficult to work with. There wasn't much chemistry between him and Harlow."

fishermen and the women they love, and while the wisecracks whiz by and there's real chemistry between Harlow and Tracy, the film gets a little preachy. There are some perfunctory and predictable melodramatics about labor troubles and union agitation—subjects that probably wouldn't have interested Anita except that around this time there was conflict over the formation of a screen-writers' guild. Thalberg was against it, and his intransigence cost him many writer friends, but in *Riffraff* Anita seems to be backing his position.

Later that year she teamed up with Robert Hopkins, who was to become a frequent collaborator. "Hoppy" came from San Francisco and had spent his youth on the Barbary Coast working at anything that brought him a nickel. For a while he etched portraits on cowhide, his favorite customers being the Barbary Coast tarts. "They always bought three," he told Anita. "One for themselves, one for their mother, and another for their pimp."

Later he was an errand boy for a gambling casino, where he met Wilson Mizner, who became his idol. They stayed in touch over the years, and when Hoppy learned that Willy was in Hollywood, he joined him there. Somehow he got a job at M-G-M as an "idea man"—a role Mizner played at Warners. He injected jokes, stretches of "ad-libbed" dialogue into scripts, talked out plots that other writers developed and refined. He was very good at this; Thalberg rarely kept him waiting, Anita noted.

Hoppy's conversation was a nonstop patter of one-liners and insults, recalls Sam Marx. About Arthur Hornblow, an M-G-M producer who was an oenophile, he commented, "Hornblow can't read a script unless it's at room temperature." And when Harry Rapf, a Metro producer encumbered with a Cyrano-sized nose, mentioned he was sailing to Europe, Hoppy said, "Harry, don't peer out the porthole or the ship may turn around."

Most of Hoppy's humor was way off-color. At a story conference, when his idea for a Gable script was tepidly received, he shouted, "Listen, this is going to be the picture of the year, so why aren't your dicks snapping to attention?" When the M-G-M story department issued an edict requiring writers to submit a daily copy of their output, Hoppy turned in the following:

CLARK GABLE STORY

Scene: Louis B. Mayer's office
Enter the hero with a cornflower up his ass.

Robert Hopkins at Anita's Santa Monica house, 1936

After Mizner's death, Hoppy and Anita got together occasionally to reminisce about their departed friend and the city all three called home. One day as they strolled around the M–G–M lot, Anita wrote later in a reminiscence of Hopkins, they hit on the idea of writing a movie about "their departed pal and (their) nostalgia for San Francisco."

Working with Hopkins was at first an unsettling experience for Anita. He had several idiosyncrasies, including phone phobia. If a call came for him while they were writing, Anita placed the receiver on her desk and he shouted from across the room. And then there was the great language barrier. Hoppy paced around, throwing out ideas. "Okay," he'd say, "there's this canary who thinks her cunt's just for piss and this cocksucker of a priest and this brass-balled gambler who get thrown together during the earthquake." Anita's job was to transcribe all this into prose that wouldn't make the M–G–M stenographers blush. It took a few weeks, but finally there was an outline Anita thought Thalberg should see. Thalberg told them to go on.

The original story was about Blackie Norton (the Wilson Mizner figure), a Barbary Coast casino proprietor, who meets Mary Blake, a nice girl so down on her luck that she applies for a singing job at Blackie's saloon. She takes a tailspin for Norton, but realizing he's a cad, she asks her priest for moral fortitude. There are many complications before the plot reaches its climax with the 1906 earthquake. Then, Blackie realizes all he needs is a woman like Mary—but will she be found among the survivors?

Heart tug and humor, nostalgia and uplift, spectacle and music— *San Francisco* had everything. When Anita and Hoppy completed a synopsis, she went to Thalberg again, this time requesting that he consider placing it on his own production schedule. He was encouraging: "It looks good," he said. "Keep working and come back when you've more to show."

Of all her M-G-M films, *San Francisco* was closest to Anita's heart, but writing it was not all fun. Hoppy kept turning up late for work, if at all. When Anita chewed him out, he cursed and walked out. She went on by herself, periodically turning in pages to Thalberg. "This looks like Gable material," he said.

Gable was "boring and temperamental," but of course, like every other writer on the lot, Anita was thrilled to get him for one of her pictures. And if you caught him off-guard, he could poke fun at his own image. Once she surprised him while he was washing his dentures in an M-G-M drinking fountain. "Well, Anita honey, how do you like America's favorite sex symbol now?" he asked. "I've never liked you better," she answered sincerely.

Thalberg thought the priest—an Irishman who had been a boxer before turning to the church—was "Spence Tracy stuff." And Mary Blake seemed perfect for M-G-M's resident songbird, Jeanette MacDonald. Anita told Thalberg she had actually had Grace Moore in mind. Grace had a *real* voice; she was glamorous, and her latest films had been very popular. She also had a wonderful sense of humor, particularly about her romantic escapades. Her latest amour, she had confided to Anita, was a Texas cattle king, so blasé about sex that "he did it with his boots on."

Thalberg explained that Moore wasn't under contract to Metro and that MacDonald was. She was also eager to play opposite Gable, and Louis B. Mayer, an ardent fan, tried to keep Jeanette happy. Diplomatically he was telling her that MacDonald was the price to be paid for Gable as Blackie Norton.

A few weeks later Thalberg informed Anita that his health and his commitment to *The Good Earth* would prevent him from personally supervising *San Francisco,* so he was passing it on to his right-hand man, Bernard Hyman. Maybe Emerson would like to co-produce with Hyman? Mr. E. liked the idea, provided he received a two-year contract at top Metro salary for a producer—around $1,250 a week.

Once Hyman and Emerson took over, everything started going wrong. Gable wasn't available, Hyman told Anita, but she could have either John Howard or Robert Young. Appalled, she insisted that the picture was doomed without Gable or, in a pinch, William Powell. What she wasn't told was that Gable didn't want the part. More precisely, he wanted nothing to do with MacDonald. She, like many actresses of the period, had a clause in her contract allowing days off for menstruation. This irked Gable, who had to go on looking lecherous and smirking even when his hemorrhoids flared up. And he wasn't Nelson Eddy—what was he to do while Jeanette shrilled her high C's? Duck the flying glass?

Anita kept after Hyman, who took the problem to Mayer; predictably, he was enraged that Gable scorned his favorite star. Threatened with suspension if he didn't accept *San Francisco* and Jeanette, Gable knuckled under.

The director was W. S. Van Dyke, or "One-Take Woody," as he was known around the lot. Van Dyke brought in big pictures on schedule and often under budget; but speed wasn't, Anita decided, the only requisite of a good director. Time and again she went to Hyman and asked for a second chance, but Hyman always replied, "Woody never reshoots."

He said it once too often. Anita tore into him where it hurt: "This would never have happened if Irving were in charge," she said for openers. "He earned his reputation by reshooting entire pictures!" What followed persuaded Hyman to order Van Dyke to refilm several scenes.

Worse was to come. The rushes of the earthquake sequence were so stagy and unimaginative that in despair Anita suggested that Mr. E. replace Van Dyke. Through him, she figured, she could keep control of the picture. Hyman rejected Emerson but agreed the earthquake scenes looked tame. On the day they were reshot, Van Dyke urged the cast to throw themselves into the spirit of the thing. "Believe it's a real earthquake. Run for your lives! Try to help your friends!" One extra got so excited that when the cameras started rolling he picked up Anita, standing on the sidelines, and carried her across Blackie Norton's saloon. "As I wasn't wearing a costume, I was cut out of the final footage," she remembered. "Which was unfortunate since nobody shrieked as realistically as I did!"

When *San Francisco* opened in June 1936, critics agreed that it was a grand show. Much to the studio's surprise, it nosed out *The Great Ziegfeld* as M–G–M's top-grossing film that year. It received several Oscar nominations, including best picture (it lost to *Ziegfeld*), best actor (Spencer Tracy, who lost to Paul Muni for *The Story of Louis Pasteur*), best director, and best original screen story—a category eliminated a few years later.

Ironically, this last citation went to Hoppy, not to Anita; she had received credit for the screenplay, and *San Francisco* wasn't nominated in that category. She didn't begrudge Hoppy his brief moment of glory (he was to lose to the authors of *Louis Pasteur*): around the studio, people knew she was responsible for *San Francisco*'s success.

Telling Ruth de Vallambrosa about the picture, Anita focused on

Gable and MacDonald in *San Francisco* (1936). "Usually you could see it on screen when Clark didn't like one of his leading ladies," Anita said, "but his smirky disdain for Jeanette actually worked to the picture's advantage."

The beginning of the earthquake sequence from *San Francisco*

Mr. E.'s contribution. "Thanks to *San Francisco,* he's been given a two-year contract as a producer. You wouldn't know him—he has gotten over all his nonsense and looks younger than any time since I've known him. He is going to produce all pictures I write which means that I won't have lousy casts in them and will also get subjects which are my speciality."

It wasn't to happen. In early September 1936, while attending an outdoor concert, Irving Thalberg caught a chill which developed into pneumonia, and less than a week later he died. His death was seen as a catastrophe which would eventually lead to the decline and fall of the M–G–M empire. This proved not to be true, but many members of the studio staff found their future plans dramatically overturned, Anita among them.

17

The Toughest
Year

THALBERG'S death led to the resignation of several assistants, including Albert Lewin, a former drama critic and professor who had been very close to Irving. Lewin and Cukor, Anita said, "bestowed M–G–M with whatever cultivation it could boast." Lewin insisted that Mayer was a crass businessman out to wreck everything Thalberg had struggled to achieve. "I'm getting out before the bum destroys everything," he told Anita. "You better do the same."

Anita had a hunch he was right. Unlike Thalberg, Mayer and the majority of M–G–M producers were "foes to entertainment." But she was too cautious to burn bridges. Bernie Hyman insisted she was secure: the studio was going to look after her, and he personally wanted to hear any ideas she had for next year's program. "Maybe another *San Francisco*," he said with a wink.

Hoppy had an idea for a racetrack comedy. "We'll call it *Saratoga*," he extemporized. "That's close to *San Francisco*. There's this society girl, so hoity-toity she's got polka dots on her toilet paper. . . . " They roughed out a synopsis which Hyman liked. "Might be ideal for Harlow and Gable."

She was also working on *Mama Steps Out,* Emerson's first solo effort as an M–G–M producer. It was low budget, beneath her caliber, but she wanted to help him prove himself and maintain his equilibrium. Work kept him steady and away from the massage parlors he visited to "relieve anxiety."

By this time she had bought a beachfront lot in Santa Monica, adjacent to property owned by Albert Lewin. His house had been designed by Richard Neutra, a celebrated Austrian architect, who was commissioned to plan Anita's home. It was nearly completed, and things were going along smoothly, when, in the last week of December, there were omens that 1937 was going to be, as she later scrawled in her diary, *"THE TOUGHEST YEAR"*: Emerson announced he was going to Coronado for the weekend; Hoppy reported for work drunk five days in a row; R. Beers went on a bender; and Clifford required surgery for a blood clot on the brain. (The operation was a success except for one unexplainable side-effect: Clifford got a case of hiccoughs that lasted for a week.)

By the end of January, she had completed a draft of *Saratoga*. Hyman said it needed more work. What didn't he like? Well, nothing he could specify; it just wasn't right. Thalberg, Anita thought to herself, would have pointed her in a certain direction. Groping to give Hyman what he wanted, she kept rewriting blindly. Some scenes he rejected; others were accepted one day, refused the next. "If you can't tell me what's wrong, how can I fix it?" she asked. She'd get it right in the end, he replied.

Meanwhile, behind her back, the script was revised by someone else. "Greasy stuff," Anita told Hyman. He agreed, and promised to go back to the original script. Then she learned he had asked Thalberg's former secretary for her opinion. "Are you so insecure you go to a stenographer for advice? Let *her* write the script!" Anita snapped. The next day Hyman backed down. Anita's script was to go into production at the end of April.

Friction then shifted to the set. Jack Conway was again directing, and, as in the past, he and Anita squabbled constantly. Hyman tried to keep both happy: "Diplomacy," Anita said, "was Bernie's only virtue."

About a month into shooting, Jean Harlow became too ill to go on working. Her condition was serious, but since she and her mother were Christian Scientists, no physician was called until Louis B. Mayer intervened. By then it was too late. On June 7, at age twenty-six, Jean Harlow died of uremic poisoning.

After funeral services at Forest Lawn, Anita and Hoppy reported to Hyman's office to discuss the fate of *Saratoga*. Several key scenes, all involving the Harlow character, were yet to be shot. Hyman suggested finishing the film with another actress, Rita Johnson, filling in for Harlow. "Don't you think," Anita asked in disbelief, "people will be confused by two actresses in the same part?" Hyman had to admit it wasn't a good idea.

The next day it was decided to reshoot the entire picture with Gladys George. George was a fine actress, but tailoring the part for her was going to be a lot of work. "I wish I was with Jean in Forest Lawn," Anita wrote that night. Later, Hyman decided it would be too costly to start from scratch. Hoppy and Anita were asked to eliminate the Harlow character from the remaining scenes whenever it was possible; when it wasn't, Harlow's stand-in would be substituted, wearing floppy hats and shot in shadow. And they had to work fast: the studio wanted the picture released on schedule. Anita took this to mean that M–G–M wanted *Saratoga* to open while Harlow's death was still fresh news. She did as she was told, but it was sick, morbid drudgery, and she refused to look at the film once it was finished.

I N J U L Y Anita and Mr. E. spent a three-week holiday in New York. She already had decided not to renew her contract with M–G–M but as yet hadn't informed Hyman. She wanted to explain she had accepted a better offer.

Sam Marx had left M–G–M two years earlier to work for Sam Goldwyn at United Artists. Knowing that Anita was discontent, he asked Goldwyn if he'd like her on his payroll. "I'll pay her anything she wants," Goldwyn replied. Phil Berg, Anita's agent, asked for $5,000 a week for her and Mr. E.'s services. Goldwyn didn't bargain; while she was in New York, contracts were being prepared for her signature.

Goldwyn's wife, former stage actress Frances Howard, had been an occasional member of Anita's Tuesday Widow parties in the twenties. "Whatever do you see in Sam?" Anita asked. "Yeah, what's the guy got?" Dutch Talmadge echoed. "He's sweet," Frances said. Some people were charmed by his legendary malapropisms, but Anita suspected that these were crafted by well-reimbursed Hollywood gagmen. But the worse thing about Goldwyn was his shrill voice: he gave her a migraine.

Things started off badly. Her first assignment was a romantic comedy about a cowboy and a society lady for Gary Cooper and Merle Oberon. Director Leo McCarey had roughed out an outline. Goldwyn handed Anita a single sheet of paper; it took her a minute to read it three times. "Honestly, Sam, I don't think there's enough material here for a picture," she said. "MATERIAL!" Goldwyn shouted. "We've got Merle and Cooper and McCarey! We don't need material! People don't go to the movies for material!" Anita spent a week arguing with Goldwyn over the hopelessness of McCarey's plot; but, getting nowhere, she resolved to pull off a tour de force. "Somehow I'll get a script out of that lousy story."

Goldwyn wasn't going to be of any help. Anita marveled that he ever got anything into production. He didn't know what he wanted and operated in a state of complete chaos. Within a month she was "anguishing" over leaving M–G–M. Albert Lewin told her he was also having second thoughts. In the past months he had worked at both Paramount and United Artists, and he was beginning to believe M–G–M was paradise compared with other studios.

T H O U G H both Emersons had been hired by Goldwyn, Mr. E. contributed nothing to *The Cowboy and the Lady* and stayed far away from her quarrels with Goldwyn. His behavior was increasingly erratic. He was either elated and fantasizing about a co-production with Goldwyn or morose and tearful over Bug's hardships.

One morning in October, he interrupted Anita while she was working on the script. He had been looking over their finances and had discovered they were destitute. Anita told him not to be foolish: they were making wonderful money. Emerson shook his head. "Soon my Bug will have to live on Campbell's Soup," he said. "I can't allow that to happen." He stretched out his hands, and instantly Anita realized he was mad: he was going to strangle her.

Shoving him aside, she ran out of the room and found her chauffeur. Together they returned to find Mr. E. slumped in a chair, weeping. She soothed him and then asked the chauffeur to drive them to Clifford's. Her brother was out, and after waiting four hours, Anita decided to take Mr. E. home. He was peaceful, as physically and emotionally drained as a child after a tantrum. That night she put him to bed and read him to sleep.

The next morning, Clifford and Anita took Mr. E. to Las Encinas Sanatorium in Pasadena. Emerson was calm until he was inside. Then he became disoriented, babbling about San Quentin, apparently believing he was to be imprisoned for attempted murder. Sedated, he regained awareness of where he was and cooperated with Las Encinas's psychiatrists.

The doctors confirmed what Clifford and Anita already sensed: Mr. E. was schizophrenic. Why hadn't the specialists Emerson had seen over the years recognized the illness? Anita asked. The chief psychiatrist agreed that his disorder might have been spotted earlier, but it wouldn't have mattered. There wasn't a cure; therapy and strict supervision could help, however, and possibly in time Mr. E. might be able to function at some level in the outside world. But relapses could and should be expected to occur; he would always require guardianship of some sort.

Las Encinas patients included some of the biggest names in Hollywood: W. C. Fields once spent time there drying out, and Kay Francis checked in periodically to lose weight. The medical staff was as competent as it was discreet, Clifford promised Anita. Mr. E. would be treated enlightenedly and humanely. Also expensively—Las Encinas was not cheap.

Anita knew how much money she made each week but was ignorant about how much was in savings and investments. Acting on Clifford's advice, she began to find out. What she discovered was first heartbreaking, then infuriating. Emerson had removed close to $150,000 from their joint savings and placed it in accounts bearing his name, though it was to revert to her in trust when he died. "He swindled me," she told her brother. Clifford dissuaded her from taking legal action, pointing out that the money Mr. E. had taken could be used to keep him in Las Encinas.

Anita now started spending her days working and her evenings visiting Mr. E. The writing was impossible, as Goldwyn kept throwing her different curves. One day he took her off the Cooper picture and transferred her to a Gershwin musical, *The Goldwyn Follies;* two days later, she was off the musical and back in the saddle with Cooper. "Woke up unsure about which picture I'm supposed to be writing," she told her journal.

The evenings were just as unpredictable. Mr. E. was in a very agitated state. Dr. Smith, Las Encinas's chief doctor, and Emerson's nurse were beside themselves: Mr. E. was pinching female patients and trying to escape the sanitorium grounds for "a massage." One visit he'd be weepy and withdrawn; the next, euphoric and boasting he'd soon be back at work as "the king of B productions." Dr. Smith thought this was a good omen. "He's not totally out of touch with reality," he told Anita. "He doesn't see himself as the king of A productions."

Anita struggled to hide her depression from family and friends. "Am pretty blue and despondent," she wrote in her diary, "but mustn't let anyone know since nobody's more unpopular than a broad singing the blues."

She resolved to unload some of the misery. In early November she informed Mr. E. she wanted a divorce. She and Dr. Smith were apprehensive about his reaction; but to their surprise, he made no protest. Then, two days later, he presented her with "a lot of pimp arithmetic" about a settlement. Anita said that that should be worked out by lawyers. "Freedom after seventeen years!!!"

A few days later Clifford called with saddening news: their mother had died peacefully in her sleep earlier that morning. Anita felt the loss, but there was consolation in knowing that Minnie, who had grown increasingly disoriented in the last years, would be spared the decline into senility. R. Beers was devastated by Minnie's death, and Anita put aside work to help him adjust.

She also used this respite to re-evaluate her professional plight. Phil Berg, her agent, said she could probably get out of the Goldwyn contract. Before telling him to begin negotiations, Anita talked to Bernie Hyman about returning to M-G-M. He was cordial but noncommittal, so she approached Eddie Mannix, one of L. B. Mayer's right-hand men. A burly, hard-drinking Irishman, Mannix had been one of Wilson Mizner's buddies, and he liked Anita. (She hadn't so much as blinked when he and Willy held a contest to see which of them could piss into a beer bottle without spilling a drop.) Hyman wasn't the only producer on the lot, he said: all she had to do was extricate herself from Goldwyn and she'd be back with Metro.

Goldwyn agreed that the contract might be bought out. Phil Berg thought Goldwyn would settle for $3,000, but he started negotiations at $1,750 and was up to twice that when Goldwyn changed his mind. He wasn't releasing Anita until she finished *The Cowboy and the Lady*.

By then Leo McCarey had left the picture and been replaced by William Wyler. At their first meeting, Wyler outlined the way he thought the plot should build. "That's not great," he admitted, "but it won't disgrace either of us. You'll probably be able to improve on it." By February 1938 Anita had completed a script which Wyler liked but Goldwyn wanted revised. In exasperation, Wyler exclaimed, "Look, the basic idea is preposterous! Why would a woman like Merle shilly-shally about bedding down with Cooper? Either accept what Anita's given you or scrap the picture."

Goldwyn accepted Anita's script. Three weeks later he replaced Wyler with McCarey and hired S. N. Behrman to rewrite *The Cowboy and the Lady* from scratch. Anita didn't care—she was *"FREE!!!!"*

18

House Guests

Just before Mr. E. entered Las Encinas, Anita moved into her Santa Monica home on Ocean Front (today part of the Pacific Coast Highway). Known as "the Gold Coast," the area was inhabited by the movie rich. To the south of Anita lived Norma Shearer, Ben Lyon and Bebe Daniels, Mervyn LeRoy, Darryl Zanuck, and L. B. Mayer; to the north was Marion Davies's monumental "beach cottage."

Anita's white stucco house had two stories. On the ground floor was a large living room with casement windows facing the Pacific Ocean; a dining room opening onto a garden and a swimming pool; a library, a kitchen, a pantry, and a breakfast nook. In the main hall was a wide, curving staircase with a chrome banister and a skylight above it. On the second floor there were two guest rooms and two master suites, each with dressing room and private bath equipped with a bidet and sauna. There was also a fully equipped gymnasium and a steam room.

The furnishing of the house was supervised by Fanny Brice, then moonlighting as a decorator: Anita called her style "early Baby Snooks." Everything was simple—good wicker, chintz, sisal rugs.

"The house was very angular, and some people considered the ceilings too low," says Mary Loos. "But that was Neutra's style. It was very luxurious, much better designed than it was ever utilized." Neutra had designed a home for relaxation and entertainment; and while Anita was hospitable, she was always working too hard to do justice to the architect's vision.

Anita's beachfront house in Santa Monica, which was completed in 1936

"This place is too big for you alone," said Howard Sturges. "You need a man to take up some of the space." Sturgie had come to Hollywood with Cole Porter, then under contract to M-G-M, and was helping Anita through the rough spell with Goldwyn and Mr. E. "A man like Mr. E. is enough for a lifetime," she answered. When Sturgie mentioned the same thing again, she repeated a French aphorism of which she was very fond: *"Qui embrasse trop, manque le train."* (A rough translation might read, "Too many kisses make you miss the train.")

But replacing Mr. E. was a thought Anita occasionally entertained even before she was officially "free." In the diaries covering the early Hollywood years there are notations about men who made passes as well as references to a man to whom she was "very attracted"—he *didn't* make passes, and the ones who did weren't as attractive. Except for Leopold Stokowski, the conductor of the Philadelphia Orchestra, whose charisma off the podium was as great as on.

They had met in Europe at a time (the late twenties) when Anita was still devoted to Mr. E.'s welfare. "I introduced them," recalls Ruth de Vallambrosa. "They were very taken with each other, and I encouraged Anita, but she wouldn't hear of it." But in 1936, when Stokowski came to Hollywood to appear in *One Hundred Men and a Girl,* she was very excited. He was, she wrote Ruth, "the only good company I've had here since Willy took a powder."

"STOKIE" was the only entry in her diary on the five days after

Stokowski's arrival. Then he goes unmentioned until a week later, when "Stokie and Garbo drop by." Three days later Stokowski called to ask a favor: Would Anita please take Greta to Bullock's Wilshire and buy her some decent clothes?

With Stokie occupied elsewhere, Anita came to depend on Sturges when she needed an escort. And when Sturgie wasn't free, she turned to another member of the Porter clique, F. Ray Goetz.

Nobody knew what the "F" stood for or much about Goetz's life before he emerged from Tin Pan Alley obscurity as the lyricist for "For Me and My Gal." In the early 1920s he married French soubrette Irene Bordoni, who looked a little like a plump Anita Loos. She starred in *Paris,* Cole Porter's first Broadway hit, which was co-produced by Goetz, who also produced and directed two later Porter shows, *Fifty Million Frenchmen* and *The New Yorkers.* (Bordoni was in neither; by then she was the ex–Mrs. Goetz.)

Marjorie Oelrichs, Leopold Stokowski, and Anita, Santa Monica, 1937

Anita described Goetz as "an overfed Buddha," though he was actually more of a hefty American scamp. Sturges told Anita that Porter's accountant once accused Goetz of pocketing royalties owed the composer. Porter stared witheringly at the accountant. "Though not as *precise* as you," he said, "Mr. Goetz is far better company."

Goetz was one of Wilson Mizner's old cronies. He wanted to *be* Willy, Anita said; but for all his weight, he was just a shadow of the man they both idolized. Goetz was good company but a bit of a buffoon, too. "Doesn't it make Ray a little ashamed that nobody gets mad when he does something stupid?" she wondered.

Goetz was clearly smitten; and while Anita didn't encourage him, she didn't dampen his expectations. She relied on him to chauffeur her, shop for last-minute groceries at the Farmers' Market, and entertain Mr. E. when she was working against a deadline.

Sometimes Emerson was stable enough to leave Las Encinas for dinner or a weekend in Santa Monica. His visits were trying for Anita, and she always had company when he was home. Clifford often came with his close friend Edgar Bergen; Sturgie and Goetz were counted on; and always there were Betty and Sandy Wendel. Mrs. Wendel, a writer, was a dear friend who was devoted to Emerson. Anita depended on her to keep him amused. He called her Beth and once told Anita, "Beth is my best medicine."

Emerson's visits to Santa Monica led him to believe that he and Anita were going to reconcile. Sometimes he'd feign sickness so he wouldn't have to return to Las Encinas. "I'll cure what ails him," a strapping Swedish maid told Anita. "Where does it hurt?" she asked Emerson. He pointed to his stomach. After a couple of chops, Emerson announced he was fine. "Just a little gas," he said.

Back at Las Encinas he became devious about the divorce. One day he'd be agreeable, the next outrageous in his demands for a settlement. When Anita pressured him to get on with it, his mood swings accelerated and intensified. Dr. Smith told her that the subject of divorce should be dropped temporarily, as Mr. E. couldn't handle it.

She followed doctor's orders, though she sensed that there was as much method as madness in Mr. E.'s behavior. She knew he was going to hang on as long as he could, using all his manipulative craft to do so. And being a man of the theater, Mr. E. knew how to dramatize his illness to maximum effect.

Anita allowed him to play out his drama, though it deprived her of

Betty and Sandy Wendel, Hollywood friends, with Anita during a New York holiday in the early 1940s

the freedom she insisted she wanted. Again, she may have done so out of guilt or possibly from a Victorian sense of obligation of wife to husband. Perhaps it was a safeguard against getting involved with another loser. Retaining her status as Mrs. John Emerson allowed her to remind gentlemen who wanted more than a cerebral affair that she was, after all, a married woman.

BY SPRING of 1938, Anita was back at M–G–M, working on a romantic adventure, *The Great Canadian,* with Hoppy. The hero was designed for Clark Gable; but Bernie Hyman said that Gable was tied up with *Gone With the Wind,* and who knew when that would be finished?

What was she to do in the meantime? Hyman told her to report each day to the studio—something would turn up soon. Anita spent three weeks "loafing on M–G–M money," sharpening pencils in the morning, roaming the back lot in the afternoon. Another writer might have enjoyed

LEFT TO RIGHT: Robert Hopkins, Anita, Eddy Duchin, Marjorie Oelrichs, and Emerson having lunch at the M–G–M commissary in 1936

the indentured leisure, but she was savvy enough to know that a writer with nothing to do was probably a writer whose contract wasn't going to be renewed.

But then she was told to report to Mervyn LeRoy, the highest-paid producer on the lot and, according to studio rumor, L. B. Mayer's chosen successor to Thalberg. LeRoy wanted her to adapt a creaky Hungarian play, *Dramatic School,* for Luise Rainer, who was, Anita thought, "fool's Rheingold." Two weeks later, LeRoy took her off *Dramatic School* and put her on a remake of Joan Crawford's *Our Dancing Daughters,* to star his protégée, Lana Turner.

This was more to her taste. She thought Turner had the look of "a new Clara Bow," and the old picture was not so out of date once the Charleston was replaced by the jitterbug. But before she had completed an outline, LeRoy told her to forget it; he had something else in mind for Turner. Anita was to report to Arthur Freed, the head of M–G–M's musical unit, who was in desperate need of someone to adapt Rodgers and Hart's *Babes in Arms* for the screen.

The show had great songs, but the book was weak, and Anita hadn't a clue as to how to strengthen it. But since Freed and the picture's two stars, Judy Garland and Mickey Rooney, were personal favorites of L. B. Mayer's, she felt she had to do her best.

Doing anything at all was difficult when Elsa Maxwell was around. With Dickie Gordon Fellows, Elsa had arrived in Hollywood to peddle a couple of scripts and to promote herself as a "character actress." If "old bats" like Constance Collier and Stella Campbell and Nazimova got movie jobs, why shouldn't she? Elsa and Dickie were staying at a residential hotel, but impulsively Anita invited them to move in with her. Elsa, the consummate freeloader, told Dickie to call the hotel and have the Vuitton sent along. Elsa then took over. Every night someone gave her a party, or vice versa, and Elsa insisted Anita join the fun. "Too much swank," Anita wrote.

Even worse were the phone bills. Elsa spent most of the day making transatlantic calls to principessas and Romanovs who didn't accept collect calls, though they often called Elsa collect, the charges billed to her hostess's account. Anita told Elsa that she needed absolute solitude to get on with *Babes in Arms.* Not unaccustomed to sudden eviction, Elsa was prepared. The next day she and Dickie transferred the Vuitton to Fanny Brice's house.

After they left, Anita was asked to take in the invalid child of a dead friend. Earlier, Marjorie Oelrichs had married the café society pianist and bandleader Eddy Duchin, and in the fall of 1937 she gave birth to a son, Peter. She died shortly afterward, apparently from an infection caused by inadequate sterilization in the delivery room. Peter was born with a serious respiratory ailment. As Eddy Duchin was too griefstricken to watch over his son, Marie (Mrs. Averell) Harriman, one of Marjorie's closest friends, stepped in and took charge of Peter.

In November 1938 Marie Harriman called Anita to report that Peter now spent most of every day in an iron lung; his doctors feared he might not survive another Eastern winter. If they could get him to California by train, would Anita look after him? Transportation would be tricky and dangerous. The child in his iron lung had to travel in a helium-filled compartment, and the train must bypass tunnels lest he suffocate. How this was to be accomplished, Marie didn't know; but her husband, the owner of Union Pacific Railroad, had promised to intervene.

The trip took over a week. Peter's nurses telegraphed Anita along the way, and the news was not good. In Los Angeles, Anita and Clifford were waiting with an ambulance, which rushed Peter to the Good Samaritan Hospital. Within a few days, he had improved slightly, but the local doctors advised moving him to a drier climate.

Anita rented a house in Palm Springs and hired nurses to look after Peter around the clock. Every Saturday she made the three-hour train trip to visit her charge. By February 1939, the doctors said that Peter could safely be moved to Los Angeles. Anita thought that taking him into her home would be unsettling for her, so she rented another house, in Studio City in the San Fernando Valley. Peter was by then able to spend several hours each day outside his iron lung, even play with other children, provided they wore surgical masks to protect him from infection.

While Peter was steadily improving, Mr. E. kept dancing on his checkered stage. At one point his doctors felt he had improved enough to leave Las Encinas, but Anita refused to have him back on a permanent basis. He was to take his own apartment with a nurse to look after him. Hearing this, he immediately went into a decline, making her feel guilty, as he intended. While not entirely immune to his manipulations, she was learning to ride them out, promising herself that neither Mr. E. nor M–G–M was going to unsaddle her.

The studio was also throwing hurdles in her direction, she decided. After putting a lot of work into *Babes in Arms,* she was ordered to do a polishing job on *The Great Canadian,* as Gable would soon be rid of Rhett Butler. Anita thought her rewrite one of the best things she had done for M–G–M, and Bernie Hyman agreed; but he then apologetically told her that the picture once more had been postponed: Gable had been promised a long vacation in exchange for appearing at the Atlanta premiere of *Gone With the Wind*.

Two weeks later Hoppy learned that the studio had dropped the ax on him. That night Anita and he hoisted a few highballs as they watched the sun set over the Pacific. She'd be the next victim, she predicted; she didn't have a single screen credit for 1938.

But instead of a pink slip, the next week she got a call from M–G–M asking her to report right away: George Cukor had a sick script he felt she could make well.

Peter Duchin enjoying Christmas and playing in the garden

19

Genius
and Goddesses

CLARE BOOTHE'S *The Women* had been one of the big popular successes of the 1936 Broadway season. Some critics found
Boothe's exposé of Park Avenue matrons uncharitable, but audiences
relished the bitchiness, and the play ran for over eighteen months. M–G–M
bought the screen rights in 1937, and for over a year staff writers worked
on the script, Scott Fitzgerald among many others. He deplored the
original material ("What gossip! What characters!" he wrote his daughter)
and tried to add some dimension to what was essentially a series of revue
sketches.

Cukor rejected his script and wasn't entirely happy with a later one
provided by Jane Murfin. He asked producer Hunt Stromberg to bring in
Anita. She was advised to stick to Boothe's play as far as possible. "You
can't muck around much with proven material," Cukor warned. "If the
weak scenes got by on stage, they'll get by on screen. And if you try to
improve on them, you may unravel everything."

Anita completed her script in three weeks. Unlike Fitzgerald, she did
not find *The Women* spiteful in its portrayal of femininity. "It's always
been men who find *The Women* offensive," she said. "They don't want
to believe that their wives and mothers and girl friends can be so catty. But
café society and the Upper East Side spawned them in the hundreds. . . . [the
characters] were cartoons, like the women in *New Yorker* cartoons at the

time; sketchy perhaps, but not untrue to what you overheard at Elizabeth Arden or in a fitting room at Bullock's Wilshire."

Cukor and Stromberg were pleased with Anita's script, but the censorship board of the Motion Picture Association disapproved of Boothe's dialogue, much of which Anita had left intact: over eighty lines were red-penciled as objectionable. There was no time for revision before the picture went into production, so Cukor asked Anita to come to the set each day and rewrite as they went along.

She was apprehensive about how this would work out. The set was certain to be tense, as the cast for *The Women* was composed of an array of top-rank leading ladies, each sure to watch competitively after her own interests. Norma Shearer played Mary Haines, the play's heroine, a Social Register Pollyanna. As Irving Thalberg's widow, Shearer was accustomed to deferential treatment, and her gracious veneer cracked when she was challenged. She was particularly fussy about camera angles. Her tiny eyes were slightly crossed, and she had to be photographed very carefully.

Joan Crawford won the plummy part of Crystal Allen, the perfume clerk who swipes Mary Haines's husband. Crawford resented Shearer, who got the roles that brought Oscar nominations while she was cast in programmers which, unlike the widow Thalberg's pictures (never big at the box office), earned money but no awards.

"How are you going to manage them?" Anita asked Cukor. "I've learned a few tricks from a lion tamer," he answered.

He started every day with a series of parodies of the stars who weren't on the set at that moment. The send-ups were malicious, but they fit the tone of the film, and convinced the ladies who were present that he liked them more than whoever happened to be absent. Cukor was at his most inspired, Anita recalled, when Norma was the target of the day.

Shearer never permitted herself tantrums, preferring subtler ways of sabotaging Cukor's intention of making *The Women* an ensemble vehicle. One key sequence took place in a dress shop, with Rosalind Russell spitting venom at Shearer as she is fitted for a gown. Cukor planned to favor Russell in a camera angle including both actresses; but Shearer appeared wearing a black crinoline of such billowing dimensions that there was no way Russell could get close to her. "Take off that dress," Cukor ordered. "You look like Mammy in *Gone With the Wind.*" When Shearer refused, Cukor brought a three-way mirror onto the set and positioned it and the actresses to Russell's advantage. "That's fine, Norma, my pet," he purred. "Now we can see *four* Rosalind Russells."

Cukor got further revenge by encouraging Shearer's inclination to play Mary Haines on one sustained note of gentility. "I'm not sure she could have been browbeaten into doing it another way," Anita said, "but George didn't even try. I think he wanted to hand the picture to Russell and Crawford."

Crawford was unctuously gracious to Anita, who sincerely admired the actress's tenacity and professionalism. "Joan learned everything she knew from the movies," Anita claimed. At a dinner party in her home, Crawford swept down a staircase as her guests were arriving. Her butler approached to inquire whether red or white wine was to be served at dinner. "Both," Joan answered, "and make sure the white is chilled." The dialogue was straight out of a Crawford picture Anita had seen not long before.

"Nothing she did was without calculation," Anita went on. "Once she invited me and a couple of other people to a dinner she was going to prepare herself. She cooked pork chops for us while a *Life* photographer took pictures."

Of the cast members of *The Women,* Anita was closest to Paulette Goddard, then living with (and perhaps married to) Charles Chaplin. "When Paulette hit Hollywood," Anita wrote, "all the other starlets lost their novelty." Paulette was clever as well as beautiful. She would never have asked H. G. Wells, as Marion Davies did, "Mr. Wells, don't you think

George Cukor with the cast from *The Women* (1939). From left: Mary Nash, Phyllis Povah, Rosalind Russell, Joan Crawford, Cukor, Norma Shearer, Paulette Goddard, Mary Boland, Joan Fontaine

Anita and Norma Shearer on the set of *The Women* (1939). "Norma was wonderfully poised," Anita said, "and had an almost naturally radiant smile."

Louis B. Mayer ought to take a trip to Russia and stop communism?" Paulette would have realized, Anita said, "that Louis B. Mayer could only have been an argument *for* communism."

Before Paulette, Chaplin had a meager social life, Anita remembered. But Paulette enjoyed company, and parties at the Chaplin home on Tower Drive became small, celebrity-studded gatherings with after-dinner entertainment provided by the host. Anita recalled one pantomime with Charlie playing an art critic (from an article later published in *Fate Keeps on Happening*):

> He would commence by examining a miniature picture that hung about three feet from the floor, then proceed along the wall, studying paintings that hung higher and higher until he reached one at the end which required the stature of a giant to appraise. To watch Charlie's contortions as he seemed to grow from three feet to well over six left everyone in stitches.

There was one drawback to these evenings:

> As author of his own movie scripts, Charlie was given to reading them aloud to guests. . . . Excellent as these scenarios

Paulette Goddard on the set of *Modern Times* (1936)

were, they failed to hold attention after several readings. So Paulette used to sit on the floor behind Charlie's big armchair, under which she stashed a bottle of Dom Perignon to help keep her alert. Even so these recitals were frequently interrupted by the snores of Mrs. Chaplin.

Paulette had a knack for saying the unexpected. Apropos of nothing, she'd remark, "I've got three yards of rubies." Trying to imagine what so lengthy a ribbon of rubies must look like, Anita was at a loss for words.

While she occasionally sounded like Lorelei Lee, Paulette was extremely well read. "She knew all about authors and books I had only barely heard of," Anita said. "But what went on in her head, I don't know; nobody did. I think that's the reason why she fascinated so many intellectuals—they couldn't figure her out. H. G. Wells was gaga about her. Aldous Huxley *adored* her."

Huxley also admired Anita. They had met in 1926 when the British novelist and essayist came to America for the first time. A *Blondes* fan, he wrote Anita requesting a meeting. Afterward he told his brother Julian that "Miss Loos was ravishing. One would like to keep her for a pet."

Their friendship did not begin until Huxley, with his Belgian wife, Maria, and their son, Matthew, arrived in Hollywood in 1938. Huxley was then forty-four, very tall and thin, afflicted with poor eyesight. Anita was struck by

> his physical beauty. He was a giant in height with a figure that provided a harmonious column for his magnificent head; the head of an angel drawn by William Blake. His faulty sight even intensified Aldous's majesty, for he appeared to be looking at things above and beyond what other people saw. But his chief trait was an intense curiosity and, while he was the greatest of talkers, he was equally the greatest of listeners.

This is about as close to purple prose as Anita ever got; and quite a few of Anita's friends suspect she was half in love with him, repressing the other half since home breaking and casual infidelity went against her moral code. And Maria Huxley was her friend.

Maria was a gifted, remarkable woman who chose a career of making life comfortable for her husband. She elected to ignore his occasional infidelities, secure that he wouldn't stray far from the ivory tower she constructed for him, wherever they happened to be.

ABOVE AND OPPOSITE: Anita, Aldous, and Maria Huxley
at the Santa Monica beach house

Anita encouraged the Huxleys to stay in Los Angeles by getting a job for Aldous at M–G–M as a screenwriter for *Madame Curie.* As a reward she was invited for dinner many times, and suffered while Maria dished up her idea of healthful cuisine. "People never cook chicken enough," Mrs. Huxley explained as she served a bird that had been in the oven for three hours. "I like a taste of earth on potatoes," she said, and hers had obviously been roasted before they were washed.

Huxley fared about as well at M–G–M as Maria did in the kitchen. He felt his *Curie* screenplay captured "the nobility of scientific curiosity," but the studio wanted less radium and more romance.

"Anita couldn't understand why he was so upset," said Christopher Isherwood, another Briton-in-residence at M–G–M at the time. "She didn't understand that we thought writing something for Greta Garbo or Ingrid Bergman was more glamorous than winning a Pulitzer. She had been around Hollywood so long that she couldn't understand the magic it held for outsiders like Aldous and me. She thought Hollywood had failed Huxley where I'm pretty sure Huxley felt he had failed Greta Garbo."

Huxley stayed on in California, working on a Hollywood novel, *After Many a Summer Dies the Swan,* and walking on the Santa Monica beach with Anita for relaxation. Usually they went out early in the morning before the sands had been raked clean of the previous day's debris. "I was with them once," Isherwood recalled, "when Aldous, then nearly blind, peered at something he saw on the beach." He said that he had never seen a white flower of that particular foliation thriving on such unproductive soil; what was it called? Anita blushed and made no response. "Well, Aldous," Isherwood said, "in America, it's known as a rubber."

IN THE early summer of 1939 Anita went east for a straw hat revival of *Gentlemen Prefer Blondes,* starring the buxom Marie Wilson (best remembered from her later role as "My Friend Irma" in movies and on television). On her return, she doctored a "Thin Man" script and then wrote the screenplay for *Susan and God,* another Crawford vehicle, directed by George Cukor. The picture was based on a play Anita hadn't much liked, and she thought Crawford was stepping outside her league by taking on a role created by Gertrude Lawrence. Anita took it on only to avoid being assigned to *The Philadelphia Story,* "a synthetic, snobbish play" that allowed Katharine Hepburn too much opportunity "to strut her mannerisms."

Work on *Susan and God* was constantly interrupted by world events.

"War is imminent," Anita wrote in her diary, "making it hard to concentrate on Susan's problems with God." The news was so depressing that she swore off the radio and the papers. But there were gloomy letters from Cecil Beaton and Adele Astaire that couldn't be pushed aside, and whenever she visited the Hubbles or the Huxleys, the gossip and chatter about movies and bargains at the Farmers' Market inevitably gave way to reflections on the oncoming storm.

On September 3, 1939, Anita made only one entry in her diary: "WAR IS DECLARED!!"

20

Lull Before the Storm

T H E   H U X L E Y S called the next day to say that they were returning to England to stand with their friends and family. Anita argued
that their first duty was to themselves and their son; and anyway, in
America they were in a better position to publicize what was going on in
Europe than if they were in Europe itself. Huxley agreed. "The trouble
with Aldous," Anita told Maria, "is he's a genius who just once in a while
isn't very smart."

She got him a job at M–G–M adapting *Pride and Prejudice,* and she
suggested that they collaborate on other screenplays. Huxley mentioned
Othello and *Lady Chatterley's Lover.* Anita doubted L. B. Mayer would
approve either, though Greer Garson might make a good Chatterley, and
certainly Cukor would know someone for the groom. . . . Huxley promised
to come up with a less fanciful project.

Letters arrived from Adele Astaire in Ireland and Ruth de Vallambrosa,
now Mme Andre Dubonnet, in Paris, both saying that all was quiet and
that people were beginning to talk about "the phony war." Cecil Beaton
wrote that he was arriving in New York soon and would probably be in
Los Angeles for the Christmas holidays.

And once the shock was absorbed, life went on in California much as
before—especially at M–G–M, which rarely reflected world events in its
yearly program. After *Susan and God,* Anita did patchwork on a film for
Crawford and Greer Garson, *When Ladies Meet,* then wrote the first of

Louis B. Mayer, Paulette Goddard, Joan Crawford, and Anita's favorite post-Thalberg producer, Hunt Stromberg, at the premiere of *The Women* (1939)

the Garson-Pidgeon pictures, *Blossoms in the Dust,* the story of a crusader for humane treatment of illegitimate children. Though more accustomed to writing about the mothers of such offspring, Anita did well by this unpromising subject, layering the uplift with as little goo as possible.

Many of her scripts in the past three years were written for producer Hunt Stromberg, and it got to be known around the studio that he had first call on her services. That was fine with Anita. "In most ways," she wrote in her journal, "this is a perfect collaboration." Stromberg was then in his forties, tall and handsome except for a dental flaw: "Apparently he went to the dentist as a kid, and didn't like it much, so he never returned," recalls Mary Loos, who worked for Stromberg some years later. "Barbara Stanwyck dubbed him Yellow Fang, and, I am ashamed to say, we sometimes called him that behind his back."

Stromberg's story sense was almost as good as Thalberg's, Anita felt. He was enthusiastic about what he liked, articulate about what he disliked, and came up with ideas she might not have thought of herself. His only failing was "last minute jitters": a week before a picture went into production, he'd wonder if "they'd like it in Peoria." Anita rewrote all day, with three M–G–M typists standing by to transcribe her manuscript. By morning, the new copy was ready for "Stromsie," who inevitably decided the original version was better.

At the start of 1940, Stromberg asked her to adapt Rodgers and Hart's operetta *I Married an Angel*. She had seen the show and adored its "irreverent whimsy." The script "almost wrote itself," and so successfully that Stromberg sent it off to be mimeographed as soon as he read it.

Then problems arose. On Broadway the leading role had been played by Vera Zorina, and Stromberg told Anita that she would star in the picture, too. But Zorina's agent was asking for terms M–G–M couldn't or wouldn't meet. Louis B. Mayer was pushing Eleanor Powell as a replacement, but Powell was a little heavy on the taps to pass for an angel, Anita and Stromberg felt. George Cukor, who was to direct, suggested Tilly Losch. "Then we'll have to call it *I Married a Tramp*," Anita shot back. Stromberg decided to postpone production till the right angel came along.

In spring 1940 Cecil Beaton arrived in Hollywood, but he cut short his visit to hurry back to London when the war news grew alarming. "Will I ever see him again?" Anita wondered. Letters from Adele and Ruth were somber, and each day more refugees were arriving in Hollywood. She struck up an immediate friendship with French director René Clair and his wife, Bronja, who came by nearly every afternoon to swim in her pool. In exchange Bronja tutored her hostess in conversational French. *"Pour la pratique,"* Anita wrote in her diary, *"J'ai décidé a écrire seulement en français."*

Elsa Maxwell and Dickie Gordon Fellows returned to America and were temporarily staying in Hollywood. Anita entertained them several times and dutifully went to see Elsa in a one-act Noel Coward play. "I doubt Noel would have survived it," she wrote the next day. Cole Porter, then living in Beverly Hills, threw a poolside fête for Elsa, where everyone, Anita noted, spoke with either a French or a British accent—or both, "like Joan Crawford."

Then Paris fell to the Nazis and the London blitz began. Anita was revising a Clark Gable–Rosalind Russell picture for Hunt Stromberg, who asked her to inject some topical references into the script. She tried, but *They Met in Bombay* was really a jewel-thief caper with Gable again playing Wilson Mizner. Gable hated the script, and at a conference in Stromberg's office which turned into a "free-for-all" she called him a "studio-cured ham." Later he backed down and apologized: "Anita, honey, forgive me. . . . " But she was fed up. There would be no more rewrites, she informed Stromberg, no on-set revisions. She was taking a vacation.

With Clifford as companion/chauffeur, she motored up the California coast. Their first stop was in Carmel, where Ray Goetz was living in the guest house on Judith Anderson's estate. Late that night, after Clifford was in bed, Goetz got down on one knee and proposed. First Anita pulled the overfed Buddha off the ground; then she refused his offer. Goetz hadn't been doing much professionally lately, and she figured he was just another pimp looking for a meal ticket. "I hope we will always be friends," she explained, "but legally I'm still Mrs. Emerson." Staying married to Mr. E. did have its advantages.

Early the next morning, Anita and Clifford left for San Francisco. They spent three days there, shopping and banqueting at Chinese restaurants. Anita bought dragon-lady pajamas and a pair of embroidered slippers—small enough for bound feet, the salesman said. On her way back to the hotel, a sailor tried to pick her up. She was thrilled. "Maybe he thought you were Clara Bow," Clifford suggested. "He was too young to remember Clara Bow," she shot back.

They went on to Siskiyou County, visiting her grandparents' house, which had passed into the hands of distant cousins. Anita picked a bouquet of wildflowers and placed them on Minnie's grave. Then she and Clifford started home.

Back at M–G–M, Stromberg said that there were front-office orders to revamp *I Married an Angel* for Jeanette MacDonald and Nelson Eddy. The Broadway show had been written for a dancer who couldn't sing; now it had to be overhauled for a singer who couldn't dance. George Cukor begged off, explaining that he lacked the skills required by a musical. As George was never one to question his abilities, Anita took this as being his way of evading MacDonald and Eddy. Eddy was impossible; but Jeanette, Anita rationalized, might be all right, if she could be persuaded to drop the bel canto hauteur.

MacDonald wasn't in a cooperative mood. *I Married an Angel* is about a rake so weary of café society beauties that he swears he'll never marry till he meets an angel. When heaven grants his wish, he is so bored with his angel-wife that she has to learn a few café society tricks to keep him interested. MacDonald didn't like the part of the role that required her to put on an apron and bake sugar cakes ("My fans wouldn't like me to be banal") any more than she liked the siren side ("My fans would disapprove if I were tawdry").

Nelson Eddy, Jeanette MacDonald, and director W. S. Van Dyke on the set of *I Married an Angel* (1942), the last film for which Anita would receive screen credit

The new director of the film, Roy Del Ruth, thought the notion of a man wanting his wife to be both angel and whore too provocative. Stromberg replied that the script had been cleared by the censors. "They're too liberal," Del Ruth complained.

"Get rid of him," Anita said. The only replacement was One-Take Woody Van Dyke, Stromberg warned. "Anything's better than Del Ruth," Anita answered.

She watched the daily rushes, saw Jeanette simpering like Billie Burke in *The Wizard of Oz* and knew the picture was doomed. For days, she brooded about how easily the best script could be destroyed by star megalomania and hack direction, and wondered whether she shouldn't pack up and get out of Hollywood. But her depression lifted when she came up with a surefire idea: Joan Crawford as Madame Chiang Kai-shek. Forget it, Stromberg said. M–G–M was pruning its celestial garden: MacDonald and Eddy were the first to go, and Crawford was next in line.

What the studio wanted was a remake of a silent Lon Chaney picture, *Tell It to the Marines*. Would she look at it and tell him what she thought? Charming, she reported back, but too dated to relate to current world happenings. Stromberg agreed but said that they were stuck with the idea until the front office saw it their way. "Play around with it," he pleaded. "Maybe you'll come up with something to prove us wrong."

For three weeks she scribbled and scratched out ideas, getting nowhere, until, returning home after a dinner party one night, she came up with something that might work. She stayed up all night and was still at it when, around eleven-thirty the next morning, a maid told her that the radio was talking about a catastrophe in Hawaii.

Moments later, Sturgie and Ray Goetz arrived, full of news about Pearl Harbor, bringing with them three marines they had met somewhere, all on leave, and one with a bride of less than three days. Anita fought back tears: they were so young, and tomorrow they would be reporting for war duty. She told the maid to uncork the champagne she had been saving to celebrate her divorce from Mr. E. The Huxleys arrived, then Mary and the Albert Lewins. "Everyone," Anita wrote that night, "feels relieved, almost exhilarated that America is forced into the war."

21
Fort
Loos

*T*HE FOLLOWING DAY exhilaration turned into "pretty general fright." The radio was blacked out for over an hour, and there were false reports of enemy aircraft over San Francisco. On December 10, a blackout was put into effect every evening until further notice, only to be lifted the next day when enemy attack no longer seemed imminent.

On the studio front, all was not so quiet. Stromberg invited Anita for lunch at a restaurant miles from the studio, and she correctly guessed he had a secret to share. Fed up with M-G-M bureaucracy, he was leaving to set himself up as an independent producer.

"When I go, I want you to go with me," he said—provided she could get out of her contract, which still had twenty months to run. This was exactly what Anita wanted to hear. She couldn't imagine staying at M-G-M without Stromberg. The other producers were "louses," and this "perfect collaboration" wasn't one she wanted terminated.

Was she in love with Stromberg? Hoppy thought so. When she told him of her distress about Hunt leaving M-G-M, Hop crowed, "You're carrying a torch for that guy." He wasn't entirely wrong, she had to admit, and it was pretty dumb: Stromberg was married, and though known to stray, he had never shown any inclination of straying in her direction. Anyway she wasn't cut out to be "a back street bride."

Possibly that was the source of her fascination with Stromberg. It was an affair of the mind, like the ones with Mencken and Mizner and Mr. E.

at the start. She had made a mistake in getting physical with Emerson, and it wasn't one she was going to make again if she could help it. Choosing men who weren't inclined to make passes was one safeguard; reminding those who were so inclined that she was still Mrs. John Emerson was another.

M–G–M agreed to let Stromberg go at the end of February 1942, just a few weeks away. Could Anita wangle her way out of her contract around the same time? She approached Eddie Mannix, the only studio executive she trusted. "Never in a million years," he replied. "We love you and you're too valuable to us."

Anita went home, had a brandy, took a swim in the pool, felt chilled and nauseated afterward, and on the advice of a maid, applied a very potent mustard plaster to her chest. The next morning she woke up with first-degree burns. Stromberg paid a sick call and advised her to relax and make the best of her "penal servitude."

Anita went back to Mannix, told him she had a few ideas, one she'd like to develop with Hoppy. Mannix told her to go ahead. Hoppy did have a Lana Turner picture in mind, something called *The Flying Blonde*. Was it about a Beryl Markham–type aviatrix, or was "flying" Anita's euphemism for Hoppy's favorite F word? Either way, the idea "started riding them rather than vice versa," she told Mannix a few weeks later.

Did she, Mannix asked, know "The Rosary," that old (1898) ballad about a man who staves off temptation by fingering his mother's rosary beads? Mayer, whose allegiance to motherhood was legendary, had always wanted a picture based on that song. How about it? Anita knew that any screenwriter who pulled "The Rosary" was a screenwriter on the way out.

But Hoppy thought they could outfox Mannix. "We'll give it a contemporary twist," he improvised. "There's this guy who thinks he's got iron balls until they shrivel on him when he's about to go into battle. . . . Then he finds Mama's rosary in his uniform pocket and as he fingers it, the lead starts filling his pencil. . . . " Mannix thought Hoppy's variation might be perfect for Gable. "Take all the time you need," he said.

W H E N not writing, Anita was contributing to the war effort. Though vegetables and fruit were always plentiful in southern California, she insisted on growing her own victory garden. As the land around her house was sandy, she constructed a huge, raised trough which was filled with rich soil. "Mention Anita," said the Mexican-born actress Margo (a close friend of Mary Loos), "and the first thing I see is a little lady wearing a big straw hat and a man's shirt tied at the waist, doubled over to inspect her zucchini." The garden flourished, and now when she stopped at the Farmers' Market, it was to pick up health foods. "The first time I ate green noodles was at Anita's," remembered Margo. "That was dinner—spinach noodles and lots of home-grown vegetables."

Anita and Paulette Goddard started knitting and crocheting socks, scarves, and sweaters for the boys overseas. One day as they worked, one of them began to hum a barracks ballad popular at the local stage door canteen:

> Hitler has only got one ball
> Goering has two but they are small
> Himmler has something similar
> But Goebbels has no balls at all.

Inspired by this doggerel, they began crocheting "peter heaters" to fit the genital deformities of all involved. These were then starched, handed out to friends, and included among the parcels sent abroad.

One night when she was expecting dinner guests, Anita opened her front door and discovered a pimply teenager bearing an impressive-looking document, whose contents informed her that her house was being requisitioned as a link in a crucial civil defense operation. All along the California coast, checkpoints were being set up to detect possible enemy invasion. Two men would be stationed outside her house each night with an interceptor and telephones giving them immediate access to Santa Barbara, the center of operations.

Fort Loos, she dubbed her house. The rotating crew of sentinels became very dear to her. Every evening she plied them with lemonade and plates of sandwiches and cookies. Once when she was giving a party, she invited them to join the guests, but they wouldn't abandon their equipment. "Haul it inside," she ordered. The boys were thrilled when they spotted Marie Wilson and Frances Rafferty. "Our friends will never believe we met movie stars," they said. "Call them up and ask them over," she insisted. The regiment arrived and soon everyone, including Anita, was jitterbugging. "The best party I ever gave," she wrote the next day.

FORT LOOS was a distraction from her growing unhappiness with M-G-M where no one seemed to appreciate her special talents. She was so blue that Marie Wilson suggested a visit to Lola, a fortune-teller of uncanny accuracy. Anita didn't need much persuasion; she was a devoted, if skeptical, reader of astrological columns, and wasn't about to dismiss any occult science since the day, many years before, when a tea-leaf reader had peered into her cup and spotted Mr. E. in the dregs.

Lola said there were three kings in the future. Forget romance, Anita said. What about her career? "Diversify!" Lola advised. "Do not put all eggs in one basket."

The next day Mannix told Anita to forget about the "Rosary" project: Gable was enlisting. Anita was furious. Mannix must have known about this for weeks—he and Gable were close friends—and yet he let her go on working on the script. Maybe Lola was right: it was time to peddle her wares in a different market.

That night she met Lionel Barrymore at a party, and they chatted about sister Ethel, then enjoying her greatest stage success in *The Corn Is Green*. Lionel said he had an idea for a play for Ethel. Go on with it, Anita urged. But Lionel didn't have the time or the stamina. He had roughed out a synopsis, and Anita could develop it as she pleased—as long as he got credit as co-author.

Within two months, Anita had completed a light comedy, *Old Buddha*, about a Chinese empress who commandeers an American dentist to look after her infected tooth. Riches will be his if the treatment is painless; otherwise his reward will be the empress's culinary specialty—poisoned apricot cream. Lionel suggested that the script be sent to Arthur Hopkins, who had staged several notable productions for the Barrymores in the past.

Meanwhile, Anita wrote a script about the WACs for a second-rank M-G-M producer, who threw it across his desk as his comment on its merit. "I feel insulted by working for cretins like George Haight," she wrote. Then, melancholy after a few highballs, she wondered if she wouldn't be better off dead. She longed to "be erased. This is a world I have decided I want no part of." But the next day she was making plans for the future. As soon as her contract expired, she told Margo, she was returning to New York. "How can you leave this beautiful house?" Margo protested. Anita waved it away. "I can be happy anywhere if I'm happy in my work."

In April 1943 she did draw an assignment she enjoyed. *The Valley of Decision*, Marcia Davenport's best-selling novel about a Pittsburgh steel family, was a good story; it was going to be an important picture; and producer Edwin Knopf was "dashing." In Knopf, tall, handsome, and heroic—he had lost an arm in World War I by snatching a grenade from the hand of a Belgian child—she thought she had discovered another Thalberg or Stromberg. Perhaps she wouldn't be leaving M-G-M when her contract lapsed. Definitely she'd stay on till *Valley of Decision* was finished.

M-G-M had prepared a different scenario. At the end of a story conference, Knopf stretched out his hand and said how sorry he was that Anita wouldn't be around to complete the job. She looked blank, so embarrassedly he went on to say that he had been informed that she wasn't picking up her option. Anita got out of the office fast, went home, poured a Dubonnet, and fumed. This was the ultimate humiliation. M-G-M was dropping her and making it look as though it were her idea. And nobody, not Mannix, not her agent, had had the good grace to forewarn her.

F R E E D from M-G-M, Anita became nervous about cutting her ties to Hollywood. Writing for the screen might still be an attractive proposition as long as no long-term contracts were required. Friends warned that free-lancing was tricky, since studios preferred contract writers to independents, even when the independent had top credentials. But Joe Schenck, now a chief executive at Twentieth Century–Fox, came up with the perfect deal. Fox was then grooming Dorothy McGuire as the next Katharine Hepburn or Margaret Sullavan and needed someone to work exclusively on develop-ing showcases for her. Anita felt that, though mousy, McGuire was adept at scatterbrained comedy: with proper handling, she might be another Connie Talmadge. Maybe some of Dutch's old pictures could be reshaped to fit her. Schenck liked the suggestion. An agreement was reached, limiting Anita's employment at Fox to McGuire vehicles and allowing her to work where she chose—at the studio, in Santa Monica, or wherever she happened to be.

That concession was important, as *Old Buddha* had been accepted by Arthur Hopkins, and Ethel Barrymore's lawyers were checking over contracts prior to signature. Hopkins thought the play overlong and urged Anita to come east to collaborate on the editing. So in September 1943 she closed up the Santa Monica beach house and left for New York.

22

Bicoastal

A N I T A checked in at the Plaza with Cagney, her Pomeranian, and a black maid who had been working for her for a few years, Gladys Tipton. The next day she had her first meeting with Arthur Hopkins, an old-school gentleman, soft-spoken and kindly. "*Old Buddha* is delightful," he said. "I'm sure you can go on from here to other Broadway hits."

This was a preface to bad news. Ethel Barrymore had bowed out, preferring to return to Hollywood to appear in *None but the Lonely Heart* (for which she would win an Academy Award). To replace her, Hopkins suggested Marjorie Rambeau, a veteran actress with a lusty voice and dynamic stage presence. Rambeau liked *Buddha* but wasn't free until several months later. Anita agreed to wait.

She filled in time by making notes for two potential McGuire pictures, the first a revamped *A Virtuous Vamp,* the other a *Kitty Foyle-*type romance, *White Collar Girl.* Nearly every night she went to the theater with Sturgie or Hopkins, cartoonist Peter Arno, or a recently acquired beau. No one remembers his name; in the diaries, Anita refers to him as "Sugar."

Sugar was a burly Irishman, with a ruddy complexion, lots of rough edges, and a sporadic drinking problem. (Soon after they met, Anita was taking him to AA meetings.) Sometime in the past, he had been a reporter, but currently he was unemployed.

"I'll never know what she saw in Sugar," says one friend. "Not at all her type," sniffs another. If Anita had been levelheaded, she might have seen that Sugar fit her category of pimp, but he simply swept her off her feet. The morning after their first date, she went to Tiffany's and bought him a pair of gold cuff links. She was not normally extravagant about choosing gifts.

The diaries suggest that the relationship with Sugar was physical. Why did she choose Sugar when she had avoided getting involved with so many other men in the past? Perhaps it was a matter of timing. She was now fifty-five, setting the foundations for a new life, and she may have figured that if there was ever to be another man in her life, this was the appropriate moment for him to make his entrance. It is clear that she wanted to marry Sugar and was prepared to force Mr. E. into a divorce to do so.

Early in 1944 Anita returned to the West Coast for a few weeks to work on the script for *A Tree Grows in Brooklyn,* an important picture for Dorothy McGuire. Sugar went with her. One evening she asked Mr. E. to dinner at the Santa Monica house. Also present were Clifford, Mary, the Wendels, and her new beau. The evening went pleasantly until after dinner, when in a private conversation Anita told Emerson she wanted to marry Sugar. Emerson moaned and wept, put on such tragedy airs that Anita, exhausted, asked Betty Wendel to calm him. His composure was restored, and he went out to face his rival. "May the best man win," he said sportingly. "He already has," Sugar replied. Mr. E. became so over-wrought that Clifford had to sedate him.

Divorce discussions started again, and as in the past, Emerson pulled out all the stops to prevent what Anita insisted was inevitable. Betty Wendel stayed neutral, but Clifford took a hard line, and Mary was outspoken. "I got on my hunkers," she recalls, "and told Emerson to butt out of Anita's life. She was entitled to some chance for happiness. If I had known Sugar a little better, I would have kept quiet."

Bringing Sugar to California created problems Anita hadn't foreseen. What was he to do while she was working on *A Tree Grows in Brooklyn*? Maybe a short-term job. Since he had experience in publicity, Anita asked Joe Schenck to find a place for Sugar at Fox. After an interview, Schenck reported that Sugar didn't seem to care much whether he worked or not. So Anita bought him a car to drive around in while she worked on *Brooklyn*. He was gone most of the day, and when he returned, he was always more eloquent about his feelings. "Sugar loves me deeply, he says," Anita noted on a Friday.

Then came Monday: "SUGAR WALKS OUT ON ME!!" That afternoon he returned drunk; she remonstrated; he said he'd do as he pleased. He was gone for the better part of a week, then turned up so abusive that Anita fled to Clifford for shelter. Sugar kept turning up at odd hours until he was "persuaded" to get out of California and Anita's life.

She was relieved that he was gone and embarrassed that she had ever been dumb enough to take him on in the first place. The whole foolish business added to her cynicism about romantic love. Years later she would title a chapter of one of her memoirs "Sex Can Make a Dunce of You," and though Sugar isn't mentioned, she must have had him in mind, as well as Mr. E., when she wrote it.

I T L O O K E D as though 1944 was going to be another tough year. All in a matter of weeks, Sugar showed his true colors, R. Beers died, and Arthur Hopkins dropped *Old Buddha* when Marjorie Rambeau backed out because of illness.

"I'm lower than a snake's vest," Anita told her diary. People advised her to forget New York and stay in Hollywood, but she resisted Joe Schenck's persistent efforts to get her to sign "a termer." She was set on returning to Broadway with a hit play—if not *Old Buddha,* then her "cocktail bar comedy," which now preoccupied her thoughts.

A year earlier she had mentioned to stage and screen director Rouben Mamoulian an idea for a play called *Blue Lounge.* Mamoulian encouraged her, but she more or less forgot about it until one day, just before returning to California, when she was having lunch with Helen Hayes and her husband, Charles MacArthur.

Hayes was then appearing in a play about Harriet Beecher Stowe after years of impersonating Queen Victoria. "I'm tired of hoop skirts," she complained. "I'd love to kick up my heels again." Anita seized the opportunity. "How'd you like to be tight for two acts?"

Anita first had met Hayes twenty years earlier when Hayes auditioned for the stage *Blondes.* "Oh, no!" Anita had said. "She's too sweet and naive." Hayes took that as a compliment, but "later I learned those were the two worst things she could possibly say about anyone."

They became close after Hayes married MacArthur. Anita adored Charlie and couldn't imagine what he saw in Helen: she was a wonderful dancer, but Charlie didn't care for the ballroom; she looked great in décolletage, but so did lots of Charlie's girls. "She had the choice of giving up Charlie or taking up with me," Hayes recalls, "and God bless her, she took me in hand and did her best to make me worthy of Charlie and the kind of person she could feel comfortable with."

Talking to Helen wasn't difficult, Anita wrote. "I came to realize that underneath her sentimental, homespun exterior she had a rollicking Irish sense of humor. How else could she have held on to Charlie, when even the world-renowned cleverness of Dorothy Parker had failed?"

Hayes had played lots of light comedy in her early career, and MacArthur encouraged her to cut loose once again. She was too professional to commit herself to an unwritten play, but obviously intrigued enough for Anita to plunge headlong into what now was called *Happy Birthday*.

The comedy was designed as a star turn for the actress playing Addie Beamis, a prim librarian who drops by a seedy Newark bar in search of her booze hound of a father. She takes a drink, gets tiddly, loses her inhibitions, and falls in love. The plot was slender, and Anita was to have trouble expanding it; once or twice she tossed it aside as hopeless, until in early 1945 she was able to tell her journal, "It's going to be all right!!!"

In reading over what she had already completed, she discovered in a character description of Addie the ingredient that made the play jell. Addie, she had said, was one of those people "who view life only with the head . . . who believe only in reality," but gradually she learns that "one of life's great realities is illusion."

The potency of illusion is the theme of the play. As the liquor flows, the drab Mecca Bar takes on a *vie en rose* glow, the jukebox lights up, and Addie, previously contemptuous of cheap music, dances and sings like a Broadway ingénue. Even the tables change dimensions, growing tall enough to shelter Addie as she eavesdrops on plot-prodding conversations.

Rouben Mamoulian was enchanted by *Happy Birthday*, agreed to direct it, and suggested that Anita send it to Rodgers and Hammerstein, then the biggest names on Broadway, thanks to *Oklahoma!* and *Carousel*, both directed by Mamoulian. Oscar and Dick, he explained, had recently formed a company to produce shows other than their own and were on the lookout for lighthearted comedies.

A week later Helen Hayes arrived in Los Angeles with the touring company of *Harriet*. She stayed with Anita during the run, and one afternoon Anita handed her a script and told her to read it by the pool. She was going off to the Farmers' Market. Hayes said all the right things when Anita got back: the play was wonderful; she'd love to work with Mamoulian; Rodgers and Hammerstein were perfect as producers.

While waiting for word from the perfect producers, Anita tinkered with the script of *Diary of a Chambermaid*, a picture starring and produced by Paulette Goddard and her new husband, Burgess Meredith. Another distraction was Mr. E., who came to dinner one night and because of heavy rains and flash floods couldn't return to Las Encinas until a week later. *"Est-ce que la vie en vaut la peine?"* Anita asked her diary.

Life did seem worth the trouble when good news arrived from Oscar Hammerstein: Dick Rodgers and he loved *Birthday* and wanted to put it on. They couldn't make a firm commitment without assurances from Hayes and Mamoulian, but he asked Anita to hang on for just a while longer.

It was not until after V–J day, August 14, that Hammerstein was able to inform Anita that everything had come together. In March 1946, he and Rodgers would be opening on Broadway Jerome Kern's *Annie Get Your Gun* with Ethel Merman. As soon as that was out of the way, they were prepared to go into rehearsal with *Birthday,* bringing it into New York by mid-May. This schedule suited Hayes and Mamoulian. Could Anita be in New York in September to sign contracts and discuss various preproduction details?

She arrived in mid-September, took a suite at the Plaza, and left the next day for a weekend with Hammerstein and his wife, Dorothy, at their country home in Doylestown, Pennsylvania. Oscar was of a height to dwarf anyone except a Harlem Globetrotter; and standing next to him, Anita felt "like David before Goliath." But he was a "honey-bear, the sweetest and gentlest" man she had ever met. He presented her with a list of improvements which he and Dick "hoped she'd consider." Though the suggestions seemed to her either picky or needless, she worked at them fitfully during the next few weeks.

She had planned to stay in New York at least through the spring opening of *Happy Birthday,* but in early November something happened to change everything. Jerome Kern keeled over in the street from a heart attack, and a week later he was dead. As less than half of the *Annie Get Your Gun* score had been completed, it was necessary to start from scratch with a new composer. Irving Berlin volunteered, and while he promised to work quickly, there wasn't any way the show could open before May. And that meant *Happy Birthday* would have to be postponed until the fall.

Hammerstein broke the news as gently as possible; but still, Anita feared the postponement meant the loss of Mamoulian and Hayes. About Mamoulian she was right—he had signed a contract with M–G–M which didn't allow him time off for stage work. Hayes promised to wait: she had been offered a summer-stock tour in James M. Barrie's *Alice-Sit-by-the-Fire* and wanted to do it because it had a nice role for her daughter, Mary, a blossoming actress.

As there was nothing to keep her in New York, Anita returned to Santa Monica, where living was cheaper. Mamoulian, whose first M–G–M assignment was *The Pirate,* asked her to work on the script, and she tried, but no one was satisfied with what she turned in. (Mamoulian was later replaced by Vincente Minnelli.) She didn't care. By then it was nearly time to return to New York for *Happy Birthday* rehearsals.

Just before her departure, she visited Mr. E. at Las Encinas. During her absence Betty Wendel would be looking after him, and of course he could always reach Anita at the Plaza. She went on to say that if *Happy Birthday* was a hit, she was going to settle in New York. Emerson took this so much better than she had expected that she guessed he was already scheming to get to New York himself. How to prevent that was something she'd think about later. Now all that mattered was *Happy Birthday.*

PART
Four

PLAYBILLS

23

Happy Birthday,
Lousy Christmas

O N   H E R   F I R S T   evening in New York, Anita visited Joshua Logan, Mamoulian's replacement as director of *Happy Birthday*. They were lucky to have Logan aboard, Oscar Hammerstein told her. His staging of *Annie Get Your Gun* had made Josh the hottest director on Broadway, with first refusal of all the best scripts.

Then in his late thirties, Logan was a big man (over six feet and weighing more than two hundred pounds) with a soft, rubbery face and just a trace of a southern drawl. But beneath this phlegmatic exterior rested boundless energy and enthusiasm. "I knew I had to do your play after reading the first line," he told Anita. "Just wait till you see Jo Mielziner's set designs—they're a glittering fairyland!"

Actually, Logan had strong reservations about *Birthday*, finding it "original but weak." He had taken it on partly as a favor to Rodgers and Hammerstein, partly to work with Helen Hayes, partly because he was a *Blondes* addict. The weaknesses of the script, he felt, could be minimized by artful staging. He had no lack of faith in his own abilities.

Rehearsals began on September 9, 1946. Anita went the first day and occasionally thereafter but generally stayed away, since she knew the presence of an author can unnerve actors. She felt very secure. Watching Logan in action, she began to share his confidence in himself.

Before the opening in Boston on October 3, there was a final rehearsal that went without a hitch—not a good omen, according to theatrical tradition. And as if to prove the rule, the first performance of *Birthday* was a disaster of flubbed lines and technical mishaps. The next night actors and stagehands hit their cues, but the public reaction was again cool, bordering on the hostile. Logan decided something was seriously wrong with the script.

In rehearsals he had realized Addie was written in an "odd, schizophrenic way": one moment she was sweetness and light, the next she was cutting and abrasive. Sensing that Anita was striving for complexity, he put off asking for clarification until he could gauge audience response. Once the verdict was in, he told Anita the character had to be simplified. "Can't Addie be bitchy or sweet, not both?" he asked. "It would make for a pleasanter evening if she was just sweet. Nobody wants Helen Hayes to be a bitch."

In Hollywood Thalberg and Stromberg had told Anita that a hero must never, even momentarily, be presented in an unsympathetic light. She had never been entirely convinced, and with good reason—Shakespeare and the other great dramatists had never adhered to Thalberg's law. But on

Grace Valentine and Enid Markey watch as Helen Hayes sings "I Haven't Got a Worry in the World" in Anita's comedy, *Happy Birthday,* produced on Broadway in 1946.

the other hand, she wasn't Shakespeare. That something was gravely amiss with *Birthday* she thoroughly understood, and she assured Logan she'd mull it over and give him her thoughts the next day.

The third performance was a Saturday matinee, attended by many theater people who had come to Boston just to see the show. At the end there was barely enough applause for curtain calls, and the comments Logan overheard froze his blood. A friend, composer Arthur Schwartz, tried to dodge him, but Logan forced a confrontation. "Oh, God, Josh, what can I tell you? I just *hated* it."

Before the evening performance, Anita and Logan were called to a conference in Richard Rodgers's Ritz-Carlton suite. Earlier in the day, both had spotted Rodgers and Hammerstein talking to their lawyer, and individually each had concluded they were arranging to close the show in Boston.

A very weary Oscar Hammerstein opened the meeting by announcing, "Well, we all know we're in trouble, but we'll fix it." There was a short pause. "By Monday," Rodgers snapped. Logan looked apprehensively at Anita, who turned thumbs-up.

"She was a real powerhouse," Logan recalls. Starting early the next morning they ripped the script apart, removing the offending lines—about half of Addie's part by Logan's count—replacing them with softer jokes. Addie Beamis was becoming very sweet—too sweet, Anita privately worried. But by midnight the chore was accomplished, the new pages typed and delivered to Hayes to memorize.

The new Addie Beamis made a hit on Monday evening. For the next two weeks, Anita continued to polish, always with advantageous results. By the end of the Boston run, it looked as though *Happy Birthday* was going to be a popular favorite.

On the day of the New York opening, October 31, Anita went to Mainbocher for a final fitting of the dress she was wearing that evening, then to lunch at Sardi's, and then back to the Plaza for a nap. After the show, there was an opening-night party, attended by cast and crew and such friends as the Averell Harrimans, Joan Crawford, Linda Porter, Cecil Beaton, and Ruth Gordon and her husband, Garson Kanin. After midnight, the reviews started coming in, and they were all cool—except the all-important *New York Times* notice by Brooks Atkinson.

In his Sunday follow-up piece, Atkinson was even more favorable. While most of his colleagues, he wrote, subscribed to Dr. Johnson's dictum that "the heroes and queens of tragedy must never descend to trifles," he had had a glorious time watching Helen Hayes cavort on the

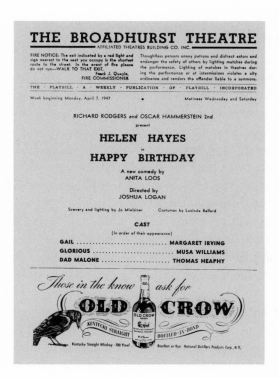

Broadhurst stage. Playing tragedy, the actress had stood "on tiptoes"; it was nice to see her with both feet on the ground. He congratulated Hayes "for giving the audience its money's worth" and Anita for writing "a popular comedy in an original vein."

Theatergoers heeded Atkinson and queued up at the Broadhurst box office. There was a lot to pick from that fall season—*Born Yesterday, Annie Get Your Gun, The Iceman Cometh,* Ingrid Bergman in *Joan of Lorraine,* Lillian Hellman's *Another Part of the Forest*—but *Happy Birthday* held its own. It started out at capacity and was still going strong two months later. Word of mouth was so good that *Variety* predicted it would last out the season. It did better than that, running close to six hundred performances, finally closing in the early spring of 1948.

A N I T A finished her Christmas duties early that year. Presents and cards were bought, wrapped, and addressed before the first of December, when she returned to California. She planned to stay no more than three months, just long enough to attend Mary's wedding to novelist and screenwriter Richard Sale, sell her house, and wind up other business.

Mr. E. fit this last category. He was thrilled about *Happy Birthday,* not so thrilled when his Bug told him he wouldn't be returning with her to New York. He started to howl and she howled back. "Blew my topper," she wrote on three consecutive days.

Some friends thought she was ruthless. Why, they inquired, couldn't she place him in an East Coast Las Encinas? Anita didn't care what Betty Wendel or anyone else thought. All the bitterness she had repressed for so many years now strengthened her determination to act tough. At age fifty-eight, she was starting a new life and career, and Emerson was one ghost that wasn't going to haunt her future. Thanks to the money stolen from her, he was now living comfortably at Las Encinas, so why move him?

During her visit, she was entertained by her friends—the Hubbles and the Huxleys, Chris Isherwood, Rouben Mamoulian, Ray Goetz, and George Cukor, the host of a small dinner party to celebrate *Happy Birthday.* Among Cukor's guests was Katharine Hepburn, who mentioned she'd like to play Addie Beamis on screen. Anita was fond of Hepburn but didn't much care for her acting, though her offputting mannerisms might suit Addie.

The next afternoon Hepburn came to tea and offered to approach certain producer friends about a package deal: herself as star, Anita as screenwriter, and Cukor as director. Within the week she was back with bad news. Reaction to *Birthday* was negative, since the censors felt the play was an endorsement for liquor—get drunk, get your man! It was stupid, she agreed, but the Production Code enforcers saw it that way. Anita made a few phone calls on her own and discovered that Hepburn was right.

By the end of February 1947, Anita was ready to return to New York. Mary and Rich Sale had bought the Santa Monica house for approximately its original cost—about $50,000, Mary remembers. Gladys was again coming east with her; but Cagney, in failing health (and soon to be "put down"), stayed behind.

O N H E R return, Anita took an apartment at the Plaza Hotel Annex on West Fifty-eighth Street. It was compact—foyer, two small bedrooms, bath, living room, and makeshift kitchen. Once in her new quarters, she got to work. "I don't know how much longer I can stand this inactivity," she had written at the end of her California stay. She returned with two theater pieces in mind. One was a musical adaptation of *She Stoops to Conquer* for Mary Martin, abandoned once Martin signed for *South*

Anita with Richard and Mary Sale on their wedding day in Santa Monica, 1947

Pacific. The second was also a musical, an original, called *Jacqueline* (or, alternately, *Montparnasse*), about a Josephine Baker–like chanteuse and her romance with a French diplomat. Interracial romance was a daring theme at the time, but it suited the somber cast the American musical was taking in those Rodgers and Hammerstein days.

Howard Dietz wrote the lyrics and Fred Alstone some melodies. When there were enough songs for a presentation, auditions were held for Rodgers and Hammerstein, who weren't enthusiastic; and then for Mamoulian and Logan, who liked it but had too much on their plates to take it on. Through persistence, Anita found a millionaire neophyte willing to make *Jacqueline* his maiden production, provided there was a star in the leading role.

Anita's first choice was Lena Horne. She was flattered but insecure about her acting ability. Hilda Sims, the original Anna Lucasta, auditioned and was rejected; she had talent and experience but no charisma. Then came Dorothy Dandridge, who had charisma and talent but little experience. After a year of Jacqueline hunting, the millionaire wearied of the game and pulled out.

But Anita wasn't content to let it rest. Over the years, whenever a new black entertainer made a splash, she got the script out of her files and put it back into circulation. This went on till 1962 and Richard Rodgers's *No Strings,* a musical set in Paris and anchored to an interracial affair. Rodgers may not have cared much for *Jacqueline,* Anita thought bitterly, but he sure hadn't forgotten its premise.

W R I T E R S, like cooks, fall into two broad categories: there are those who complete one dish before going on to the next, and others who thrive on keeping all burners going at once. Anita was a member of the second fraternity. Halfway through *Jacqueline* she was trying to develop something for her friend ZaSu Pitts, the skittish film comedienne who had just scored a personal success in *Ramshackle Inn* and was looking for a follow-up Broadway vehicle. Anita wanted to help but couldn't come up with an idea.

It was Esta Silsbee, a part-time secretary, who provided the thread of a plot. Often after finishing her typing, the outgoing and chatty Silsbee stayed on for a cup of tea, and one afternoon she told Anita a little about herself. Reared by a series of foster parents, none kind and a few abusive, she had nonetheless made a good life for herself. Her mother, she eventually discovered, was a second-string opera soprano with a social pedigree. "I was the by-product of an indiscretion Mama's family wanted erased." But when the diva gave a concert in Chicago, where Esta was working as a publicist for orchestra-leader Vincent Lopez, the daughter went backstage to take a close look at her mother. "I didn't tell her who I was," Esta recalls. "I didn't need help then. All I wanted was that moment of contact."

Anita was intrigued. Served up with tears, this might be another *Stella Dallas,* but told with humor, it could be ideal for ZaSu. Right off the bat she came up with a wonderful title—*Mother Was a Lady.*

ZaSu was then sharing an apartment with Frances Marion, whom Anita had known for years; she had, in fact, been a bridal attendant at the Emerson wedding. Like Anita, Marion was a veteran screenwriter; she had worked on many of Mary Pickford's most celebrated films and accumulated over 136 screen credits between 1915 and 1936. During the sound era, like Anita, she had worked mainly at M–G–M, and occasionally, one was put on a script the other had started. When this happened, neither felt resentment or any need to apologize, as Anita had felt with Fitzgerald. She and Marion were pros, who knew such shifts had nothing to do with their abilities but were a reflection of studio insecurity.

Marion had given up on Hollywood at about the same time as Anita

ZaSu Pitts, best remembered for her comedy roles, though her greatest screen performance was in Erich von Stroheim's *Greed* (1923). In 1948, Anita wrote an unproduced play for her, *Mother Was a Lady*.

and for the same reason—they weren't breeding Thalbergs out there anymore. She was planning to live in retirement, but writing something for her old friend ZaSu was appealing. When she learned that Anita had the same notion, she suggested they collaborate.

Esta Silsbee says the partnership went beautifully. The authors started early each morning in Anita's apartment and were finished by noon. Marion left and Anita changed into leotards and did her daily calisthenics, using a straight-backed chair to stretch her legs. By the time Silsbee arrived to type the morning's output, she was dressed for lunch or shopping.

By four she was home waiting for Marion to stop by to check over Silsbee's typescript. Sometimes ZaSu would join them, often with a young actress she had befriended, Nancy Davis, who recently had played a small part in *Lute Song* with Mary Martin and Yul Brynner. ZaSu kept hinting about a role for Nancy in *Mother Was a Lady*. The future Mrs. Ronald Reagan was a nice girl, Anita thought, but "a little too reserved to make it as an actress."

Some evenings ended with ZaSu volunteering to cook dinner. This was a mixed blessing: Pitts was a "tragedienne of the kitchen," always burning her fingers, losing her grip on saucepans, moaning about the inadequacies of Anita's spice rack. But the ordeal invariably ended in a meal worthy of Lucullus.

Most evenings Anita went out for dinner, to the theater, or to a movie. Around this time, she saw a lot of Maurice Chevalier, then appearing on Broadway in a one-man show. They had known each other for twenty years, but Chevalier had recently separated from his second wife, and the time was ripe for romance. Anita never said as much to friends, but two or three believe a close attachment developed between them. When Chevalier took his show on the road, Anita pasted his itinerary in her journal and called him at least once a week. He played a brief return engagement a few months later and then returned to France. They were not to meet again for years, and when they did, Chevalier was very cool.

Anita also had a bad crush on rhinestone hustler Mike Todd, then married to Joan Blondell, the star of a touring edition of *Happy Birthday.* Blondell told her Todd was a bastard; he had bilked her out of money her former husband, Dick Powell, had put aside for their son's education. And Anita's friends were appalled. "He wasn't what you'd call a prince of a gentleman," says one. "The original slime was still sticking to him." He was one of those scalawags Anita found so attractive and yet was smart enough to keep at a distance. When Todd died in a 1958 plane crash, Joan Blondell exclaimed, "That's bullshit. No plane could've wiped out that

Frances Marion, Anita's collaborator on *Mother Was a Lady,* wrote over 130 movies between 1916 and 1953, including many of Mary Pickford's most successful films, as well as *Dinner At Eight* and *Camille* for Greta Garbo. She was a bridal attendant at Anita's wedding in 1920.

son of a bitch!" Anita, who knew him less intimately, went into "mood indigo" on hearing of his death. "I've been carrying a torch for that guy for years," she wrote in her diary.

But she never was to ask Todd, whose specialty was high-class burlesques like *Star and Garter* and *The Naked Genius,* to produce any of her plays. When *Mother Was a Lady* was finished in June 1948, she went immediately to George Abbott, Broadway's leading author, producer, and director of farces, who put it on his calendar for December 1948.

Anita revised the play several times, never to Abbott's satisfaction. Finally he dropped the show from his schedule. The holidays that year were "the lousiest ever"; she was "bluer than Gainsborough's boy." Broadway was starting to look as chance-of-the-draw as Hollywood, and Abbott was as smug and constipated as any studio producer it had been her misfortune to encounter.

Her Gainsborough period didn't last long. As *Mother Was a Lady* was falling apart, a Broadway producer was assembling the pieces for a musical *Gentlemen Prefer Blondes.* A song-and-dance Lorelei was not a new idea—Florenz Ziegfeld had wanted to do it in the late twenties—but now, with a surging interest in the flapper era, it was an idea whose moment had arrived.

24

Siren's Song

HERMAN LEVIN admits he wouldn't have thought of it himself. In the summer of 1948, between marriages, he passed a Cunard office on Park Avenue and, on a whim, went in and bought a ticket to Europe. On the crossing he bumped into music publisher Jack Robbins, who during some shop talk said, "You know what'd make a swell musical? *Gentlemen Prefer Blondes.*"

Levin was skeptical. "I hadn't been in the business long," he recalls, "but already I'd had everything suggested as a musical." But looking at *Blondes* again, he decided Robbins was right. As it would have to be a lavish production, he felt he'd need a partner in taking it on. So he called Oliver Smith, his co-producer on an earlier show.

The two men were a study in contrasts. Levin, a former lawyer, was short, jolly, and outgoing, younger than the tall and elegant Smith, who had been in the business much longer. Smith's decors for Ballet Theatre had established him as one of America's great set designers, and he had gone into production when the Jerome Robbins–Leonard Bernstein ballet *Fancy Free* became Broadway's *On the Town.*

When Smith expressed enthusiasm, Levin set up a lunch meeting at the Colony. Anita arrived, Levin recalls, "looking as young as when she wrote for Griffith." Smith was "captivated. She was marvelous, wonderful, so vital, bright, funny, enthusiastic. The three of us hit it off right away and became good friends for as long as Anita lived."

At this initial meeting, the question of the libretto came up immediately. Anita wanted to do it herself, but Levin was nervous about that.

"Since, as far as I knew, she had never written a musical, I was not anxious for her to do it alone. I suggested tactfully that maybe she'd like to have a collaborator. She understood my apprehension and wasn't at all offended."

For co-author, Levin suggested Joseph Fields, responsible for such smash successes as *My Sister Eileen* and *Junior Miss*. Fields hadn't written any musicals; but he was known to be a solid craftsman, and Levin hadn't been impressed by the structure of *Happy Birthday*. Levin's first choice for composer was Jule Styne, who'd written some of the best of the Sinatra songs and one Broadway hit, *High Button Shoes*. Mike Todd also endorsed Styne, and when Anita learned he had written her favorite song, "I Don't Want to Walk Without You," she was sold. "That was the kind of music she liked best," Styne says. "Teary barroom ballads."

Determined to open the show before the end of 1949, Levin started looking for a vacant theater and settled on the Ziegfeld, owned by his friend Billy Rose. "Saying Billy was a friend needs clarification," Levin explains. "He *terrorized* me into becoming his friend. Billy wasn't one of nature's noblemen — you never knew what the bastard might do next — but he had power and could be very useful."

Rose felt he had a proprietary interest in the shows booked at his theater, and he kept asking Levin to see the script for *Blondes*. "I told him it wasn't finished," Levin says, "but that didn't deter Billy. He wanted to read whatever there was. And what there was, was lousy."

Though Levin hadn't realized it, Anita was miffed at having a collaborator forced on her and decided that Fields could do the job alone. She gave him her earlier dramatization of *Blondes;* and thinking she wanted as few alterations as possible, he did little except excise dialogue to make space for songs.

Eventually Rose bullied Levin into letting him see the script. "It stinks," he said. "I can do better than that." A week later he handed Levin a ten-page outline for the book. Levin and Oliver Smith had to admit it was good. They showed it to Anita and Fields, who were also impressed.

"Billy specifically asked for no credit," Levin remembers. "He was so unlikeable that it was easy to hate even the good stuff he did. So I wouldn't tell them who wrote it. I got the impression they thought I had done it."

With Rose's synopsis as a guide, Anita started on a new script, working fast and mainly by herself, though Fields's participation continued to irk her. One day she called Levin and said she wanted out. Then she hung up and failed to return calls.

Levin and Smith parked themselves in the Plaza Annex lobby, waiting for her to arrive or depart. When she came through the door, she greeted them civilly but pointedly did not ask them upstairs. Levin was ready to have it out in public, if that was the way she wanted it. "You can't do this, Anita, you're ruining—"

She stamped her foot. "She really did," Levin insists. "I've heard about people stamping their feet, but I had never seen it before. And while the foot was small, it was still very impressive."

"I can't work with Fields," she said. "I've met studio executives with more upstairs than he's got."

Levin was painfully aware that if Anita walked out, it would look terrible for the show: she could disown this *Blondes* as a travesty of the original. "Probably she was too much of a lady to have done that," Levin says. "But I wasn't taking any chances. I told her that she didn't have to see Joe Fields again. And as far as I know, until opening night in New York, they never spoke again."

Before Anita completed the book, Levin was looking for a director. Oliver Smith suggested George Abbott. Knowing a little about Anita's troubles with Abbott over *Mother Was a Lady,* Levin was hesitant, but Anita told him to go ahead: after all, Abbott had done a bang-up job on the best of the Rodgers and Hart musicals. After an exploratory meeting with Abbott, Levin told Smith it wouldn't work. "I know he's a great director, I know he's great at comedy; but for me he's about as funny as the clap. I have no ability to talk to him."

Smith then mentioned John Wilson. Levin was enthusiastic. "When I'm asked 'What are your favorite musicals?' *Kiss Me, Kate* is one of the top five. A great show, beautifully directed by Wilson, impeccably cast and designed. So Oliver and I met with Jack and we got along great. The only way you couldn't like Jack was if he took a hate for you."

Born to a well-to-do New York family, educated at Andover and Yale, in his prime John Wilson looked the way Fitzgerald wanted readers to imagine Jay Gatsby. On vacation from the New York Stock Exchange, he met and fell in love with Noel Coward. After a few years the affair ended; Wilson married and, just prior to World War II, returned to America to stage a string of Coward comedies, some plays for the Lunts and Tallulah Bankhead, and two musicals, *Bloomer Girl* and *Kiss Me, Kate.*

His wife was Natalia ("Natasha") Paley, the daughter of Grand Duke Paul of Russia and a morganatic wife. At the onset of the revolution, when she was fourteen, Natasha managed to escape with her mother and sister down a drain pipe and with a few Romanov jewels sewn in their petticoats.

Natasha Wilson, a Russian princess and café society beauty who had a brief Hollywood career (she appeared with Katharine Hepburn and Cary Grant in *Sylvia Scarlett* in 1936) before marrying stage director and producer John S. Wilson. Anita and she became close friends when her husband directed *Gentlemen Prefer Blondes* in 1950.

They joined the White Russian enclave in Paris, where Natasha worked for and later married couturier Lucien Lelong.

The Wilsons made a handsome couple, and their marriage endured until Wilson's death in 1961, though it was often troubled by outside romances and by a mutual drinking problem (his predating and possibly triggering hers). Usually urbane, Wilson could become vicious when drunk or around anyone to whom he took an (often inexplicable) aversion. (About Coward he once said, "Dear Noel, so blessed, he never had any looks to lose.") But he never turned on Anita, who adored him and, to a lesser degree, Natasha. She was to spend many weekends at the Wilsons' home in Fairfield, Connecticut, over the next fifteen years.

Though Wilson's drinking was later to interfere with his career, Levin says it wasn't a problem at the time of *Blondes*. The major collaborators got along beautifully, disagreeing only about the casting of Lorelei. "Herman and Jule and Jack Wilson had very grandiose ideas," Oliver Smith remembers. "They wanted Ethel Merman, who turned it down flat. She was smart. Can you imagine Merman in a blond wig?"

Then they started auditioning every pretty blond actress (and some who weren't blond) who could sing and had some kind of name value. Marilyn Maxwell, Vivian Blaine, Janet Blair, tried out; but there was, Levin remembers, "no flame, no spark, no 'oh boy, she's the one' feeling."

Anita suggested Gertrude Niesen, a torch singer who had made a hit in a so-so 1944 musical, *Follow the Girls*. But there was a coarseness about her that displeased Smith. "Herman and I thought she would be seriously miscast, and I don't think Anita was all that enthusiastic, either. She wasn't dejected, though the rest of us were pretty discouraged. Anita possessed endless optimism; on the surface, at least, she was always sanguine. She had mastered the hard lesson that gloom is contagious, particularly in show business."

In hindsight, Levin believes the problem of casting centered on indecision about how Lorelei should be played. "We were looking at gorgeous blond seductresses when what we really wanted, though we didn't know it till we spotted it, was a girl who could make fun of a gorgeous blond seductress."

"Anita and I became soul mates during the struggle to find a Lorelei," says Oliver Smith. They were both keen on the yet-unknown Carol Channing and put up a hard battle to get her the part. Channing was then appearing in *Lend an Ear!,* a musical review that had originated on the West Coast. "Separately we had both seen it," Smith says, "and we were both entranced by Miss Channing. We tried to convince Jack Wilson, but he wouldn't listen. He had his own pet dark horse and persuaded us to see her in a stock production at Westport, Connecticut. We went on a Sunday evening, and by coincidence sitting behind us was Carol." The actress on stage, they agreed, couldn't hold a candle to the actress sitting behind them.

Anita called Levin and insisted he see *Lend an Ear!* She went with him, as did Smith and the Wilsons. They all agreed Channing was "a knockout," though physically far from an ideal Lorelei. Channing then looked much as she does today, though she was much heavier, a Valkyrie of a woman; there was no resemblance to the Lorelei described in the novel or drawn by Ralph Barton. But Anita insisted that Channing's size was a comic advantage: "She can play Lorelei like a Great Dane under the delusion it's a Pekingese."

When the role was offered to Channing, her agent, Baron Poland, made demands that sounded outrageous to Levin. And Poland refused to negotiate. Levin told his press agent, Richard Maney, to get something in the papers suggesting that Betty Hutton was about to sign for *Blondes.* The next day the squib appeared in the theater column of *The New York Times,* and within twenty-four hours Baron Poland surrendered.

B Y midsummer 1949, Levin and Smith had a book, a score, a director, a set designer (Smith), a costume designer (Miles White), a Lorelei, and a Dorothy (Yvonne Adair, another *Lend an Ear!* alumna). What they didn't have was backing. Getting the show to Broadway was going to cost $200,000 (Levin estimates that today it would cost over $4 million), and since there was no star, investors weren't rapping at the door.

There were countless backers' auditions, Levin remembers. "Each cost a grand total of thirty-five dollars, ice water included. Oliver asked about liquor and I said no—we can't afford getting them drunk on our money." Anita came to all the auditions, and she was "wonderful," Levin recalls. One night she played both Lorelei and Dorothy while Wilson and Styne took on the other roles in a mini-version of the show. "Everybody loved it," Levin says, "but when it was over, we hadn't raised a dime."

Levin informed Billy Rose about the difficulty, and Rose took over. He told Levin to bring Jule Styne to Oscar Hammerstein's apartment the next evening. "We get there and meet Oscar, Dick Rodgers, and Josh Logan—the whole *South Pacific* team," Levin remembers. "After Jule played some of the score, they said they'd each take a five-thousand-dollar share." The next morning an item appeared in the *Times* about the *South Pacific* investment in *Blondes*. By late afternoon, Levin had closed his subscription book, though calls were still coming in from prospective buyers.

B L O N D E S started rehearsals in September 1949. Anita attended run-throughs, revised dialogue, took a lively interest in the costumes. Miles White was encouraged to emphasize Channing's Junoesque figure. "In one scene," Channing remembers, "I wore a costume with a pheasant's tail. 'Make that tail longer,' Anita said. 'Give Carol a tail like the girls wore in the Folies-Bergère.' Because Anita was so tiny, she thought nothing was more wonderful than being big."

Anita also kept busy playing backstage cupid. Ruth Dubonnet had recently divorced her third husband and returned to America. Though Ruth neither needed nor asked for help, Anita resolved to find her friend a new beau.

"She set her sights on me," Levin says. "But I was already involved with one of the dancers in the show—she was hired before we got involved, let me emphasize—and we were keeping it secret. But Anita had a nose for that kind of thing, and she was thrilled. She saw me as a sugar daddy, and I never bothered to set her straight, 'cause I think she liked me better that way."

Ruth Dubonnet did her own picking. "The big romance of the show was Mme Dubonnet and Jule Styne," remembers Carol Channing. The affair was a blessing because it distracted Styne, if only momentarily, from nagging Anita and Levin about the musical's shortcomings. "Jule is an adorable guy," Levin says. "If he's got a fault, it's that he's always worrying about the entire show, not just his songs, but *everything*. I suppose that's not bad, but it gets to be a pain in the neck in the final week of rehearsal. He said the first-act finale didn't work. I knew that, Jack knew that, Carol knew that, and I thought Anita knew it, too. But it's five days before the out-of-town opening, and I tell Jule we'll solve it then—that's why we go out of town. But I take the precaution of booking Jule into one Philadelphia hotel and Anita and me into another, so that he won't come up and bang on our doors when we don't answer the phone."

GENTLEMEN PREFER BLONDES opened in Philadelphia, Levin's hometown, on November 1, 1949. "We were booked for three weeks, then straight into New York," Levin says. "If you can't fix what's wrong with a show in three weeks, it can't be fixed."

The local reviews and audience response proved that Styne had been right to worry. Channing was a sensation, and there was praise and applause for score, sets, costumes, and direction. Only the book was found wanting. The chief problem was the end of the first act, so wordy it slowed down the momentum until the second act was too far under way.

Anita refused to admit there was a problem, possibly because she had no notion of how to correct it. Egged on by Levin, she made small alterations, which were tried out and discarded after one performance. Then Jule Styne came up with a maybe-it'll-work solution: end Act One with Lorelei reprising a couple of songs, cut the start of Act Two to the bone, get rid of that awful apache ballet, and the show would come in a winner.

Anita agreed to try it Stein's way; and the first time out, the show held together. The closing week in Philadelphia the *Blondes* company was high on the euphoria of coming into New York with a solid hit.

FRIENDS from California came East for the Broadway opening, December 8, 1949—Clifford and the Wendels (who were investors in the

Anita and Carol Channing, *Gentlemen Prefer Blondes,* 1950

show). Mr. E. begged to join them, but Anita insisted the excitement would be too much for him.

After the performance, Levin hosted a party at the St. Regis. "Anita wanted me to make a spectacular entrance," Carol Channing remembers. "She arranged for me to wear a tiara that once belonged to Empress Josephine." But with the tiara came a security guard with instructions never to leave Channing's side. "When I went to the loo, he'd tag along. And if I went on the dance floor he had to partner me or walk next to me. So Anita said she'd dance with him and there we were stuck together all night like Siamese twins on a double date."

All the reviews were favorable, though there was some quibbling about *Blondes* looking old-fashioned after *South Pacific.* Even if the notices had been harsher, the praise lavished on Channing, soon elevated to star billing, would have assured a healthy run for the show. It was to stay at the Ziegfeld for more than ninety weeks and went on tour for another year. Levin was planning a London production when Channing told him she was pregnant. "So I canceled it," Levin says. "I was convinced the show wouldn't work without Carol, and in my opinion, it never has."

Anita appreciated Channing's contribution, but she didn't feel the show couldn't go on without Carol. When the musical was eventually staged in London in 1961, Anita was delighted by Dora Bryan's Lorelei, and felt it was unfair that the British critics compared Bryan (best known in America as Rita Tushingham's mother in the film version of *A Taste of Honey*) unfavorably to Marilyn Monroe in the 1953 film version.

Anita made no contribution to that film. The script was written by Charles Lederer, Marion Davies's nephew, and Anita felt Charlie had done a grand job; his script, she admitted, was an improvement on her own libretto. And though she had no hand in the casting, she felt Monroe was an inspired choice. Marilyn was the most "luscious" of all Loreleis.

25

From
the French

B L O N D E S really had two stars. One was Carol Channing; the other was its author. The show brought Anita more attention than she had received since the publication of the novel back in the twenties. She was interviewed extensively; she and Channing were photographed by Richard Avedon; her picture was in all the papers and on the cover of *Theatre Arts*. She appeared on radio and made her television debut as narrator of an adaptation of F. Scott Fitzgerald's "Bernice Bobs Her Hair," starring Julie Harris. For *The New York Times*, she wrote a short history of *Blondes* and later a review of the Kinsey Report in the style of, and signed by, Lorelei Lee.

Nostalgia for the twenties was now in full flower, and bemusedly Anita heard herself described as "the last of the flappers." She was flabbergasted. "Me—a flapper!? The only thing I ever flapped was the pages of a yellow legal pad." Sometimes she felt like a fossil from a prehistoric era; but the publicity was good for the show, and what was good for the show was good for her bank account.

Shortly after the opening of *Blondes*, she left the Plaza Annex and moved to a more spacious apartment in the Langdon Hotel at the corner of Fifth Avenue and Fifty-sixth Street. She bought a car, and since she didn't drive, chauffeuring was added to the list of Gladys's chores. They went to Fairfield, Connecticut, to visit the Wilsons, to Cape Cod to see Paulette Goddard in a stock production of *Caesar and Cleopatra*, to the Hamptons, and often to Atlantic City, particularly off-season, when the resort's magnificent Victorian hotels were virtually deserted.

IN JANUARY 1950, Anita started work on *A Mouse Is Born,* a novel about Effie Huntriss, a film star confined to bed while awaiting the birth of her first child. To pass the time, Effie starts writing a memoir of her checkered career. She wants her "mouse" to know Mama's side of the story.

By July the book was finished and accepted by Doubleday for publication. On August 5, Anita sailed for Europe on the *America,* her first transatlantic vacation in twenty years. The ship docked briefly at an Irish port, where she was met by Adele Astaire. In the early 1930s, Adele had married Charles, Lord Cavendish and since then had lived at his estate, Lismore, outside Dublin. Anita spent a fortnight with Lord and Lady Cavendish, attending several performances at the Abbey Theatre and "too many horse fairs." Then she flew from Dublin to Paris, where a group of New York friends were vacationing—Natasha and Jack Wilson, Ruth Dubonnet, Howard Sturges and Linda Porter.

Lismore, the Cavendish castle in Ireland

Thanks to Ruth Dubonnet's connection with the Parisian fashion world, she got to see all the fall collections. For *Elle* and *Paris-Match* she was photographed in Balmain gowns, several of which she purchased at reduced rates. Balmain's favorite model was a tiny Burmese girl, so petite that almost no one except Anita could fit the dresses designed for her. But even if she had had to pay full price, Anita would have done so. Couturier clothes were made from fabric that lasted a lifetime; and anyone handy with a needle, as both she and Gladys were, could rescue a démodé gown by lifting the hem or removing a ruffle.

On her return to New York, Anita began work on a stage adaptation of Colette's 1945 novella *Gigi.* Ninon de Tallon, Colette's American agent, had approached her about this some months before, and at that time she had done her own translation of the book, not an easy task since, she later wrote, "Colette employed the widest vocabulary, loved to use words with which even the French were unfamiliar." By the time the translation was finished, she was convinced there was a play in *Gigi,* but she put it aside while finishing *A Mouse Is Born.*

Anita had felt an affinity for Colette ever since she read the *Claudine* series years before, though the two writers could not have been more remote in style. Colette's greatest strength was in her sensuous, almost erotic descriptions of both the simple and the deluxe pleasures of life, while Anita, as Oliver Smith once accurately commented, "cut everything to the bone." But the two women shared many similar convictions, especially about sexual bonding, perhaps because their personal histories ran along parallel lines. Colette had received little formal education, passed her youth as a touring vaudeville performer, and married a hack novelist who published her first works under his pen name, Willy.

Gigi is a Belle Epoque version of the Cinderella story. The coltish sixteen-year-old heroine is the youngest member of family in which all the women are trained to become courtesans. Gigi's grandmother and her great-aunt Alicia have chosen sugar king Gaston Lachaille as the girl's initial protector, but Gigi outwits them by getting Lachaille to marry her.

Anita started *Gigi* in early October 1951 and completed it before the end of the year. Meanwhile, *A Mouse Is Born* was published to tepid reviews, many critics finding it too reminiscent of *Blondes.* Self-imitation is a legitimate charge, but there are some wonderful scenes, including a visit to a nudist colony so vivid and funny that it suggests Anita must have had firsthand experience in one of those bare-it-all enclaves. And for Hollywood gossip fans, there's the fun of unlocking this roman à clef to discover who's really who. Thalberg and Mayer and the legendary M–G–M

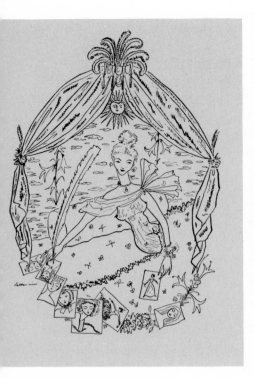

A
Mouse Is
Born
BY ANITA LOOS

DRAWINGS BY PALLAVICINI

Doubleday & Company, Inc., 1951
Garden City, N.Y.

Title page and illustrations from *A Mouse Is Born*

publicist Howard Strickling are unmistakably there, and contributing to the composite portraits are two powerhouse agents, Greg Bautzer and Charles Feldman. Effie Huntriss, the heroine, is unfortunately no more than the generic Hollywood star with more bust than talent, not an original like Lorelei Lee.

IN EARLY 1951 Anita went to California to write a film version of *Happy Birthday* for Columbia. Judy Holliday wanted to play Addie Beamis so badly that she had persuaded Harry Cohn, Columbia's chief executive, to finagle censorship clearance for the play. After three weeks, he shifted ground and told Anita he was shelving *Birthday* indefinitely. Holliday explained that Cohn didn't like the play and had taken it on only to get her off his back for a while.

But the trip wasn't a total loss. While in Los Angeles, Anita talked to George Cukor about directing *Gigi.* Halfheartedly he committed himself, though, as he later admitted, he didn't care much for the original novel or for Anita's adaptation—both were too "ooh-la-la." For the role of Gigi's grandmother he suggested a mutual friend, Constance Collier. "Perfect!" Anita exclaimed. "Yes," Cukor agreed, "provided Constance can still see enough to avoid bumping into the scenery."

Back in New York, Anita showed the script to a close friend—"maybe the funniest man I ever met"—Sandor Incze, a Hungarian-born publicist and publisher then toying with becoming a producer. He liked *Gigi* but felt it should be mounted by someone more experienced than he was. "Show it to Gilbert Miller," Incze said. "If he turns it down, I'll do it."

Then in his mid-sixties, Miller was esteemed on both sides of the Atlantic for his tasteful productions of literate entertainment. He was, wrote a 1943 *New Yorker* profiler, "kind, generous, intensely loyal to his friends" but also "abrupt, occasionally rude, moody." Former aides remember him fondly despite his total lack of humor.

Anita had known him for years. They had many friends in common, and she was very fond of his wife, Kitty (the daughter of banking titan Julian Bache). She lunched with Kitty at least once a month and dutifully attended the Millers' annual New Year's Eve gala. But Gilbert viewed Anita with suspicion. He didn't comprehend most of her ripostes, and those he did, he found too fresh.

Miller didn't much like *Gigi,* but he took it on in proverbial dog-in-the-manger fashion. Morton Gottlieb, his assistant at this time, explains,

"He didn't want Incze to produce it—why I don't know. I don't think he ever wanted to put it on himself; at least, he had no commitment to it himself. He wanted it out of the marketplace, and maybe, if everything fell into place, he'd go ahead."

But Miller went through the motions of getting the show ready for a fall opening. Actresses were auditioned for Gigi, among them Grace Kelly, Rita Gam, and Vanessa Brown. None was ideal, but Brown ("a little too knowing," Anita thought) was the best of the lot, and it was decided to go with her unless someone better came along.

Every spring Miller went to Europe for a lengthy vacation, leaving Morton Gottlieb in charge of the office. "I was naive," Gottlieb recalls. "I guess I should have guessed Gilbert didn't really want to produce *Gigi*, but since I didn't, I put all the machinery in operation for a fall opening. I sold theater parties months ahead, which was easy, since it was Anita's first show since *Blondes* and it was the only comedy so far announced for the new season. I had the show sold out nearly every night for several weeks. And that's how *Gigi* got produced by Gilbert Miller. Gilbert hated turning down all those theater parties, so he decided to do the play, though he was still looking for an out."

Miller was hoping Colette might reject the adaptation, but instead she sent her blessings. Anita was, she later wrote, "the most subtle and friendly of collaborators." And then she provided another favor (though possibly to Miller it was a disfavor): she discovered an actress who looked exactly like the Gigi she had visualized while writing her novel.

Part of every summer, Colette lived at the Palace Hotel in Monte Carlo, and one day in the hotel lobby she noticed a young actress who had just finished a British film shot on location in Monaco. Immediately she wired Anita in New York and Miller in London, urging them to sign no one until they looked at Audrey Hepburn.

Soon Anita heard from Miller: he had seen Hepburn in London, and would Anita please come immediately? With Paulette Goddard (now divorced from Burgess Meredith) as companion, she sailed on the *Ile de France* a few days later. When they arrived at their suite in the Savoy Hotel in London, they found a portfolio of Hepburn photographs left by Miller for their inspection. Paulette studied them carefully. "She's too perfect. There's got to be something wrong . . . maybe she lisps."

Arriving for tea, Miller said he had been apprehensive too. Miss Hepburn had appeared in a few films, but her stage experience was limited to the chorus line of West End musicals; so he had asked actress Cathleen Nesbitt to listen to her read from the stage of a London theater.

238

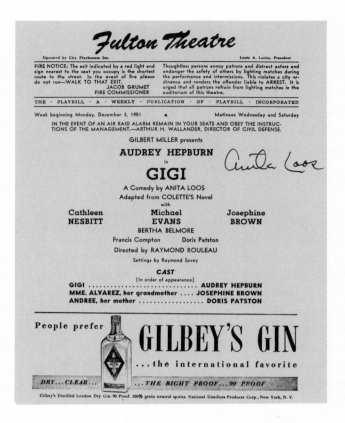

"She couldn't be understood even from the middle of the stalls," Nesbitt remembered. "But voice projection is something that can be learned quite quickly. What she could project, and this is something that can't be taught, was personality. I told Gilbert I foresaw no difficulty."

There had been one other hitch. Earlier a talent scout from Paramount had noticed Hepburn and put her under contract to the studio. Miller had checked with the company and learned that as there were no immediate screen plans for Hepburn, there were no objections to her appearing on Broadway for eight or ten months.

Hepburn appeared at the Savoy the next morning, looking nervous but every bit as good as in the photographs, and she was charming, with perfect manners, poised despite the awkwardness of the situation. Anita was delighted and told Miller to proceed with Hepburn's contract.

He then suggested Cathleen Nesbitt as Gigi's Aunt Alicia. Nesbitt was an accomplished actress who had been one of the great beauties of the Edwardian stage and, now in her sixties, still looked the way dowager empresses ought to look but rarely have. Anita agreed that Nesbitt would be ideal as the former queen of the demimonde.

From London Anita and Paulette flew to Paris, where Anita was to

meet Colette at the restaurant Le Grand Vefour. The novelist and her third
husband, Maurice Goudeket, were already seated when Anita arrived
punctually. She had prepared a gracious tribute, but before she spoke more
than a few words, Colette interrupted to ask where she had discovered
those adorable shoes. The conversation drifted to fashion, then to the
menu, Colette accepting some and rejecting many of the chef's recommen-
dations while Anita and Goudeket sat silently until the ritual ended.

The next day Anita went to Colette's apartment, where her hostess,
suffering from crippling arthritis, received her propped up in bed, sipping a
tisane and thumbing through the manuscript of *Gigi.* Gently she pointed
out a few discordant Americanisms. Then she tossed aside the playscript
and got down to more interesting business. Where, she inquired, had
Anita discovered that alluring gray *tailleur?*

George Cukor had withdrawn as director, and to replace him Miller
suggested Raymond Rouleau, a Belgian living and working in Paris. Anita
saw one of his productions, an indifferent play beautifully staged, and
afterwards met Rouleau for supper.

He would be perfect, she reported to Miller, if he spoke English; but
he didn't, *pas un mot.* Miller thought Anita was making too much of very

Anita and Colette at the Restaurant Le Grand Vefour in Paris. At the time of their meeting to discuss the stage adaptation of *Gigi,* Colette was seventy-seven and in failing health. She was to die four years later.

little. After all, he spoke French, and so did she, Hepburn, Cathleen Nesbitt, and Constance Collier. One of them would always be at hand to help out Rouleau and other cast members less bilingually gifted.

Miller was now prepared to start rehearsals in early October and open *Gigi* by Thanksgiving 1951. It was then late August. Anita and Paulette had intended to spend at least two months in Europe, but those plans were now revised. Anita had to return to New York in two weeks; but in the meantime she was going to enjoy herself—an easy matter with Paulette as her partner.

Paulette was then being courted by Claude Terrail, the proprietor of the fashionable restaurant Tour d'Argent. Goddard kept her distance, but Terrail was so persistent that she finally agreed to visit his restaurant on the condition that she bring along, as chaperones, Anita and Miles White, the costume designer for *Blondes,* who also was vacationing in Paris.

Terrail sent a silver Rolls-Royce to pick them up. Paulette looked at it disdainfully. "In California, I had a car like that, but the engine never turned over so I gave it to the milkman." Anita and Miles stared at each other in suspended disbelief: anything was possible with Paulette.

After escorting them to a table, Terrail withdrew discreetly. He assumed that Paulette and guests would order the house specialty, pressed duck, but when a waiter passed by bearing a huge bowl filled with Beluga caviar, Paulette grabbed it from his hands. "Forget the duck!" she whooped. "Caviar is the healthiest thing anyone can eat." Also the most expensive, Anita thought, as she watched Goddard shovel thousands of fish eggs into her mouth.

B E F O R E rehearsals began on October 10, Anita met several times with Gilbert Miller to discuss the script and other production details. At the first conference, Miller riffled through the pages of *Gigi* and said unenthusiastically, "Well, Anita, there are some funny things here." With no hesitation Anita shot back, "Don't worry, Gilbert. We'll get rid of them in Philadelphia." Miller smiled but wasn't amused. It was just that kind of crack that made him chary of Anita. She was, he said, "a minx."

In the days ahead Miller was to have ample reason to regret his involvement with *Gigi*. Bad omens started with Audrey Hepburn waddling off the boat from Europe. During the Second World War, Audrey and her mother had nearly starved to death, and the girl had never put on weight—until this voyage. Not at all sure she could handle a starring role in her first New York play, she had worked out her anxiety by eating her way across the Atlantic. The sprite Miller had hired in London was now a very tubby gamine.

Even after she started to diet diligently, Miller remained displeased with his protégée. "Gilbert had been looking forward to introducing Audrey to his society friends," recalls Morton Gottlieb, "but she wasn't interested in that." Shy and very insecure, she wanted to stay close to her mother and her English boy friend.

During the first weeks of rehearsal, Miller continued to think about replacing her. Vocal projection remained a problem, and overall her performance looked tentative at best. Anita told Miller to stop badgering the girl. Cathleen Nesbitt offered to tutor her privately if only he would treat Audrey with respect. Miller agreed to a truce, but then other problems arose.

Constance Collier became confused as to whether she was acting in French or English and withdrew from the cast. She was replaced by Florence Reed, who also couldn't adjust to bilingual direction. Finally Gigi's grandmother was played by Josephine Brown, an actress who wasn't anyone's ideal third choice for the role.

By the Philadelphia opening on November 8, Hepburn had gained assurance, and the local critics were enchanted by her, though cool about the production, which was, aside from Cathleen Nesbitt's glittering performance, very shaky. A week later in New Haven, with some of the wrinkles ironed out, the show was, Anita wrote in her diary, "terrific."

The New York critics didn't agree. *Gigi* got a lukewarm Broadway welcome, many reviewers implying that there was something distasteful about this winking account of a teenager's narrow escape from concubinage. Theater people thought *Gigi* one of Miller's weakest productions, badly mishandled by Rouleau, whose lack of English perhaps accounted for the wide range of diction among the cast, everything from Borscht Belt to Oxonian.

But Hepburn's personal notices were love letters, and Richard Maney, Miller's press agent, advised that the show would only catch on if the actress was heavily promoted. Paramount Pictures had a similar idea. A company representative told Miller that the studio would contribute money to a publicity campaign for Hepburn. In exchange it asked only that when she reported to the studio for her first assignment, she check in as a star.

Up to this point no one in *Gigi* received star billing, and below the title, Nesbitt's name preceded Hepburn's. If either was to be raised to elite status, by rights it should be Nesbitt, and not only because of rank and experience. Hepburn was adorable, but Cathleen Nesbitt was the show's pièce de résistance.

Anita, Miller, and Maney hated to ask her to bow before Hepburn, but Nesbitt said she understood. A week later, with appropriate ballyhoo, Audrey Hepburn became a Broadway star. *Gigi* went on to run profitably until May 31, 1952, and might have continued longer if Paramount hadn't needed Hepburn for *Roman Holiday*.

Anita's adaptation of *Gigi* was to have a healthy after-Broadway life. It was produced several times in Paris, and the 1956 London production, directed by Peter Hall and starring Leslie Caron, was, Anita felt, superior to the New York version. Though she received $35,000 for the rights to her play, she did not participate in the making of the 1957 movie musical. As many of her friends were part of the show (Alan Jay Lerner, Cecil Beaton, Maurice Chevalier, among others), she was careful to speak kindly of it for the record. Privately she admitted she didn't much care for it: Charm had been sacrificed to production values—"it was too M–G–M."

26

Unity
and Disharmony

*A*NITA never kept copies of her letters; the rare exceptions were those she sent Mr. E. at Las Encinas. Shortly after the opening of *Gigi,* finding herself "in the peculiar situation of not having any pressing work," she seized the opportunity to tell Emerson of a surprising development in her life:

> . . . Your Bug, in the last year, has "got religion" . . . and of all things, Unity. . . . [A friend] subscribed to their little magazine for me and it started me on a career of reading the Bible and I suddenly found myself able to handle all problems with such ease and confidence that it was a revelation. I've heard some people say Unity is a servant girl's religion, to which my answer is that religion should not be sophisticated; when it is, it loses all humanity. . . . I would not think of starting off my day without my *Daily Word* [the Unity magazine], and while sometimes the messages are a little corny, the Bible text is always *great.* . . .

In *A Mouse Is Born,* Anita had referred to Unity, a latter-day version of Couéism supported by highly selective uplift quotations from the Old and New Testaments. Effie Huntriss, *Mouse*'s heroine, believes in "the Great Law of unity, which teaches that when people hold their thoughts very, very strongly the Thoughts materialize, and Thinkers ultimately receive what they demand."

Anita obviously felt uncomfortable about sitting in a pew alongside Effie and "servant girls," and she never mentioned Unity to friends (unless she knew they too were believers). But her faith was firm. Until her death she kept up her subscription to *The Daily Word* and clipped and pasted into her diaries those messages which pertained to her life.

Mr. E. was so overwhelmed by Anita's Unity epistle that he couldn't answer it himself. Julie Butterworth, his nurse, wrote that it had indeed cause a great upheaval—Emerson had to be sedated after reading it. Then she approached practical matters. Anita had mentioned sending Mr. E. a subscription to *The Daily Word* as a Christmas gift; that was fine for his spiritual well-being, but what he needed was a foam-rubber pillow: he had recently developed an allergy to feathers. And what Mr. E. *really* wanted for Christmas was a trip to New York.

Anita replied that she was too busy with *Gigi* to entertain him. But on December 11, she opened the door and there were Mr. E. and Mrs. Butterworth. Somehow Emerson had convinced the Las Encinas staff that Anita wanted him home for the holidays. The next morning Anita left for Fairfield, Connecticut, to visit Jack and Natasha Wilson. This was nothing she could cancel, she explained. There was business to discuss with Jack, and it couldn't be put off. On her return three days later, Emerson "had gone into a nose dive." He was suffering constantly from gas, had shooting pains in all his extremities, and was, Mrs. B. summed up, "a general mess."

Anita resigned herself to devoting all her time to diverting Mr. E. She took him to *Gigi* and, afterwards, backstage to meet Audrey Hepburn ("Adorable," said the entranced Emerson); to lunch at her favorite restaurant, Quo Vadis; to supper at El Morocco; to the Gilbert Millers' New Year's Eve party.

At last, on January 8, 1952, he and Mrs. B. returned to Pasadena. Two days later an emotionally drained Anita went off with Ruth Dubonnet for a vacation in Sarasota, Florida (where she met and wrote an article about circus clown Emmett Kelly). Back in New York, she found this letter waiting for her:

Darling Bug—

I cannot write you myself, but will try and dictate a few lines to Mrs. B. I hope all your projects are coming along okay. I wish I felt more enthused about everything but life is too complicated unless one is well enough to fight the elements. All my love to my darling little girl and take good care of yourself.

It was signed "Boy."

T H E   P R O J E C T S   Emerson referred to were two adaptations of French plays by a team of prolific boulevard playwrights, Pierre Barillet and Jean-Pierre Grédy (best known in America for two comedies written some years later, *Cactus Flower* and *Forty Carats*). The first was *Ami-Ami* (*Darling-Darling* in Anita's translation), an intricately plotted bedroom farce; the other was *Le Don d'Adèle,* a whimsical comedy about a young girl born with second sight, a gift that will vanish once she loses her virginity.

Two years earlier Garson Kanin had adapted the play, which, as *The Amazing Adele,* had been produced at a Connecticut stock theater with Ruth Gordon in the leading role. It was a fiasco, but Anita and Jack Wilson agreed that in a freer translation and with a more youthful star the comedy might work. "When a girl of Ruth's age hasn't lost her ESP, she probably never will," Wilson quipped. They both thought it would be ideal as a musical for Carol Channing, who thought so too. Morty Gottlieb, increasingly restive as Miller's right-hand man, wanted to produce the show on his own.

In April Anita sailed on the *Ile de France* to confer with Barillet and Grédy. As companion, she chose her secretary, Florence Edwards, known as Eddy. She was, recalls Ruth Dubonnet, "a drab creature, her clothes always in disarray, but very nice, very sharp and astute about people." Anita placed absolute faith in Eddy and relied heavily on her judgment.

The meeting with Barillet and Grédy was a great success—they all became close friends. After a few days in Paris, Anita and Eddy went by train to Florence, where they were met by Howard Sturges, who drove them to Montecatini Terme, a fashionable spa about forty miles away. For months Anita had suffered from arthritis, and Sturgie had suggested she try the cure at Montecatini, where the mud and waters were reputed to soothe any number of ailments.

In the next years Anita was to return frequently to Montecatini, always staying at the Grand e La Pace, one of the most gracious of all European hotels. Designed on palatial lines, with a massive porte cochère, lots of topiary, caryatids, frescoes, mosaics, and a magnificent formal

Pierre Barillet with Anita at a square dance in Fairfield, Connecticut, where they were spending a weekend with John and Natasha Wilson

garden, La Pace was celebrated for its luxury, for the painstaking attention of its staff, and for its cuisine. There were two menus: one for cure patients, limited to boiled fish, fresh vegetables, and fruits; and another for guests who could stomach elaborate pasta creations and rich desserts.

On her first morning at Montecatini, Anita was scheduled for a consultation with the spa's star specialist, Dr. Pisani. Her pains, he diagnosed, were caused by either a liver ailment or maybe her heart, which was "a hundred and forty-eight years of age." But not to worry—by following the cure faithfully, she would leave Montecatini feeling as young as she looked. Every morning she must spend twenty minutes in a mud bath, then rest for thirty minutes, then drink two liter-bottles of water, glass after glass, until the flasks were empty. Food was to be taken only from the restricted menu.

Getting that water down was the worst part. The mud baths were soothing, the poached fish superb, but she craved ice cream. Giving in to temptation, she ordered a tutti frutti, only to see Dr. Pisani pass by her table. Shaking a warning finger, he said, "Tomorrow your heart will be a hundred and fifty years of age." She pushed the dish away.

Another guest at La Pace, Clementine Churchill, invited Anita to tea. At the appointed hour, she arrived and found a lavish spread (her heart would be 175 the next day), though there was only one other guest, the duchess of Marlborough. "Winston will be delighted we've met," Mrs.

Churchill said. "*Gentlemen Prefer Blondes* is one of his favorite books." He had, she continued, kept it on his night table during the worst months of the war, reading it over and over when he couldn't sleep. Anita remembered something Napoleon supposedly said about women being the diversion of conquerors.

B A C K in New York, Anita pushed ahead with *The Amazing Adele,* shaping it around Carol Channing's distinctive personality. The locale was shifted to 1930s Atlantic City, and Adele became more Orphan Annie than the French sprite of the original. Anita was nearly finished with a rough draft when Jack Wilson, "half-pissed," called to report that Carol was "definitely cool about *Adele.*" Anita was very hurt: why didn't Channing have the class to call herself instead of letting Jack be the messenger of bad news?

Putting *Adele* aside for a while, Anita concentrated on her personal life. For some time she had been thinking of leaving the Langdon for more spacious quarters. When the mother of one of Jule Styne's friends died, Ruth Dubonnet urged her to take over the vacant apartment at 171 West Fifty-seventh Street, directly across from Carnegie Hall. It was big, well laid out; and due to the former occupant's long-term tenancy, the rent was, considering the location and size, a steal—under six hundred dollars a month.

Anita's new home consisted of an entrance hall, a living room, a dining room which she transformed into an office, a pantry, a kitchen, three bedrooms, and two baths. That added up to a lot of space needing furniture. "Anita was like a bachelor about living," says Stanley Simmons, a former dancer turned costume designer, who helped her resettle. "She wasn't interested in decor and was very guarded about spending money on it." Many pieces were picked up at a Salvation Army thrift shop and refurbished by Alvin Colt, a costume designer. One of Anita's few extravagances was a child's bentwood rocker, picked up at F.A.O. Schwarz, which became her favorite chair.

Even before moving in, Anita, who was now in her sixties, was apprehensive about spending every night alone in an apartment arranged to accommodate a family. At the Plaza and the Langdon, there had been hotel staff to call on in case of emergencies. She tried to persuade Eddy and Gladys to live with her, but both declined; they had their own lives to live. But just when Anita was thinking about interviewing prospective housekeepers, Gladys changed her mind and accepted the job.

This was a significant turning point in their relationship. From here on, they were like Ruth and Naomi—where one went, the other lagged not far behind. Anita's friends understood that Gladys was not a servant but "family"—a funny, motherly, upbeat lady generous enough to put aside her own life to look after Miss Loos.

Anita says in her memoirs that Gladys had started working for the Emersons in the 1930s, but the diaries (specific about the entrances and exits of domestics) mention only one Gladys at that time—a maid fired for filching bills from Mr. E.'s wallet. Mary Loos doesn't remember Gladys until after the start of the war, and the Mexican gardener at the Santa Monica house says it was later, around 1944—which fits the diaries, where Gladys becomes prominent just as Anita is leaving for New York and *Happy Birthday*.

Gladys Tipton was born around 1903, probably in Tennessee. She married a Mr. Turner, then a Mr. DeKalb, and before joining Anita she had traveled around quite a bit. Producer Charles Hollerith knew a Wisconsin family she had worked for in the 1930s, and cartoonist Peter Arno remembered her from Chicago.

Gladys has always been vague about her past, not necessarily because she had anything to hide—nothing except, perhaps, a prosaic life history. Maybe all that was important was the years after she started working for Miss Loos.

JACK WILSON had lost interest in *Adele*—"a blessing," since Wilson was now "a hopeless dipsomaniac"—but Morty was still eager to produce with a partner, Albert Selden, who in exchange for a hefty investment was going to write the score for the show. Anita convinced herself she liked his score, but no one else shared her enthusiasm. "I designed the sets," Oliver Smith says, "as a favor to Anita. The book was promising, but the songs weren't up to Broadway standard."

Adele was turned down by every name actress who read it, so the collaborators were forced to look for an unknown. Anita had an unbeatable record as a star maker—Channing in *Blondes*, Hepburn in *Gigi*—and who said lightning couldn't strike thrice?

Someone suggested Tammy Grimes, a student at the Neighborhood Playhouse, where the faculty spoke of her in glowing terms. She could act, she could sing in a scratchy sort of way; she had poise, presence, and an offbeat, 1930s-type glamour—Jean Arthur and Carol Lombard combined.

Though still some months away from graduation, Grimes had already attracted Broadway attention.

Anita saw her in a Neighborhood Playhouse production and was impressed by her individuality. She invited Tammy to tea. "I was very impressed," Grimes remembers. "Not so much by who she was, but of a certain attitude, a statement of *what* she was. Today anything goes; but she and ladies of the same age group, like Lillian Gish and Ruth Gordon, made an event out of appearing in public. You present yourself in the way you want the world to see you. It has to do with self-respect, pride in your profession, and a kind of discipline I certainly didn't possess when I met Anita. But I knew enough to want to emulate such assurance."

Rehearsals for *Adele* started the last week of November 1953, and the musical opened in Philadelphia on December 26. The first night was, Anita reported, "wonderful," but the reviews the next day were "as bad as any I've ever seen."

Anita and Gladys in 1952

That afternoon there was a production conference in Anita's suite in the Bellevue-Stratford Hotel. Gottlieb announced that he was bringing in someone to help Selden with the score and asked if she'd accept similar assistance with the book. She didn't much like the idea; but in the past she had done some doctoring on shows with out-of-town problems, and she realized a fresh point of view could be helpful.

By opening night in Boston, the new material was in place, with results that pleased the public and the producers but not Anita. "They've gagged it up with a lot of Borscht Belt one-liners," she wrote. The local reviews were mixed—three pretty good, two dreadful. Gottlieb and Selden told her they were closing the show after the Boston run.

That night she went with them to break the news to the cast. "No, no!" they shouted. One of the showgirls said that if money was the problem, she had a friend with lots of cash; borrowing a dime, she went off to call him. The actors believed in the show, and Anita sided with them. What was at fault was the amateurism of her producers, Gottlieb and Selden. "They're not in my class."

The reason *Adele* closed in Boston, Morton Gottlieb says, is that the Shubert Organization, after reading the out-of-town reviews, reneged on its agreement to book *Adele* into the Winter Garden. "So we're out of town with no theater and, with those notices, no chance of getting one. *Adele* had great sequences, but it needed a different approach. People who saw it thought it should be done more kiddingly—not camp exactly, but as a spoof of the Busby Berkeley musicals. But Selden didn't want to do another *Boy Friend,* so the show was half spoof, half straight, and audiences didn't know how to respond."

Anita left Boston once the closing notice was posted but returned for the final performance, bearing presents for the cast. For Tammy Grimes there was the special gift of lasting friendship.

"Every so often Anita would ask me to tea," Grimes recalls. "Usually there'd be just the two of us, and she'd want to know about my career and, later, about my daughter, Amanda [Plummer]. Once I mentioned how I *longed* to own a Fortuny gown, and a few weeks later, she called to say a friend had one and wanted to pass it along to me.

"Her friend was Lucy Rosen, who was the first woman—maybe the *only* woman—to play the theremin. She lived in this gothic stone villa near Caramoor, New York. We drove up to see her, and Lucy Rosen made a truly spectacular entrance. She was wearing a Grecian robe and carrying a staff. She had very pale skin and hennaed hair that stood out on end as though it were electrified. Perhaps the electricity from the theremin went straight up into Lucy's coiffure. She looked like a Burne-Jones lady caught in a wind storm. We had this magnificent dinner—nine courses with sherbet in the middle—and at the end Lucy presented me with my Fortuny. And Anita was responsible. Without her I never would have gotten a Fortuny or the chance to meet a *divine* eccentric like Lucy Rosen."

27

Writer's Cramp

*E*VEN before *Adele* went into rehearsal, Anita was working on a new play with Charles MacArthur for Helen Hayes. Based on a Ludwig Bemelmans novel, *To the One I Love the Best,* it was a lightly fictionalized account of the final years of Anita's friend Elsie de Wolfe.

In the late twenties Elsie raised café society eyebrows by marrying Sir Charles Mendl, a press attaché to the British embassy in Paris. The marriage was platonic, an arrangement that suited both partners: Elsie got a titled husband, and Sir Charles, a celebrated wife unperturbed by his compulsive flirtations.

At the outbreak of World War II, the Mendls fled France, leaving most of their assets behind. Eventually they settled in California, where Elsie transformed a modest Beverly Hills house into a fantasy villa of wicker and striped awnings. After the war, they returned to her beloved Villa Trianon in Versailles, which had been occupied and ransacked by the Nazis. Bemelmans' novel begins at this point, telling of Elsie's struggles to restore her house beautiful.

The work on the play went slowly. MacArthur was frequently ill, and Anita was involved with getting *Adele* launched. When the musical closed, she was eager to get back to the Hayes comedy, tentatively titled *Daisy* after its heroine, and asked the MacArthurs to invite her to Palm Beach, where they were vacationing.

She arrived in Florida in mid-January 1956. Hayes was appearing in

Lady Mendl's home, After All, in Beverly Hills

a local production of *The Glass Menagerie,* and the collaborators worked mainly in the evening when she was at the theater. MacArthur was so weak that Anita did as much nursing as writing. One evening she had to call a doctor, who suggested last rites be administered at once. "What's his faith?" he asked. "I'm a phallic worshipper," MacArthur managed to say.

Despite the jest, MacArthur's condition was very grave. Taken to a hospital, he was fed intravenously for two days but then made a miraculous recovery. A week later, he and Anita were back at work. When *Glass Menagerie* closed, the MacArthurs treated themselves and Anita to three days in Havana. They stayed at the Hotel Nacional, ate at the Florida Café ("better than Maxim's"), and visited Ernest Hemingway.

A week later Anita returned to New York, arriving on March 6. That evening she learned that Mr. E. was critically ill and might die at any moment. The news was not unexpected: before leaving for Palm Beach, she had been informed that Emerson was failing and couldn't be expected to rally. Betty Wendel called to say that he wanted to see her, but Anita refused to come until the funeral.

The next day, March 7, Emerson died at age eighty-one. Whatever Anita wrote in her diary that night, she thought the better of it, snipping out the page and attaching a new sheet bearing only the factual information that Mr. E. was gone.

On March 10, she flew to Los Angeles for the funeral, attended by Clifford, Mary and Richard Sale, the Wendels, Aldous Huxley, and Mrs. Butterworth. She stayed on for ten days, talking to lawyers about Mr. E.'s will, which left everything to her. And, surprisingly after all his twenty-odd years at Las Encinas, there was something to bequeath: it had been left in a trust fund, and it wasn't a lot, but it brought Anita a few thousand dollars each year.

Anita stayed with the Sales, now living in Beverly Hills. Aldous Huxley visited often, and people (Mary Loos, Betty Wendel, and Christopher Isherwood, among others) have speculated that Anita may then have seen in Aldous a mate for her twilight years. He too was free, as Maria Huxley had died of liver cancer a few months previously.

Huxley had other plans. Three weeks later, Anita was shocked to read in a New York paper that he had married Laura Archera, a woman twenty years his junior. The Italian-born Archera had many talents. As a teenager, she gave violin recitals at Carnegie Hall; later on, she worked as a film editor. At the time of her marriage, she was practicing psychotherapy, a field in which she was largely self-taught.

Anita considered Laura a fraud, but she was biased, said Isherwood: "Laura was in many ways a remarkable woman." Betty Wendel (who collaborated with Huxley on a play) agrees. "I can see why Anita disliked Laura, but she was perfect for Aldous. She shared his interest in the metaphysical—'the doors of perception' and all that, which I strongly doubt would have interested Anita *at all*. And Laura took very good care of Aldous while going on with her own career—something Anita failed to manage with Mr. E."

O N   T H E   train back to New York Anita started answering condolence notes, and by dawn she had finished eighty-six letters. The next morning she awoke with writer's cramp. Her hand was twice its normal size and so sore her doctor put it in a sling. She tried writing with her left hand, then a Dictaphone, and bought a portable typewriter, which was slow going on five fingers.

A few weeks later Charles MacArthur became seriously ill; within a matter of days he was gone. Anita spent a week with Hayes at the MacArthur home in Nyack. Helen insisted that Anita go on with *Daisy,* and Anita advised Helen to accept the role of the dowager empress in the film version of *Anastasia*—work was the best cure for grief. Hayes felt that she lacked the hauteur of a Romanov, but Anita reminded her, "Mary of Scotland was tall, and you did all right by her!"

Throughout the spring of 1956 Anita worked on *Daisy,* then went to England for a few days with Hayes, who was filming *Anastasia* in a studio outside London. From London Anita went on to Montecatini. Her hand continued to trouble her, and the specialists in New York disagreed as to whether the pain was caused by writer's cramp or arthritis. Perhaps Dr. Pisani could help.

Pisani couldn't believe his eyes: never before had he seen a condition "only recently detected by the German scientist Steinbocker." Though the connection might seem remote, the pain in Anita's hand stemmed from calcium deposits on the vertebrae of her neck. These could be dissolved by electric mud treatments in conjunction with daily doses of the Montecatini waters. Every day she was to drink "one glass Tamerici, two glasses Regina, one glass Tettuccio."

The libations tasted worse than the witches' brew in *Macbeth* sounds, and Anita feared for her life each time she stepped into her electrified mud bath. But she followed the regimen faithfully, and after two weeks she felt well enough to go off to Switzerland and Paris before returning to New York in September.

With her writing hand once again functioning, Anita completed a new version of *Daisy* and then a second draft before the new year. Both incorporated changes suggested by Helen Hayes, who had strong reservations about the earlier script. But the hand-tailored amendments didn't please her, either. What did Helen want? Anita wondered. She was ready to abandon the play.

But then Hayes called to say "she couldn't live without the play." Anita started another revision of *Daisy* "with added humanity": Hayes felt that the leading character was unsympathetic.

Her concentration was interrupted by a domestic upheaval. After a vacation in Tennessee, Gladys returned to New York with her mother, too frail to live alone. As there was no other place for her, Mrs. Tipton moved in with Anita and Gladys. The old lady was good-natured and spent most of her time reading the Bible, but Anita found her presence distracting. A short while later, Gladys bought a house in Teaneck, New Jersey, for her mother, quite possibly with money supplied by Anita.

This proved a mixed blessing. Gladys had to drive to Teaneck every evening and often slept over. Anita was planning another vacation in

Montecatini that summer, with Gladys as her companion, but who was to care for Mrs. Tipton? Anita stewed over this until Valentine's Day, 1957, when she found a letter pushed under her bedroom door. Gladys wrote about the distress she felt each night when she left her "little friend" alone in that big apartment to look after Mrs. Tipton. But what could she do? Now things were to be different. She had found a "God-respecting" lady to live with her mother, and she and Anita could go to Italy and enjoy themselves. "Happy Valentine's Day, Mrs. Emerson!"

Helen Hayes was to join Anita in Montecatini for two weeks so they could work out the problems with *Daisy*. But just before they were to leave, Hayes announced that she had committed herself to appearing with Richard Burton in Jean Anouilh's *Time Remembered* that fall. Anita had been hoping to see *Daisy* on Broadway by the beginning of the new year, but now it couldn't open until late 1958 at the earliest.

The trip went on as scheduled, though little work was done in Montecatini or in Nice, Avignon, or Paris, other stops on the summer tour. But back home in early September, Anita stayed with it, and by November 30 she was able to write, "LICK DAISY!!!!"

Helen felt, on the other hand, that much work was still to be done. And there was lots of time, since she had been pressured into appearing in Eugene O'Neill's *A Touch of the Poet* the following season. So *Daisy* was going to stay on a back burner for another year.

To keep busy, Anita started thinking about new projects. Some months earlier, two young men approached her about a musical version of *Happy Birthday*. Their songs were pedestrian, but the idea was valid. With the right collaborators, it might go over. She called Carol Channing, now married to TV producer Charles Lowe, who doubled as his wife's business manager, and she was thrilled. Why not Jule Styne for the score?

Styne and Anita were both planning European vacations that summer, so why not spend a few days together in Montecatini knocking around ideas? Just before leaving, Anita heard rumors that Carol was dickering with a major network about a TV series, but Channing insisted that her heart belonged to Broadway. Anita remained uneasy, and with good reason. A week into her Montecatini stay, she received a letter from Lowe saying Carol was regretfully withdrawing in favor of TV. Styne told Anita not to lose sleep over it. "I've got a hunch," he said, "Carol wasn't right for it, anyway."

• • •

M E A N W H I L E, back in New York, stage director Robert Lewis (best known for *Teahouse of the August Moon* and *Witness for the Prosecution*) was planning a dramatization of Colette's *Chéri*. Colette had died four years earlier, but with the aid of Ninon de Tallon, the American agent for the estate, Lewis obtained stage rights to the novel and its sequel, *The End of Chéri*.

To adapt the books Lewis had three people in mind: Thornton Wilder, Terence Rattigan, and Anita Loos. When the first two pleaded prior engagements, Lewis arranged through Tallon to meet Anita on her return from Italy.

She was charmed by Lewis, "a middle-aged *amoretto.*" *Chéri* was one of her favorite books, she told him; once she had mentioned it to Tallulah but, not much of a reader, Bankhead couldn't place Colette or Chéri—did they run one of those checkered-tablecloth bistros on Third Avenue? She went on to reminisce about her first trip to Paris when the great cocottes were still highly visible, elegantly dressed by Poiret and Worth, as they drove through the bois de Boulogne every morning.

The *Chéri* novels are a demimonde variant of the *Der Rosenkavalier* story. Lea, a courtesan in retirement, is having a last fling with Chéri, the teenaged son of her best friend. As in the Strauss-Hofmannsthal opera, Lea surrenders her cavalier to a younger woman, but here the results are tragic for everyone but herself. Chéri is seductive and sensitive, but so spoiled and self-centered that he needs a mother-mistress to survive. Deprived of Lea, he eventually commits suicide.

Chéri is one of Colette's masterpieces, but it presents many problems for the would-be stage adaptor, particularly when its less successful offspring is part of the bargain. The two novels cover a span of twenty-six years, not easily reduced to the two-hour traffic of an evening's entertainment without too much condensation on the part of the playwright and a heavy reliance on makeup by the actors. Even worse, *Chéri* has almost no plot. All the drama is internal, filtered through Lea's highly active consciousness. She is one of many Colette heroines who derive as much pleasure from analyzing their emotions as other women find in fingering an expensive jewel or a sinewy thigh. Perhaps that's what drew Anita to Colette: the Frenchwoman was an erotic *cérébrale*.

Externalizing the murmurs of Lea's mind was no easy task, but Anita moved along swiftly. Mornings were devoted to *Chéri;* then after lunch she polished yet another version of *Daisy.* Hayes read it, and in February 1958 arrived at Anita's apartment and said that though she hated bestowing a "Judas kiss," she just didn't think the play was ever going to be right for her.

Or for anyone else perhaps. None of the many drafts of the comedy is promising. Elsie de Wolfe, Anita once said, "was not admirable, just irresistible"; but Daisy is very resistible, and her obsession with Louis Seize armchairs might seem excessive even to a fellow interior decorator.

There was a "squall" over *Daisy,* but it didn't last long. Anita felt too indebted to Hayes for *Happy Birthday* (would it ever have run so long without Helen?), and nursing grudges wasn't her style. Her diaries were a graveyard for hostilities. By writing the evil she thought of people in the heat of the moment, she purged herself of festering resentments. Though she never realized it, her journals brought more peace of mind than any passage in *The Daily Word.*

A N I T A finished the script of *Chéri* by spring of 1958. Robert Lewis liked it and was already talking about actors. And actors were talking about *Chéri.* At Sardi's one afternoon, Anthony Perkins (still some months away from his first major stage role in *Look Homeward, Angel*) introduced himself and asked Anita for an audition. She made no promises, as she had someone else in mind. A year earlier she had seen a German actor in a film adaptation of *Felix Krull* and was convinced he was born to play Chéri. Robert Lewis agreed, provided Horst Buchholz spoke English. Reliable sources reported that not only was he fluent, he also was eager to appear on Broadway.

For Lea, Robert Lewis suggested someone so inappropriate, Anita gasped—Marlene Dietrich. "With two krauts in the play, we'll have to rename it *Schatzi.*"

But Lewis was serious, so they met Marlene—"boring as always," Anita wrote—who agreed to read the script. A week later she reported that she found Lea, Colette, and *Chéri* "démodé."

The top candidate then became Simone Signoret, riding the crest of her *Room at the Top* success. She was interested, on the condition that her husband, Yves Montand, could be with her during the *Chéri* engagement. And since he was contemplating a one-man Broadway show, that might be possible.

One day it was *oui,* the next *peut-être,* until late June when Lewis, committed to an early-fall opening night, told Anita that Kim Stanley had read the script and "cried over it for days." She had read lots of plays, didn't really want to do a play, but *had* to do *Chéri*.

Anita wasn't overjoyed. Stanley was the most indulgent of method actresses. Anita was told horror stories about her shenanigans during *Touch of the Poet,* when Stanley changed her interpretation nightly, rattling other cast members with her whims. There was also the question of Stanley's plausibility as Lea: could an actress so introverted, so very modern American in temperament, so lax about the spread of her *poitrine* and *derrière,* be convincing as an enticing, if aging, *poule de luxe?*

Lewis thought so. Anita gathered that he would be as happy with Stanley as with Signoret; and when Signoret kept vacillating as rehearsals grew near, she went along with his choice.

Rehearsals, which started in August 1959, were reassuring. Anita grew fond of Stanley, asking her and her children to tea, often with Horst Buchholz and his wife, Myriam. The show opened its only pre-Broadway engagement in Washington, D.C., on September 21, to mixed reviews. Richard Coe, the highly regarded critic for the Washington *Post,* wrote

Anita, Horst Buchholz, and director Robert Lewis discussing *Chéri* (1959)

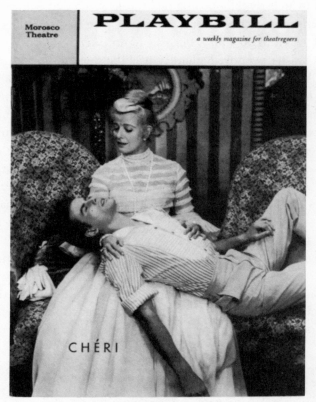

Kim Stanley and Horst Buchholz on playbill for *Chéri*

what Anita described as a rave notice, though Coe remembers it more accurately as "moderately good."

That things were amiss should have been obvious to anyone listening to the audience tittering at the wrong times. The worst unintentional laugh came as Stanley entered as the elderly Lea, padded, wearing tweeds and a wig that made her look like Benjamin Franklin. Earlier the dialogue stirred up ripples of derisive giggles. Anita had taken many speeches directly from Colette, translating them into an English that sounded stilted or peculiar.

These blemishes, so easily remedied, mystifyingly went uncorrected. The real problem was the lead actors, who had no rapport and were individually wanting. Kim Stanley looked all wrong, while Horst Buchholz, who looked great, walked through the play as though he were always waiting for the next close-up. Anita went backstage and delivered a gentle lecture on professionalism. He received it indignantly, but the next night he gave "a great performance," and *Chéri* got "its best audience reception to date."

Chéri opened in New York on October 12, 1959. After the performance, Anita went to Sardi's and then to a party at Robert Lewis's apartment. En route, Morton Gottlieb broke the news that the first review had appeared and it was very bad. Written by Walter Kerr of the *Herald Tribune,* it was mainly a blistering attack on Kim Stanley. Gottlieb recalls that Anita became visibly distraught, while she remembered little about the rest of the evening except her inadequate attempts to console "poor Kim."

The next morning she surveyed the damage, which was extensive. All the reviews were bad save the one in the *Times,* and the *Times* critic during this period was widely considered the weakest in the paper's history. *Chéri* had a moderately good advance, and the day after the opening another $5,000 worth of tickets was sold—very encouraging considering the notices. Hoping to build business through word of mouth, Lewis and Anita made cuts and adjustments; and while the changes pleased them, audiences continued to laugh in the wrong places.

Chéri did build up a small but distinguished corps of fervent admirers before its closing on November 28. Though initially Maurice Goudeket, Colette's husband, had raised a number of piffling objections to the script, he ended by calling it "an exemplary adaptation." Simone Signoret, in New York for the opening of Montand's one-man show, told Lewis that on stage she could never have played Lea as sensitively as Stanley. Joshua Logan said it was Anita's best play and urged her to rethink it as a movie, maybe with himself as director.

Anita latched on to Logan's notion and ran with it—or maybe it ran away with her. In a flash, she saw *Chéri* as Garbo's comeback film. The actress agreed to attend a matinee performance; she sneaked in after the show had started and watched from the back, obscured by a pillar. The next day she called and said how much she admired Colette. Anita waited for her to comment on the play, but nothing was forthcoming. After a prolonged pause, Garbo said wearily that she was off for Gstaad in a few days, and perhaps they could get together on her return, though the Lord alone knew when that would be. Anita interpreted this as Garbo's way of saying she wasn't interested in *Chéri.*

This did not discourage her from plotting further about a picture version of *Chéri.* For several years, she kept George Cukor interested, and they talked of Simone Signoret or Vivien Leigh as Lea, Robert Wagner or Tony Curtis or Sal Mineo for Chéri. And twice the picture came close to production, only to fall apart at the last minute.

Even before *Chéri,* Anita had started to sour on the stage—just as much a rat race as the movies. She wondered if there was any longer a place on Broadway for the kind of civilized entertainments that were her specialty. Each year the American theater grew progressively more witless, more tasteless, more simpleminded. She disliked all of Arthur Miller, enjoyed few of Tennessee Williams's plays after *The Glass Menagerie;* and while an occasional musical brought pleasure, she never cared for the Rodgers and Hammerstein mix of saccharine and uplift, and later, she liked even less the Prince-Sondheim school of cynical razzle-dazzle.

Nonetheless, for the remaining twenty-odd years of her life—perhaps out of habit as much as anything else—she went on writing new plays and reworking old ones. One was produced in London, a few others came to life in out-of-the-way places in New York and other parts of the country, but none was staged in the hub of the American theater. *Chéri* marked the close of her career as a Broadway playwright. In the final years of her life her most fruitful work was to be in another field of literary endeavor.

PART
Five

A LADY
OF MEMOIRS

28

A Strange
Exhilaration

O N D E C E M B E R 3 1, 1 9 5 9, after working all morning on yet
another rewrite of *Daisy,* Anita dressed for lunch. She walked to
L'Aiglon, a hospitably elegant restaurant on East Fifty-fifth Street, where
she met Natasha Wilson and Madeleine Sherwood, a former Sennett
bathing beauty and widow of playwright Robert E. Sherwood. Mado was
in one of her fretful moods, worrying about nothing, and Natasha ordered
a vodka stinger instead of dessert, on top of martinis before and during the
meal. But she had good news about Jack, steadily sober for weeks and
thinking about writing his autobiography.

Returning to the apartment, Anita dictated some letters on her
machine for Eddy to type later. These she wanted out of the way since
Eddy was leaving at the end of the week for a fine new job at the MCA
talent agency. She was down to the last "Yours devotedly" when the
doorbell rang. It was her friend Stanley Simmons, bringing a book he had
just finished and was sure Anita would like. Slender, stylish, and so
sympathique, Simmons was just about the kindest person she knew.

At four-thirty, when Simmons was about to leave, Helen Hayes
arrived from Nyack. Since she and Anita both were going to Gilbert and
Kitty Miller's New Year's Eve soirée, they had arranged to spend the early
evening together. Immediately they got out the sewing basket and started
making final adjustments to their party ensembles. At eight, they had

dinner (Cornish game hens beautifully prepared by Gladys), then watched a bit of TV before dressing and leaving at eleven.

As usual, the Millers' Park Avenue apartment was resplendent, its crowning glory being Goya's *Red Boy,* a gift from Kitty's father. As stipulated in Julian Bache's will, *Red Boy,* like a child of divorced parents, changed hands every six months, living half the year with the Millers, the other half at the Metropolitan Museum. Claudette Colbert was present, looking so youthful there might have been dew on those apple cheeks.

Forty-five minutes past the New Year, Anita and Hayes left the Millers', picked up Cathleen Nesbitt, and went on to a second celebration, hosted by Daniel Blum, the editor of the *Theatre World* yearbooks. It was a huge, rowdy bash of a party, stage gypsies cheek-by-jowl with theatrical eminences, many of them pretty liquored-up. Normally Anita loathed free-for-alls, but this one had too much going on to leave as quickly as she otherwise might have done.

She watched Diana Barrymore plunge off the wagon, winding up spread-eagled on the floor while Tennessee Williams moaned about her lapse. Diana had been in such good shape, he thought she was ready to play Blanche in a revival of *Streetcar.* "Well," Anita commented, "I saw her father stagger through the greatest performance of *Hamlet* I've ever seen!"

When Anita spotted the husbands of two good friends petting in an alcove, she decided she had had enough. Outside waiting for a cab, she watched Mary Martin's son, Larry Hagman, roar off on a motorcycle, wearing jeans and boots but no jacket. "He'll die of exposure," Cathleen Nesbitt gasped. "There's more brandy inside him than around a St. Bernard's neck," Anita said reassuringly.

Back home, Anita read a few pages of Stanley Simmons's book, fell asleep, but woke up before six after a grisly nightmare featuring Mr. E. She made herself a cup of tea, wrote New Year's letters to Gladys and Mrs. Tipton, then chatted with her early-rising friends, Morty Gottlieb and magazine editor Leo Lerman.

That afternoon, with Gladys still in Teaneck, she prepared a lunch of toast and Lipton's chicken noodle soup and started her new diary with a list of New Year's resolutions:

1. NEVER TO WEIGH MORE THAN 90 POUNDS. [She then weighed about 92 and could rarely get below that. When she weighed two or three pounds more, she reduced calories to a thousand daily. She drank only an occasional split of champagne, and once in a while she went to Jolie Gabor's health spa in upstate New York.]

2 . TO KEEP EXPENSES UNDER $1,000 A MONTH . [Her work in recent years had not garnered much money, though royalties kept coming in from *Blondes,* other past writings, and continuous magazine articles. There was a comfortable sum in savings, but her accountant suggested self-restraint would be prudent.]

3 . TO FIND A HOUSE SOMEWHERE AND RELAX WITH GLADYS, MRS. TIPTON, DOGS, A GARDEN, ETC. [She had heard rumors that the owner of 171 West Fifty-seventh Street was planning either to raze the building or turn it cooperative. Either way, she might have to move. If forced to buy, she wanted a house, not an apartment, preferably in the country or, better still, Italy.]

The chief attraction of a house was to provide separate quarters for Gladys's mother. A few months earlier the woman looking after Mrs. Tipton moved to another state, and three or four times a week Gladys was again driving to Teaneck. Short-term substitutes were found, but until Mrs. Tipton's death a few years later, Gladys was always running off to New Jersey. Every absence took its toll on Anita, who fretted until "her household manager, guide, and religious consultant" returned.

Never had Anita depended on anyone as she did on Gladys—not even Mr. E. in the happiest years of their marriage. Gladys took immaculate care of Anita's wardrobe, always knowing which accessories went with each dress. She cut, washed, and arranged Anita's hair. She paid the household bills out of a joint checking account. She provided spiritual uplift when Anita was blue. She was an excellent nurse, once curing Anita's bursitis with applications of hot turpentine—a smelly but effective remedy, better than anything the doctors prescribed.

By now Anita was asking Gladys's advice on professional as well as personal matters, and there were occasions when Gladys told Anita's collaborators what Miss Loos was too exhausted to say herself. And there is reason to believe that Anita turned against collaborators because Gladys mistrusted them.

Naturally, there were people who didn't care much for Gladys. Though no one said it to Anita's face, some friends thought that she delegated too much authority to her companion, who was frequently charged with being possessive. And there was friction between the women. Twice Gladys quit; then after Anita had stewed in misery for a few days, she returned, explaining it was all a joke.

"Sadism," Anita wrote. "Why am I such a schmuck? Why can't I get some self-respect and authority?" Anita did form relationships with people who took advantage of her docility. While it is certainly no more than coincidence that Gladys bore the same name as Anita's sister, who died so many years before, she did become a sister substitute.

Anita attacks the biological family unit in work after work, but the idea of family was appealing to her—only it shouldn't be built along bloodlines but from spiritual kinship. A family was formed from those people who shared your interests and attitudes, who overlooked your failings as you passed over theirs, who loyally saw you through your troubles as you supported them through their own. The cornerstone of Anita's family was Gladys.

Anita shared in all her friend's special interests—it seems likely that it was Gladys, not Unity, that got Anita into reading a few verses of the Bible each morning. When Gladys's relatives celebrated anniversaries or birthdays, Anita was among the invited, and if she couldn't attend, she sent presents. And she gave her support to Gladys's favorite charity, a club called Les Seizes. This Harlem-based organization helped black women earn college and nursing degrees. Each spring the club held a fund raiser at the Renaissance Casino, and each spring Anita was there with a group of friends: Morty Gottlieb; Natasha Wilson; interior decorator and jewelry designer Ted Peckham; Stanley Simmons; Cris Alexander, the photographer and actor, who had appeared in *The Amazing Adele*. "They were great evenings," Alexander says. "Once Natasha got herself up in full Romanov regalia, but she wasn't nearly as spectacular as Gladys and her friends in their cyclamen and iridescent taffeta gowns."

Through Les Seizes, a third person entered the Loos household. A fellow club member told Gladys about Charles and Willie Moore, who had been burned out of their Harlem home and wanted to farm out some of their children until they could resettle. Gladys was captivated by the youngest child, a two-year-old baptized Annette Gladys but known by her middle name. "If she has no place to stay, bring her here," said Anita, thinking it would be a matter of weeks. But once she saw little Gladys— soon dubbed Miss Moore to distinguish her from the older Gladys—it became a matter of years. With her parents' blessing, Miss Moore was to stay on and on and on.

T H R O U G H O U T 1 9 6 0 , Anita kept revising old stage properties, especially *Jacqueline,* now retitled *Montparnasse.* The original role was revamped for a French musical star—Juliette Greco, Zizi Jeanmaire, Leslie

Caron, or Geneviève—and the Dietz-Alstone score scrapped for new music by Claude Léveillée, a French-Canadian with several Edith Piaf songs to his credit. Anita had high hopes for *Montparnasse.* "I feel strangely exhilarated, as though something wonderful is about to happen," she wrote. But it never did.

Finally she put *Montparnasse* out of her mind to revise a novel, *The Better Things in Life,* serialized in *Cosmopolitan* in 1930. Though never issued in book form, it had been praised by Edmund Wilson as "intrepid satire . . . the novel about Hollywood with the most teeth in it." This comment, included in a collection of Wilson's literary essays, caught the attention of Ray Pierre Corsini, then an editor at McGraw-Hill.

Anita barely remembered the novel and couldn't find a manuscript in her files, but when *Cosmopolitan* provided a copy, she read it with delight. Revisions were needed to weed out dated references, but the body of the story could stand pretty much as originally written. She accepted McGraw-Hill's offer of $2,500, a reasonable advance for the time, considering there was a risk involved in issuing a thirty-year-old magazine story.

The revisions were nearly finished when, at three a.m. on August 30, 1960, she was awakened by a phone call from Mary: Clifford, at age seventy-seven, had just died. Anita sat up the rest of the night with Gladys—"a pillar of strength"—reminiscing about her brother. People knew more about her than about him, and that was unfair, since he had accomplished so much more. She had written a few amusing novels, but he had founded group medicine in California.

She flew to the West Coast for the funeral, staying with Mary and Richard Sale. They had done well writing movie and TV scripts, but were going through a dry spell, and Anita worried about the emotional and financial cost of looking after their son, Edward, who had been born with cerebral palsy and required constant, expert care.

But their money problems were soon alleviated. Clifford's will bequeathed an estate valued at $900,000 to Mary and Anita in equal shares. After taxes, $600,000 would remain, from which the co-heirs would receive an annual income of between $10,000 and $12,000.

O N H E R return from California, Anita worked on the proofs for her novel, now retitled *No Mother to Guide Her,* and helped in its prepublication promotion. There were many interviews, and always the talk gravitated toward her years as a Hollywood scenarist. The so-called "film explosion" had long since shattered the intellectual snobbery about movies, and suddenly all the cultural pacesetters were discovering the new European directors and re-evaluating upward the product of the Hollywood dream factories.

At first Anita was vastly amused by the fascination, sometimes bordering on reverence, for the likes of Mary Pickford and Douglas Fairbanks. But then she started attending the screenings of silent films at the Museum of Modern Art and was amazed by the vitality of what she saw. Lillian Gish was superb! Doug looked great—even in the films she hadn't written for him.

Some of this affection colored her rewriting of *No Mother to Guide Her,* which was published in April 1961. The original story was based on an incident in the life of the "It" girl, Clara Bow. Clara thought her best friend was her hairdresser and general factotum, Dorothy Devoe, until Devoe threatened to tell about Clara's escapades unless paid $100,000 in hush money. Instead of shelling out, Bow took Devoe to court on charges of extortion.

Anita's heroine is Viola Lake, filmland's foremost flapper. Like Clara Bow at the beginning of the sound era, Viola can memorize lines only by using dope as a stimulus. Like Bow, she is man crazy, and she too has an indiscreet confidante. When Viola's housekeeper is slain by a Bluebeard husband, her diary is seized by a district attorney, who threatens to read its most lurid passages into the court record.

For advice, Viola turns to Elmer Bliss, a columnist dedicated to writing only "of the good, the true, the beautiful." He agrees to take on a rival columnist, Lansing Marshall, who promotes himself by defaming Hollywood and its illustrious inhabitants.

Lansing Marshall lives at the Ambassador Hotel, hangs out at the Brown Derby, and talks like a clean-mouthed Wilson Mizner. When Bliss accuses him of being anti-Hollywood, Marshall/Mizner denies the charge. No real man, he says, could dislike a place inhabited by so many "negotiable ladies," where there is so much food for conversation and reflection on the human condition.

Marshall's cynicism loses out to Bliss's sentiment. The closing pages of the book, in which an elderly Elmer glances back at his travails with Viola, are misted with a nostalgia for the old Hollywood which created "fairy tales for adults." There are no fairy tales to believe in today, Bliss muses, which is possibly "a reason for the universal prevalence of mental crack-up. . . . If we were childish in the past, I wish we could be children again."

The reviews for *No Mother to Guide Her* were largely favorable, though there was quibbling about the concluding chapter. "It is clear that Miss Loos' heart still belongs to Hollywood," wrote one San Francisco critic. True, but possibly the comment wouldn't have been made except for the dust-jacket copy, which included Edmund Wilson's evaluation. Certainly there are Hollywood novels with more teeth; in its revised form, the book is no longer "intrepid satire." It's a spoofish valentine to a bygone never-was land—a little faded, perhaps, but still diverting.

S H O R T L Y after the publication of *No Mother,* Anita got a phone call from Judy Holliday, who wanted very much to do *Happy Birthday* as a Broadway musical. This came as a surprise, since it was rumored that Holliday was thinking of giving up performing. It was more a question of not wanting to limit herself only to acting, Judy explained over lunch at "21." Her chief ambition was to write songs with her current beau, jazz saxophonist and composer Gerry Mulligan.

She asked Anita to listen to what they had written, and maybe if she liked it, she'd let them do the score for the show. She'd star in it, naturally—but oh, how grateful she'd be to sing her own lyrics!

Anita liked Gerry Mulligan better than his music, which was too jazz-oriented for her taste, though not inappropriate for a play set in a bar. About Judy's lyrics she couldn't find enough good things to say. Holliday blossomed forth with all sorts of crazy ideas—maybe a Christmas background and *Merry Xmas* for a title. Gleaning the good suggestions from the bad could wait; the important thing was that Anita had agreed to do the book for their music and words.

They were going to summer at Bridgehampton, Long Island, and since there were lots of rooms in their rented house, wouldn't Anita be their guest? If they worked together every day, the show might be ready by mid-September. Three months was too long to be a house guest, Anita said; but yes, she'd like to join them in mid-July.

The first weeks at Bridgehampton were idyllic. Anita was up every morning by six, reading or working in her room till eleven. Then she had a late breakfast with her night-owl collaborators, who afterward went off by themselves to write words and music. Anita spent the day at the beach, then, after an early dinner, listened to what Holliday and Mulligan had accomplished.

Once again Anita experienced that strange exhilaration which suggested something wonderful was about to happen. Everything was moving so smoothly that by mid-August, Holliday got a promise from Max Gordon, the producer of her first great success, *Born Yesterday,* to take on *Happy Birthday* as soon as it was finished. "It's all so simple when you're working with pros," Anita wrote.

Two days later she came down to breakfast and found Judy alone and looking as gloomy as the weather outside. Gerry was in a dry spell, she explained, and had gone off for a day or two. During a long, rainy afternoon, Holliday started confiding in Anita, talking of her troubles with men, particularly Peter Lawford, who had ditched her for Pat Kennedy. Mulligan wasn't mentioned, and Anita didn't feel it was her place to ask. She merely listened. Like most writers, she was a very good listener.

Later Gerry returned, and for about forty-eight hours everything seemed fine. Then came another tense breakfast, with Judy announcing she was too exhausted for more work that summer. Anita packed her bags and called Gladys to pick her up.

Holliday phoned a month later and talked as though nothing had happened. Gerry and she were making progress and soon they'd get together so Anita could hear the new material. A week later there was another call. Depressed, almost sobbing, Holliday said she couldn't go on—there were health problems, money problems, Gerry problems.

Anita didn't sleep that night, thinking about "dear, desperate Judy" and occasionally about herself. It was easier getting a camel through a needle's eye than getting a show on Broadway. Why put oneself through all the punishment? She couldn't think about that or she'd never get on with her adaptation of Jean Canolle's *La Jument du roi.*

29

The Needle's
Eye

T HE KING'S MARE is about the misalliance of Henry VIII and
Anne of Cleves. It's not heavy history like a Maxwell Anderson
drama, and it's not exactly a romp like the famous Charles Laughton film
biography. It's a bit of both, with a dash of Chekhov thrown in.

Ninon de Tallon, Canolle's American representative, circulated Anita's
adaptation among New York producers. An immediate response came
from Fred Coe, who recently had moved to Broadway after a distinguished
career in original TV drama. He saw the play as a historical romance with
Kim Stanley as Anne of Cleves.

Anita had already shown the script to Morty Gottlieb, who was
equally enthusiastic but urged Anita to "camp it up a bit." That might suit
Carol Channing, who loved the play—and had lots of ideas about improving it. Since Anne of Cleves spoke no English when she married Henry,
Channing thought the heroine should speak only German in the first act.
That might be rough on the audience, Anita felt, but a touch of Deutsch
might add color. She bought a bilingual dictionary.

When Coe learned about Channing's interest, he too began to see
The King's Mare as a comedy. What about Stanley, who had already been
approached? Tallon volunteered to handle that situation, and Coe was
ready to go ahead with Channing. But so was Gottlieb. "What to do?"
Anita asked her diary. She decided to do nothing and hope for things to
sort themselves out.

During her indecision, Anita received an excited phone call from Tallon. A letter from the Bristol Old Vic in England had arrived with news of a production of *The King's Mare*, using a translation made by a staff stenographer. Tallon cabled back urging the Old Vic to hold everything until Anita's adaptation arrived. Not much money was involved, Tallon explained to Anita, but this was a chance to see the play on stage. And possibly the production could be transferred to the West End with the same cast or with star replacements as Anne and Henry. Kenneth Wagg, a former Horlick's Malted Milk executive who entered the theater after marrying Margaret Sullavan, was interested in producing the play in London with Margaret Leighton as Anne.

The King's Mare opened at the Bristol Old Vic in mid-October 1961. Morty Gottlieb flew to England for the opening, but Anita waited two weeks until the production was fine-tuned. With Carol Channing as companion, she arrived in London in late October. After checking in at the Grosvenor House Hotel, they went immediately to Bristol. The Old Vic production was slowly paced, shabbily designed, and indifferently acted. It definitely needed stars in the lead roles and a lighter, brighter approach.

Carol and Anita weren't disheartened, but Kenneth Wagg was. He wouldn't bring the play to London without extensive revisions and Margaret Leighton as Anne. What this meant was that he was dropping the show, since, as Anita already knew, Leighton had other commitments.

Back in New York, Anita started referring to the show as *The Royal Schnork*. All her pals loved the new title, but eventually she regained her senses and went back to the original. She was not the only one with dumb ideas. Carol Channing suggested her dear friend George Burns as director. "There are times," Anita wrote, "when Carol seems to know very little about anything."

One problem resolved itself in January 1962 when Morty Gottlieb came to her with what he thought was bad news. His partner, Helen Bonfils, had lost interest in *The King's Mare*, and he wasn't prepared to go it alone. So the field was free for Fred Coe. *"Quelle relief!"*

Anita now had absolute confidence in Coe, "a real activator." He planned to tour the show that fall and open on Broadway in January 1963. Either he or his assistant, the youthful and personable Earle McGrath, talked to Anita nearly every day about prospective theaters, set and costume designers, and the hefty problem of finding a Henry. Among the actors discussed were Walter Slezak, George Sanders, Walter Matthau, and Zero Mostel.

No decision had been reached by the first of June, when Anita and the two Gladyses were to leave for Italy. No reason to cancel the trip, Coe insisted: he or Earle would stay in touch, and no Henry would be signed without her approval.

Arriving in Montecatini, Anita discovered many friends staying there, several on her recommendation: singer Gladys Swarthout, Howard Dietz, screenwriter Nunnally Johnson. They were pleased with the spa, but Anita sniffed too strong a scent of *la dolce vita,* though some of the indolent rich guests were, she admitted, quite diverting.

One minor member of the Italian nobility was there on his honeymoon, though he had booked separate rooms for himself and his bride. One glance at the aristocrat and Anita realized he was a *signore* who preferred other *signori.* Apparently his wife was not so perceptive. One night Anita was awakened by shouting in the corridor. Peeping outside, she saw the bride, carrying a crucifix, pounding on her husband's door. "*Caro,* in the name of the Catholic Church," she pleaded, "let me in!"

The next day King Saud of Saudi Arabia arrived with most of his court. While he and his adult retainers remained sequestered in their rooms, the children marauded over the Pace grounds, polluting the air with a stench of unwashed flesh. Anita decided to move on.

Cris Alexander, Anita, Miss Moore, and Gladys vacationing in Europe, 1960

She and her companions went to another spa, Acqui, some fifty miles further north. Here they relaxed in luxurious solitude until Anita heard from Alice B. Toklas, then living nearby in a rented villa. Crippled by arthritis and often confined to a wheelchair, Toklas was attended by Donald Sutherland, an American professor with a passion for Gertrude Stein. Anita went to tea, and though there was too much adulatory chatter about Stein for her taste, she promised to stop by again before leaving Acqui.

Quite late that evening, as she was preparing for bed, Sutherland barged into her hotel room, shouting that Toklas was dying: Anita should prepare for a last visitation. If Alice was dying, why had she been left alone? Anita wanted to know. Sutherland told her to sit down and await the final phone call. Would Alice be calling to say she just heard her own death rattle? None of it made sense. Finally Anita persuaded Sutherland to leave; but, greatly disturbed, she was unable to sleep that night.

The next morning she went to the villa and found Toklas walking around the garden on two canes. She was feeling fine, she said, though the previous evening she had been a bit dyspeptic. Maybe it was something she ate. Anita wondered if she might have prepared her celebrated brownies for supper.

F R O M Acqui, Anita and the Gladyses went to Rome, spent a few days there, then took an express train to Paris, where they went on a shopping binge. Miss Moore made a big hit at Guerlain. "She looks just like a French girl with her little white gloves," said a saleslady. "Without my gloves, I look like a French man," Miss Moore replied. Such winsomeness deserved a reward, and little Gladys left Guerlain loaded with complimentary gifts of soap and perfume.

As soon as she got home, Anita tallied up the expenses for the trip, close to fourteen thousand dollars. *"Quelle splurge!"* But she refused to feel guilty, as money was coming in from the first London production of *Blondes* and a production of *Gigi* in Paris, and soon *The King's Mare* would be touring cross country.

While she was away, Coe had discovered a British actor, Anthony Newlands, who was perfect for Henry, though he had no marquee value. Newlands auditioned for Anita, who decided *The King's Mare* would make him a star. Rehearsals were scheduled to start in late September.

Anita was spending a pleasant Labor Day holiday with Coe and his family on Long Island when—"CATASTROPHE!" Newlands's agent called saying the actor was withdrawing because of ill health. A new Henry would have to be found tomorrow if rehearsals were to begin anywhere near schedule.

Someone suggested Peter Lawford. "He's the world's worst actor!" Anita gasped. No one disagreed; it was merely pointed out that he was available—available, but not interested unless *The King's Mare* was turned into a musical. "What chutzpah!" Anita exclaimed. "His singing's worse than his acting!"

Rehearsals were postponed while the search for another Henry went on. Anita occupied herself with plays and movies, read a lot, entertained guests from out of town: Adele Astaire, then living in Middleburg, Virginia, with her second husband, Kingman Douglass; Cecil Beaton; Christopher Isherwood and artist Don Bachardy, who took her to a birthday party for W. H. Auden. "An incredible assortment of intellectual queens," she wrote afterward, "of which I am the Queen of queens."

By the start of 1963 there was no Henry and therefore no possibility that *The King's Mare* would be staged until spring at the earliest. Anita was losing confidence in Coe. Her phone calls went unreturned, and even Earle McGrath, while reassuring, seemed vague about what his boss was accomplishing.

She decided to call a showdown meeting at her apartment, attended by Coe, McGrath, Carol Channing, and Charles Lowe. Coe begged forgiveness for being "irresolute." Sometimes he was a slow thinker and a slow mover, but now he had a lead on several possible Henrys. From here on, he'd keep everybody informed on his progress.

Everyone felt reassured but Gladys, who insisted Coe was "coming apart at the seams, worse than Mr. E. at his worst." As the weeks passed and nothing happened, Anita suspected that, as usual, Gladys was right. Then one morning she read in *The New York Times* that Channing was going into a touring production of Shaw's *The Millionairess.* Immediately she called Charles Lowe, who explained that it was an interim booking, that he and Carol were still committed to *The King's Mare;* but they'd like to see Coe pick up the pace.

Anita understood. She herself was already at work on two new projects: the first, an adaptation of a 1916 French play, *L'Ecole des cocottes;* the second, a volume of memoirs. The latter was an idea originating with Ray Pierre Corsini, the editor of *No Mother to Guide Her,* now working on a free-lance basis for several publishers, all eager for book proposals. Why not write your autobiography? Mrs. Corsini asked Anita. Oh no, was the reply, repeated several times. Raking up the past would bore her and couldn't interest anyone else.

As further urging might only irritate Anita, Ray Corsini dropped the subject. Then one day Anita asked her to tea and showed her an item in *Variety* reporting that Beatrice Lillie had received an advance of $100,000 for her life story. "Do you think I could get that much?" she asked. Corsini doubted that Lillie actually had been paid that much—it was all publisher hype—but was confident she could get a tidy sum for Anita's reminiscences. Anita told her to proceed, not only for the money but because alone with her memories, she would be liberated from "a lot of deadbeat collaborators."

Corsini presented the idea to three publishers, all highly receptive and quick to respond. The editor in chief of Macmillan sent an enthusiastic letter, enclosing a contract with the clause naming financial terms left blank, implying that Corsini could fill in any figure she pleased. Tom Guinzburg, then president of Viking, asked Anita and Ray to lunch. Anita had known and esteemed Tom's father, the late Harold Guinzburg, one of the founders of Viking, and the son was every bit as agreeable, Anita decided. When he offered a $25,000 advance, with a favorable royalty scale and other generous terms, she accepted with pleasure.

Before starting to write, Anita revisited the scenes of her childhood. She spent a few weeks in Siskiyou County and Los Angeles, staying with Mary and Richard Sale, who had sold the Santa Monica beach house and moved to Clifford's hacienda. On her first night, a fire broke out mysteriously on the grounds, a candelabrum dropped from the mantel, books cascaded from shelves. Was Clifford trying to spook her? All week she was subject to nightmares about Mizner, Mr. E., and other departed friends. Was the hereafter warning her to abandon the memoir? Probably she had indigestion from too many Mexican dinners.

Back in New York, she phoned Fred Coe, McGrath, and Lowe to find out what was happening with *Mare* but couldn't reach anyone. "I'm depressed that no one is minding the store," she wrote, "so I'm leaving for Italy."

Waiting for her in Montecatini was a letter from Madeleine Sherwood with a clipping from *The New York Times*: Carol Channing had signed for a new musical, *Hello, Dolly!* Anita couldn't blame Carol, but how aggravating show business could be!

30

Walpurgis Nights

REMINISCING was more enjoyable than Anita had anticipated, though she got off on a wrong tack. Her original plan was to use Gladys as a narrator, just as Lorelei had told Dorothy's story in *Brunettes*. This approach seemed to have several advantages. First, it signaled the reader that the book was playful, not a full-dress biography. It allowed Anita to tell only as much of the truth as she might have confided to a close friend. Finally, it served as a tribute to her beloved companion.

But she soon realized that doing it this way was coy and imitative of her own past work and Gertrude Stein's *The Autobiography of Alice B. Toklas*. So she resigned herself to telling her story as she wanted to remember it.

Perhaps because of her Hollywood training, Anita had developed an unusual method of working. She wrote out of sequence, revising and polishing small fragments of the book until they "flowed." Unlike many writers who prefer not to show work in progress, she passed along these small sections to editors and advisors, who, accustomed to judging large chunks of a manuscript, were initially confused and sometimes frustrated by Anita's system. But they learned that she welcomed criticism and knew how to use whatever suggestions she received to full advantage. And they were impressed by the labor and patience that went into that breezy, seemingly tossed-off style characteristic of Anita at her best.

She spent nearly two years on the memoir before she was satisfied it was ready for the printer—two years of on-and-off concentration, as she was also promoting two stage projects. Fred Coe had dropped *The King's Mare* after Channing's defection, but there were nibbles of interest from other producers. And her adaptation of *L'Ecole des cocottes* had grown into a small-scale musical called *Gogo, I Love You*, with music and lyrics by Claude Léveillée and Gladys Shelley.

She had her doubts about *Gogo*; she had written the book while under the spell of Bertolt Brecht, but she knew that she and her collaborators, who had *Irma la Douce* in mind, hadn't come up with even a one-penny opera. Could they get by with it? No—*Gogo* closed off-Broadway after a single performance.

GETTING back to the memoir, where there were no collaborators to encumber her, no producers to be courted, was always a relief. But there were mischief makers to plague her in her private life. Gladys sometimes got very high-handed—"Madame la Cuisine," Anita dubbed her in the diaries—and when she came down with the flu, she preferred melodramatics to aspirin and hot tea. A bad case of the sniffles was enough for her to bring out the dress put aside for her funeral.

And then there was Miss Moore, generally "a bundle of joy" but occasionally "a holy terror." The child was now kindergarten age, and by pulling strings to circumnavigate a waiting list, Anita placed the girl at the Ecole Française, a school with elite appeal and firm academic rating. But Miss Moore started repeating naughty words she heard on the school bus, and she didn't much care for the cafeteria cuisine, depositing most of it behind a water cooler.

Little Gladys was deprived of her TV privileges for a while, but when another lunch was found moldering behind the fountain, Anita took desperate measures. If Miss Moore kept throwing away good food, she would return to her family in Harlem. The child screamed and sobbed that she would eat everything, even the prune whip.

And she was obedient except when Gladys was away for an evening. Then Miss Moore couldn't sleep, asked for water, then the bathroom, then for Mommy. When Anita said she was Mommy that night, Gladys moaned and sobbed. Anita read *Oz* books and crooned "Over the Rainbow," but the child didn't release herself to sleep till Gladys was home. These "Walpurgis nights" ended only when Gladys resigned temporarily from her charity work for Les Seizes.

. . .

B Y J U N E 1 9 6 5 , Anita had finished a draft of the memoir, now titled *A Girl Like I,* and also had found a producer for a West End production of *The King's Mare.* Keith Michell was set to play Henry; Peter Coe, acclaimed for his staging of *Oliver!,* had agreed to direct; but there was still no Anne. Everything short of salaaming was done to entice Margaret Leighton, but she had just turned down a Noel Coward play to concentrate on films, and she had to be consistent or Noel would never forgive her.

Arnold Weissberger, a lawyer specializing in theatrical matters and with a luminous and adoring list of clients (Anita among them), suggested Glynis Johns, who was available and looking for stage work. Anita thought Johns too pretty and "tea cozy" to make the perfect Anne, but who was she to look a gift mare in the mouth?

With the two Gladyses she sailed for England, arriving a week before *The King's Mare* was to start its provincial tour in Liverpool. She attended the final rehearsals, was pleased with Coe, Michell, and Johns, not so pleased with the way the script played. Corrections had to be made.

The first performance in Liverpool was ragged, and while the audience was "enthusiastic," the reviews were "not so good." Coe wanted a play doctor, and, though offended, Anita agreed until Gladys insisted she put her foot down. Anita issued an ultimatum: she walked if anyone else was brought in. On her own, however, she wired Jean Barillet to come to England at once. If there was to be a play doctor, she'd choose him herself.

Meanwhile, she revised several scenes, which Coe, "behaving schizophrenically," first praised and then behind her back said would be staged over his dead body. Then Barillet arrived, and both he and Ninon de Tallon supported Anita about the revisions. When Coe refused to budge, Tallon threatened that both Jean Canolle and Anita would publicly disown the production unless he cooperated.

Coe made the changes, but, as Anita admitted, they weren't any great improvement. The script had two vivid characters but no specific point of view, so it played like disjointed scenes in need of an organizing idea. What Anita seemed to be striving for, but never quite achieved, is history seen as a comedy of manners, a Shavian comedy minus Fabianism, or a *Lion in Winter* (written after Canolle's play) without trendy aphorisms.

The London opening had to be postponed at the last minute. A few hours before the curtain, Glynis Johns slipped in the shower, breaking a toe and chipping an elbow. It would be a a week before she was able to walk normally. Anita had been planning on leaving London the next day and decided not to change her schedule. *The King's Mare* could open without her.

On schedule she boarded the Golden Arrow for Paris with the Gladyses and Dickie Gordon Fellows. It wasn't a pleasant trip. Since Elsa Maxwell's death two years earlier, Dickie had been querulous and so very helpless, acting as though never in her life had she opened a door or made a phone call for herself. Worst of all, she treated Gladys as a servant, expecting her to carry baggage without so much as a thank-you for acknowledgment.

After five days in Paris, the ladies went on to Florence, where a rental car was waiting for them at the train station. Dickie imperiously seated herself in the backseat, allowing Anita to decide whether she or Miss Moore would ride up front with the chauffeur, Gladys.

Once installed at La Pace in Montecatini, Anita felt that her responsibility to Dickie was absolved, and she was happy to see among the spa guests such familiar faces as Whitney Warren from San Francisco and Lillian Gish, relaxing between visits to sister Dorothy, then living (and gravely ill) in Rapallo.

She had known Lillian for almost fifty years, but for the first time they struck up a real friendship. Both were enchanted with John Wayne, just back from a safari in Africa with lots of slides and adventure stories. Both were upset by William Holden, who dropped by La Pace, always a little drunk and looking for girls he could entice to a Florentine disco. One night on the way back to the hotel, there was an accident that ended with Holden being charged with manslaughter. Anita tried to console Mrs. Holden, who flew to Italy for her husband's court appearance, with tales about Mr. E. and the massage parlors of Pasadena.

Two weeks into her stay at Montecatini, Anita received news about the critical response to *The King's Mare*. Five out of ten reviews were mildly negative, the other half mixed, most of the praise going to Johns and Michell. England was then anti-American, her producer, Stanley Gordon, explained, which accounted for the *Evening News*'s swipe at "foreigners [intent on] deprecating British history."

The split reviews for *The King's Mare* were bound to be overcome by good word of mouth, Gordon felt, so would Anita waive royalties until the show caught on? She agreed—wisely so, since *The King's Mare* was to have a moderately successful run in London, long enough to qualify it as a possible Broadway import for the forthcoming season.

31

A Girl
Like I

A NITA returned to New York only a few weeks before the publication of *A Girl Like I* in September 1966. To launch the book, Viking threw a 1920s party at the Terrace Room in the Plaza Hotel. "What a night!" Too many people to recall, but of course Paulette and Tallulah and Helen Hayes, Mado Sherwood and Natasha and Ruth Dubonnet, Stanley Simmons, Ted Peckham, and Cris Alexander, as well as celebrity acquaintances like Glenway Wescott, Truman Capote, Virgil Thomson, and Edmund Wilson.

A Girl Like I received a full-page review in the Sunday *Times* book review, and down the line the notices were raves. "Anita Loos is now over seventy," said the *Times*, "but . . . she sounds as young and gay as her Lorelei." Robert Sklar, writing in *The Nation*, felt the book was "perhaps the most remarkable Hollywood memoir ever written for its candor, its wit and its intelligence." Arthur Knight in *Saturday Review* found it "downright refreshing to read the reminiscences of a lady who not only has lived long enough to have something worth recalling, but has the literary ability to confide her thoughts to paper unassisted." *The New Yorker* hoped a second installment would be forthcoming, "the sooner the better."

There were personal notes from Wilson and Capote. Wilson urged Anita to get Viking to issue an omnibus of her novels: "Your books," Wilson wrote, "will always be classics."

A Girl Like I once again elevated Anita into conspicuous public prominence. The Museum of Modern Art announced a retrospective of her films; Eugenia Shephard and Suzy, her favorite columnists, mentioned her frequently in their reports of fashionable parties. Anita was going out a lot then, though she protested that she'd rather be at home or with Stanley Simmons, who served the best chili she had ever tasted.

One party she wouldn't have missed was Truman Capote's controversial black-and-white masked ball in fall 1966. "Truman seems to have found his level as another Elsa Maxwell," Beaton said, and other friends agreed that the party was an anachronism in the Vietnam era. Anita felt otherwise. "A little glamour might do everyone good just now."

As soon as she got the invitation, she started planning her ensemble. Halston agreed to design a mask, and Kenneth Lane lent her several pieces of expensive costume jewelry. She was going to wear a black lace Balenciaga and, over it, an ostrich-feather bedcover which once had belonged to Linda Porter. Cole had passed it on when his wife died in 1957, but Anita never had known what to do with it. It was a little tarty for her spartan bedroom; but draped over the black Balenciaga, it made a smashing evening wrap.

At six-thirty on the evening of the party, she was dressed and ready for the photographers from the *Times,* who took pictures with her wearing the mask and without. Stanley Gordon, her escort, arrived at eight-thirty with a limousine to take them to a dinner party at Glenway Wescott's, where the other guests included Virgil Thomson, Janet Flanner, Natasha Wilson, and Christopher Isherwood. At ten-thirty they left for the ball and were jostled about until they found a table on a balcony where they could watch "the terrific spectacle."

W I T H Thanksgiving and Christmas not far off, Anita put off launching any new project, as there were presents to be bought, cards to address, and the future of Miss Moore to consider. A year before, Miss Moore had showed an aptitude for dance and was enrolled as a beginner at the School of American Ballet. Her instructor, Diana Adams, a former Balanchine ballerina, had said that Miss Moore definitely showed promise.

Now Adams felt the girl was ready to audition for Balanchine as one of the children in the New York City Ballet's annual *Nutcracker Suite* festival. It was wonderful that Diana Adams had such confidence in little Gladys, but Anita wasn't sure the girl could handle the pressures and problems of an stage career. She turned to friends for advice, and

Anita dressed for
the Capote ball,
November 1966

Cris Alexander told her to talk to his "mate," Shaun O'Brien, who danced
Herr Drosselmeyer in *Nutcracker*.

What O'Brien said wasn't reassuring: Balanchine was rough on the
kids. Well, Anita countered, Miss Moore was so fetching she'd immediately win him over. Don't count on it, O'Brien warned; Balanchine was
immune to charm. Anita decided to leave it to fate: if Miss Moore was
accepted, fine; it not, so be it. And Balanchine did reject Miss Moore, and
all the other applicants in her age group. "It's for the best," Anita wrote.
"Next year she'll be better prepared."

Miss Moore took the rejection less philosophically, and to cheer her
up, Anita organized a special gala Christmas Eve party: a big tree, lots of
guests, and Shaun O'Brien decked out in his Drosselmeyer regalia to act
as master of ceremonies for the opening of gifts. On the morning of
December 24, Anita did some last-minute shopping at Caswell-Massey
and Lamston's, picked up Nova Scotia salmon for hors d'oeuvres, and
was on her way home when outside the Drake Hotel on Fifth Avenue she
met Connie Talmadge.

Miss Moore on Christmas, 1966

She hadn't seen Dutch, now in her late sixties, for years, though of course she had heard about the marriages and divorces and dypsomania. Although it was still before noon, Connie was already unsteady on her feet, but she insisted Anita join her for a prelunch cocktail. "A sad experience," Anita wrote. Dutch was "a lonely lost soul, too lacking in resources to function as a living woman."

The party that night was truly festive; so many presents were under the tree that Miss Moore was put to bed before half of them were unwrapped. The next morning, before the girl was up, Anita and Gladys put aside some of the remaining gifts for orphanages. It was a quiet Christmas, and what was left of 1966 was by choice just as uneventful. Anita turned down all invitations during the interim week, and on New Year's Eve she went to bed at ten-thirty.

THE new year opened with light snow and a flurry of unsettling developments. In early January Mary called to say that she and Rich had separated and she was starting divorce procedures. The news came as no surprise, but Anita was deeply concerned about Mary and her handicapped son. How would they live? One of the sources of strife in the marriage was Sale's extravagance. They were heavily in debt, and Mary could expect only minimal financial support. But Mary said not to worry— she felt optimistic about the future.

The relationship between Mary and Anita was, at least as it emerges in the diaries, always a little prickly, a bit schoolmarmish on the aunt's side. Though she unquestionably loved Mary and possibly felt duty-bound to act as surrogate mother-to-guide-her when Mary's own mother left Clifford, and though they were very close, Anita frequently disapproved of Mary's conduct and friendships.

She had been faintly scandalized when in the mid-1930s Ernst Lubitsch started squiring Mary about Hollywood, simply because no one was ever going to believe that the relationship between a beautiful twenty-year-old girl and a forty-plus mogul was all above the sheets, as this one definitely was. Then and on other occasions, Anita warned Mary about what gossips might say of her independent behavior in taking up with beaux like the widowed Eddie Duchin, Rouben Mamoulian, and Francis Lederer. After all, Hollywood *did* have a dirty mind.

Anita felt Mary was being a Pollyanna about her postdivorce future, but within weeks Mary found a good position as assistant to producer Mike Frankovich. Anita was happy about the salary and perks, but worried about Mary working in "that Augean stable," the new Hollywood. Helen Hayes and George Cukor relayed horror stories about what was happening now that the industry was controlled by drugs and conglomerates. These tales were passed along to Mary who listened patiently and respectfully.

Which was more than could be said for Miss Moore, whose return to school after the winter intersession was "Disaster!" First came word that she had offered a classmate three dollars for a cupcake, leading the principal to believe that either Miss Moore didn't know the value of a cupcake or she had too much spending money.

Anita blamed it on the new math. Who could understand it? Not she, not Gladys, not Edgar Scott, her financial advisor. And if they couldn't grasp this diabolical variation on an old theme, how could a child of eight cope? The principal replied that Miss Moore alone among her classmates was unable to grasp the fundamentals, perhaps because she was willful or perhaps she lacked application.

Anita was deeply concerned. At this time she was convinced that the girl had real theatrical talent, but she wanted her to have a thorough education, not so much as something to fall back on if her career failed but as a foundation to help her lead a sane and productive life. She didn't want to see her ending as unresourceful as Dutch Talmadge or as "nutty and self-indulgent" as Judy Garland.

She tried to help the girl with her lessons by making a game of them. For arithmetic, she brought out several pairs of shoes, tried them on, and when a "purchase" was made, Miss Moore, playing clerk, made change from the bills Anita handed her. The money returned was always too much or too little.

Besides math, Miss Moore was also lagging behind in science and English. Anita glanced over the science homework and decided it consisted of "things pertinent only to a medical school." English was another matter. Anita selected poems for memorization, and in classroom presentation, the child was brilliant. Her true forte was stage presence.

B Y M A R C H 1 9 6 7 Anita realized that she had been on holiday for too long. It had been months since she picked up her legal pad and pen and started to work. There were reasons for her to do so now, money among them—lots going out and not much coming in—but more importantly, she was getting bored with what might be called outside distractions if there had been anything to be distracted from. It was part of the writer's syndrome—the longing to be released from one book and the uneasy biding of time till the next one comes along.

32

Mining the Past

*B*U T W H A T to write? *The New Yorker* had requested a sequel to *A Girl Like I*, and the idea was appealing at first. Then problems arose. The first memoir had sold well, particularly in New York, Chicago, Boston, Los Angeles, and other cities boasting a sophisticated audience, but not well enough to earn out its large advance. Viking applied money from Hamish Hamilton for British rights to the unearned debit, an action that enraged Anita, who felt she was entitled to part of those English pounds.

She never read contracts, relying on her agent or lawyers to do so. Two decades ago, it was standard procedure (and in general still is) for publishers to apply subsidiary funds against unearned advances. When the contractual terms were explained to her, she understood and calmed down.

Viking was genuinely interested in a second memoir, as it would cover her years at M-G-M, with Thalberg and Harlow, Garbo and Gable among its cast of characters—personalities people knew about through the TV late shows—and so quite possibly it would sell better than the first. But Anita had a hunch that she wouldn't get much of an advance just then, so she decided to push ahead without a contract. Once she had put together a few chapters, she'd show them to Viking and see what kind of money they talked.

Temporarily disenchanted with the world of publishing, she returned to the theater. The big money made on Broadway all stemmed from musicals, so she started looking over past shows, hearing distant melodies in her head. At the top of the slate was *Happy Birthday,* but not with Gerry Mulligan's score or Holliday's lyrics. Holliday had died in 1965, and no one liked Mulligan's music very much. She approached a few producers with the idea, including her friend Charles Hollerith. "It's all there," she said. "All you have to do is slip the songs in." Hollerith disagreed, insisting that the original script must be totally revamped if the show was to work as a musical.

Meanwhile, she was making progress with a musical version of *The King's Mare,* retitled *Something About Anne.* Her collaborators were James Gregory (music) and Ralph Blane (lyrics—he is best known for "The Trolley Song"). The three worked steadily until June, when Blane returned to his home in Broken Arrow, Oklahoma, and Anita went off to Montecatini and Acqui.

In Italy that summer, she started work on the second memoir, starting with a chapter about Wilson Mizner. Finishing that, she went on to another about her return to Hollywood in the early thirties and completed a draft before her vacation ended. But she wasn't entirely satisfied and put aside the manuscript for many months.

That fall she was preoccupied with domestic events. Miss Moore again applied for *The Nutcracker* and was accepted by Balanchine. What about schoolwork and Miss Moore's already inflated ego? Anita worried. But the child was so delighted, it would be cruel to deprive her of the experience.

For Miss Moore's debut, Anita arranged a theater party, with Helen Hayes, Natasha Wilson, Stanley Simmons, and Morty Gottlieb among the guests. "Miss Moore stands out!" Anita wrote the next morning. She couldn't help but stand out, says Gottlieb: the soles of her Capezios had been varnished with crimson nail polish.

One person missing at the opening was Gladys, whose mother had been taken to the hospital a week earlier. Specialists hired by Anita performed a biopsy and reported that Mrs. Tipton, then in her nineties, required surgery for cancer. If the operation was a success, she might live for months. Anita was appalled. Perform surgery on a very old lady so she could survive a few months? It was as inhumane as the bleeding procedures practiced by seventeenth-century *médecins imaginaires.* But there was no need to urge Gladys against following doctors' orders, since Mrs. Tipton died peacefully that same night.

There were too many deaths. Anita's diaries were becoming a list of names circled in black: Mae Marsh, Dorothy Gish, Tallulah Bankhead, Peter Arno were among the recent departed. The grim reaper was making a lavish harvest from her friends, and since she was now close to eighty, the constant reminder of mortality weighed heavily. Depression always triggered physical illness, and throughout the winter of 1968 Anita was down with the flu more than she was up at her desk.

"Realize I must find something to write," was her own prescription. *Something About Anne* was now far enough along to hold auditions for prospective producers and stars. Rex Harrison and his then-wife, Rachel Roberts, listened to the Gregory-Blane score and asked for encores. The next day Harrison called to say Rachel was so enthusiastic that she wanted to start voice lessons with James Gregory that very afternoon. She had appeared in musicals, but *Anne's* songs were so demanding that she wanted Gregory to know she could handle them.

Gregory's report on the ensuing meeting was not encouraging. Roberts arrived unsteady on her feet and fiddled around for ninety minutes until she felt sober enough to sing. After some squawking, she asked for a reprieve: tomorrow she'd be in better vocal and physical condition. At the second meeting, Roberts was in control, though her voice still seemed to have a hangover. All *Anne's* songs would have to be rewritten to cover her vocal limitations, Gregory told Anita, or else they'd have to be half-sung — Harrison's method in *My Fair Lady*. But would a musical sound like a musical with two nonsingers in the leading roles? Gregory didn't think so, and Anita agreed. The Harrisons were out.

Through Stanley Simmons, Anita met opera and theater director Frank Corsaro, who was enthusiastic about *Anne* and felt the effervescent Beverly Sills would be perfect in the leading role. Anita encouraged Corsaro to approach Sills, who reported that she was committed to Rossini and Donizetti for the next few seasons.

Disillusioned with the theater, Anita went off to Montecatini for two months, spending every morning polishing the first chapters of the second memoir. Before returning to New York, she had a considerable chunk of manuscript completed to her own satisfaction.

In September 1969 the manuscript was sent to Viking, where it collected dust, or so Anita surmised. Her calls went unreturned for days, and when someone did get back to her, it was only to stall about a decision. After six weeks Tom Guinzburg offered $6,000 as an advance, the best he could do since *A Girl Like I* hadn't been a best-seller.

Unaccustomed to bargaining, Anita turned to Ray Corsini and asked her to intervene. In the interval between the two memoirs, Corsini had opened her own agency, and she informed Anita that this time she would have to charge an agent's fee, but she felt sure she could better the advance. She got Guinzburg to raise his offer to $15,000, with foreign and

first serial rights retained for Anita. This proved not to be excessive, since
the second memoir, *Kiss Hollywood Good-by,* not only was to earn out its
advance but brought about as much in royalties.

N O   S O O N E R had she settled down to *Kiss* than Anita came up with
another promising book idea. It started with a long phone chat with Helen
Hayes, recently returned to New York after several months in Los Angeles
shooting a TV movie. The new Hollywood was unbearable—how grateful
she was to be back in civilization!

Anita mentioned that New York wasn't all that civilized just then, a
remark that raised Helen's Irish dander. New York City's reputation as an
Eden for muggers, addicts, derelicts, and porn pushers was so infuriating!
While admittedly such undesirables did blight the skyline, the city was as
wonderful and exciting as it had been when they both were in their salad
days. People were too brainwashed to explore its wonders; they restricted
themselves to their own safe neighborhoods and went out of town as often
as possible, weekending in the Hamptons, summering in Montecatini. Or
hibernating in Mexico, Anita interjected—Hayes spent every winter in
Cuernavaca.

Eventually they agreed to forgo their annual holidays to investigate
New York City and write about its diversified pleasures. It was tacitly
understood that Anita would do most of the writing, but she would have
the benefit of Hayes's gift of gab. And Helen's name on a book jacket was
money in the bank: Hayes's earlier books had all been best-sellers.

Anita asked Ray Corsini to present the book to publishers. Corsini
agreed, though she had reservations about its reception. Books about New
York rarely sold well outside New York, sometimes not even within its
boroughs. But the Loos-Hayes names might overcome the resistance to
such special material.

The first responses to the proposal were not encouraging. Anita was
"drained" by the rejections. "Feel I am of no value to anyone." Typically
she was her own worst critic, and she was ready to drop the project. "Not
yet," said Corsini, and with good reason: the next day came an offer from a
Macmillan editor who said, "Loos and Hayes could write about Podunk
and it'd be fun." He had offered $25,000, but Helen Wolff, with her own
imprint at Harcourt Brace Jovanovich, bid $30,000. Apart from the money,
the prospect of having such a renowned editor led Anita and Helen to sign
with Harcourt.

Still to be worked out was a possible conflict of interests. Anita was under contract to Viking for her memoir, but she wanted to set that aside to go straight ahead with what she was always to call "Helen's book," confident that she could complete it in eight months. Viking agreed to wait on the memoir until she finished her guide to New York, which as it took shape became another chapter in the history of Dorothy and Lorelei.

33

Friendship

PREPARING the book, Anita went through the New York Yellow Pages searching for out-of-the-way places to investigate: academies for astrologers and bartenders, a charm school for black girls, a prep salon for barbers. Looking over these academic outposts as well as revisiting the sanctioned city landmarks took more time than expected and was one reason the book went over schedule.

Another hitch was Helen Hayes. Humble with apologies, she went off to Mexico for her annual winter vacation. (Just before boarding the plane, she called Anita for "a final mea culpa.") Later she spent several weeks in Washington, D.C., playing Mary Tyrone in *Long Day's Journey into Night*.

Though exasperated by her collaborator's hyperactivity, Anita took advantage of her absence to visit a few hot spots Hayes probably would never have entered. With an unidentified male companion, she inspected the Times Square porn theaters, was dazzled by the physical beauty of the on-screen exhibitionists and depressed by the clientele, middle-aged John Does in three-piece suits and carrying briefcases.

Since Anita was doing most of the writing, Helen's absences were not a serious obstacle, though material did have to flow back and forth so Hayes could touch up or expand as she saw fit. And in the final stages of polishing, she did make a considerable contribution to the book. But the most engaging part of *Twice Over Lightly,* which like all good travel literature depends less on the place visited than on the perceptions and sensibility of the visitor(s), is all Anita's handiwork.

She sets up a dialogue between the authors. As they sight-see, they chatter, wisecrack, philosophize, and disagree, and the Hayes and the Loos who emerge are crystallizations of their real selves, as stylized as the personas Anita created for Fairbanks, Harlow, and Gable in the past. And they bear more than a passing resemblance to Lorelei and Dorothy—older now, but still as feisty and argumentative as the not-so-innocents Anita launched on a European tour in 1925.

Twice Over Lightly was completed in early 1972. Anita returned immediately to her memoir, and she was still working on it when she sailed on the *Leonardo da Vinci* in June. She wrote every morning during her two-month stay in Italy, and by her return to New York in September the book was virtually complete. Two months later it was delivered to the printers, and simultaneously, *Twice Over Lightly* was issued by Harcourt Brace Jovanovich.

Anita and Helen made a cross-country promotion tour. Ray Corsini was worried—Hayes was in her seventies, Anita in her mid-eighties—and so was the publicity director for Harcourt, who asked, "Shall I send an oxygen mask along?" She explained that there had been so many requests for personal appearances that she'd had a hard time cutting them down to even this overloaded itinerary.

The tour was exhausting, but Anita reported to both Gladys and Corsini that she was enjoying it, and she sounded full of pep, as though the junket had pumped up her adrenaline. She said it was Helen who brought out the crowds who lined up for autographs, among them people who had seen *Victoria Regina* and wanted signed books for their grandchildren. But there was an equal number who had read *Blondes* and wanted Anita's autograph for similar reasons.

The tour was worth the effort, since the book, which received excellent reviews, eventually sold over fifty thousand copies.

Harcourt was eager for a follow-up book by Anita, and she was already discussing another literary collaboration with her friend Paulette Goddard, who after the death of her third husband, Erich Maria Remarque, spent part of every year in New York. When in the city, she and Anita saw each other several times a week for shopping or a movie, tea or a stroll through Central Park. For years Anita had wanted to write something about or with Paulette, who knew a good deal about everything. She recently had studied with a world-renowned master of Zen Buddhism, and she then was introducing Anita to the artistry of the Zen tea ritual as well as to the cuisine of New York's only Zen restaurant. (Anita felt guilty about omitting this curiosity from *Twice Over Lightly.*)

Their first notion was to tour the French château country and write about what they saw—or more precisely, on what they had missed out on. Anita wanted to concentrate on the erotic intrigues that had transpired when those pleasure estates surged with hot Bourbon and Orléans blood. Harcourt's response was lukewarm, so Anita tentatively suggested that she tell Paulette's story, just as Lorelei had related Dorothy's in *Brunettes.*

Harcourt was enthusiastic. Anita didn't kid herself into believing that writing *The Perils of Paulette* (a title that popped immediately into her head) was going to be easy. For years, publishers had been after Paulette for a memoir, and she had refused, saying she didn't want to do one of those "tell all" books. That was fine, Anita agreed, but of course she had to tell *something*. Paulette promised to be unguarded, so contracts were signed, each author guaranteed an advance of $30,000, payable in three installments.

That summer Anita was returning to Montecatini, and Paulette decided to join her there after a short stay at her home, Casa Remarque, in Porto Ronco, Switzerland. By the time of Goddard's arrival, Anita already had something on paper, drawing on memories of past adventures with her friend. She worked alone in the morning; then, every afternoon by the pool, Paulette reminisced discreetly while Anita stored up mental notes.

For five days they went off to Rome, a city Paulette adored but Anita had never taken to. Goddard's guided tour produced no reappraisal: Rome was unspeakably expensive, hot, dirty, crowded with Cinecittà riffraff, and, like all Italy, simmering with social unrest. This was one summer Anita returned to New York with no regrets.

Getting off the boat, she got "the biggest compliment of my life." Someone asked her, "Say, aren't you Louise Brooks? I've seen *Pandora's Box* twelve times." And another thrill came two weeks later, when Paulette lost a contact lens during a matinee and the gentleman who aided them in their search said, "I'd do anything to help *you*, Miss Loos." Paulette was very put out at going unnoticed.

Less amusing was Paulette's minimal cooperation on the book. She was being very reticent, and Anita worried that she never was going to pull anything juicy out of her friend. She had gotten one chapter from their adventures in Rome, but very little about Paulette's past. Finally, Goddard announced she didn't want to say anything about Chaplin. "But, Paulette," Anita gasped, "people will ask 'Where's Charlie?'" Goddard wasn't to be joked out of her silence, so Anita told Harcourt there could be no book and returned her share of the first third of the advance.

It didn't hurt her bank account, since a steady trickle of cash was flowing in from other sources. Some months earlier Charles Lowe had put together for his wife an updated version of *Blondes* in which Channing as an aging Lorelei looks back on past triumphs. Named after its heroine, the show utilized some of the old book, added new material by various hands and new songs by Jule Styne and Betty Comden and Adolph Green. Anita was hurt that she wasn't asked to contribute; but since some of her material was retained, she received a small percentage of the weekly gross. During *Lorelei*'s extensive pre-Broadway tour, that percentage yielded about a thousand dollars a week.

At approximately the same time, Alan Jay Lerner adapted his film musical of *Gigi* for the stage, and that show was also working its way across country. Anita received a percentage for the musical, amounting to a few hundred dollars every month. (It would have totaled more if the stage *Gigi* had been a bigger hit.) "Thank heaven for little girls like Lorelei and Gigi!" They paid for her trip to Barbados during the Christmas holidays of 1973.

In late January 1974, *Lorelei* opened at the Palace Theatre in New York. Anita attended the premiere, adored Channing ("masterful . . . the best thing she's done so far") but liked little else. The show looked as though it had been put together "on the cheap—summer stock hits Broadway!" Critics echoed her verdict, but box-office sales were, Lowe reported later that week, "brisk—$20,000 every day."

A few months later, *Kiss Hollywood Good-by* was issued by Viking with appropriate fanfare. Though not so rich or closely knit as *A Girl Like I,* the second memoir sold better and got just as good reviews. Again Anita traveled around America promoting the book, and when it was published in England that fall, she went to London for two weeks.

While on a scouting trip to New York, Jeffrey Simmons, editorial director of British publisher W. H. Allen, read *Kiss Hollywood Good-by* over a weekend and made an offer the following Monday. He asked to meet Anita, found her "adorable," and then and there suggested she come over for promotion. Where did she usually stay? The Ritz, she answered. Simmons said fine but mentioned that W. H. Allen had offices in the old Rothschild mansion on Hill Street and kept a four-room flat on the top floor, complete with a stocked kitchen, bar, and maid service. She might find it more convenient and cozier there. Of course she could bring Gladys and Miss Moore along.

Her London visit was a triumph, like the return of a royal favorite: full-page interviews in the London *Sunday Times,* a champagne party in the former Rothschild ballroom, appearances on the leading talk shows. Foyles, a leading London bookshop, gave her a luncheon at the Dorchester, attended by Diana, Lady Cooper; Dame Edith Evans; Irene Handl; Douglas Fairbanks, Jr.; Cathleen Nesbitt; Barbara Cartland; and several duchesses, among many others. Bobby Short played and sang songs from *Blondes,* and Anita gave a short speech.

During her stay she saw a lot of Cecil Beaton and bumped into Shirley MacLaine, who confided that she was thinking of returning to Broadway and had heard something about a musical version of *Happy Birthday* with a Gerry Mulligan–Judy Holliday score. Anita said there was

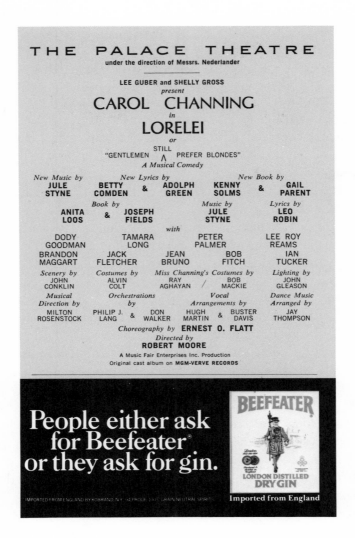

a tape of the music she could hear once they were back in New York.

MacLaine listened and turned thumbs down. Over the years Anita kept coming up against resistance to Mulligan's music, but she was so fond of Gerry: "What to do?"

Arnold Weissberger, Anita's lawyer and very good friend, urged her to start fresh with a new score. Loyalty went only so far, he argued. A week later, on his recommendation, Hugh Martin and Timothy Gray came to see Anita. They had written songs for *High Spirits,* an adaptation of Noel Coward's *Blithe Spirit,* and for a long-running West End musical, *Love from Judy.* Though his output was small, Martin was highly admired by his peers, and Anita had worked with him briefly some twenty years before when she doctored his charming and underrated *Make a Wish!*

Martin and Gray were enthusiastic about *Birthday.* Anita was perplexed. She didn't quite know how to tell Mulligan he was being cashiered, and since he was away on a tour, she postponed the chore until she saw what Martin and Gray came up with.

Timothy Gray read the libretto Anita had fashioned for Holliday and Mulligan and felt it needed revising. "Anita was too close to the original material to see how it should be reshaped as a musical," he recalls. She consented when he suggested he might make a few alterations. When he had finished, the script was totally overhauled, and Anita was delighted by his revisions. "Nothing for me to do but change a few words."

In the diaries Anita refers to Gray as "darling Timmy." Gray explains that his charm consisted mainly of speaking clearly and loud enough for Anita to understand what he was saying. Her hearing was very poor, but out of vanity she delayed getting a hearing aid, making conversation difficult for those who, unlike Gray, lacked a booming voice and stage training. "If I can hear Timmy, why can't I hear you?" she'd ask Gladys. Gray and Gladys would then exchange glances of mutual amusement.

For a while things looked promising for the Gray-Martin-Loos version of *Birthday.* Producer Robert Fryer thought it would be ideal for Mary Martin, but when Gray went to Palm Springs for a presentation, Martin got restless after a few songs. "Oh, honey, I'm too old and tired to take on such a strenuous role," she told Gray. "Maybe if Addie didn't have so much to do . . . "

Anita then suggested Dorothy Loudon. Loudon listened to the score and didn't say no, which convinced Anita she would soon say yes. Instead she took on another show, a fast flop, leading Anita to wonder why actors didn't recognize a good thing when it came their way.

Actors weren't the only exasperating people. Hugh Martin unexpectedly announced that his health, never very good, was now rotten, and he had to return to California to look after a friend in even worse shape. He doubted whether he'd be able to contribute anything further to the show.

"Without a composer, how can we go ahead?" Anita asked Timothy Gray. He didn't have an answer, so once again *Happy Birthday* went into limbo. Would she never learn, Anita asked her diary, that the nicest people made lousy collaborators?

34

Striving
for Transcendence

ANITA didn't fret long over the collapse of *Birthday;* she had plenty of work to occupy her. Viking had put on its future list a book she had wanted to write for some time, a reminiscence about the Talmadge sisters, their mother, and Norma's husband, Joe Schenck. And Grosset and Dunlap had taken on a coffee-table "scrapbook" (eventually titled *A Cast of Thousands*) using photographs from Anita's private collection accompanied by brief chapters about the people and events they depicted.

Progress on these books was delayed by a long, nagging siege of illness, the first Anita had experienced in some years. At first she thought it was the flu, but after forty-seven days of queasiness she consulted her doctor, Shephard Aronson, who felt an ulcer might be the root of the problem. Anita feared it might be something worse: though she never mentions the word in the diaries, it seems clear that she was worried about cancer.

She went to Doctors Hospital for a battery of tests, including a barium X ray, a "humiliating" procedure, indelicately executed. On the morning after the X ray, further tests had to be postponed since the barium had not been thoroughly eliminated from her system. Anita demanded to go home, and Dr. Aronson agreed.

By then he was convinced the distress was psychological. "Don't worry so much," he advised. Worrying about not worrying made Anita worry more. Aronson prescribed tranquilizers, which served only to increase the anxiety. Anita distrusted any substance that might alter that spot of gray matter on which she prided herself.

She took Aronson's capsules, but only after he presented a documented account of the drug, its efficacy and possible side effects. The medication was never controversial, and the dosage always lower than six milligrams per day. Nothing worked well, possibly because Anita didn't want anything to work. The medication curbed her appetite, and soon her weight was under ninety pounds: "I need a solid meal." She pushed herself to go out to lunch with friends, and regretted it: "I know I'm not good company."

She went on with the pills but believed willpower was the only crutch she needed. *The Daily Word* told her, "I transcend myself and all my affairs, for I am spirit." And that very afternoon, Gladys said the same thing, more colloquially: "Rise above it!"

After months of exploration, Aronson prescribed Ativan, which did diminish the anxiety for short periods. But usually Anita took only half the prescribed dosage, and then only when she felt distraught, generally after the death of a close friend—and so many were passing on! Better than the pills were a small glass of wine and a chapter of Thomas Aquinas before bed. They made all the difference between a black and a white night, made writing all the easier the next morning. Within a few weeks, she had finished *A Cast of Thousands* and was poking along with *The Talmadge Girls.*

Writing about Dutch, Norma, and Peg was a trial for Anita. Her personal memories of the Talmadges, often charming and evocative, weren't enough to fill even a slender volume. Later, Irene Mayer Selznick and other people who knew both the Talmadges and Anita wondered why so much meaty material had been omitted. But Anita had never been one to publicly air other people's dirty laundry, and just then she couldn't bring herself to speak unkindly of departed friends. (It is characteristic that the version of her final meeting with Dutch Talmadge as it appears in the book is far softer than the account given in the diaries.)

Each death brought not only the inevitable sense of personal loss but also a fear of isolation. Was she going to outlive everyone? end up with no one to turn to for support and comradeship? There were Ruth Dubonnet and Ted Peckham and, whenever she was in town, Paulette, and of course Gladys, who wasn't all that much younger than Anita. She could—any of them might—go first, and then where would Anita be?

She started dropping by for a chat with her editors or at Ray Corsini's for tea, always calling to set up a date, never wanting to interfere with the flow of the business day. She was always welcome, since whatever depression she might have been feeling was pushed aside to reveal the amusing and amusable person she wanted to be. But that she was creating distractions from a growing loneliness was apparent to many of the people she visited, and quite probably to herself as well.

Work was always the best means of staving off anxiety. *The Talmadge Girls* was eventually fleshed out by including the screenplay for *A Virtuous Vamp*, which Anita had happened to find while sorting out a file drawer of forgotten material. Meanwhile, the Mulligan-Holliday *Happy Birthday* was produced in Birmingham, Alabama, with such success that Broadway producers got wind of it. Among them was Elliott Martin, who had an "inspired" idea for the perfect Addie Beamis: years before he had put together a stock production of the original play with Imogene Coca, who could still be perfect in the lead role.

Anita was elated, but Mulligan refused to cooperate. He didn't like the terms of his contract, and he thought Coca was too old to play Addie. "He is unaware that his music has been turned down by everyone but Elliott Martin and that a new score must be contrived to bolster his songs," Anita wrote in exasperation.

There was talk of getting Marvin Hamlisch to write new tunes for some of Holliday's lyrics, keeping a few of the Timothy Gray–Hugh Martin songs and all of Gray's revision of Anita's book. But doubting whether anything good could come from stitching together such diverse odds and ends, Elliott Martin regretfully withdrew.

Anxious to have something to do, Anita came up with a book idea, *The Hollywood Nobody Knows*. Publishers reacted favorably to the prospect of a new Loos project but wondered if she hadn't had her say about Hollywood in her two memoirs, *A Cast of Thousands*, and *The Talmadge Girls*. Anita was very disappointed by the reaction.

Puzzled by her drive to get something under contract, Ray Corsini urged her to relax and enjoy this respite. There was continual magazine interest in anything she cared to write, so why push herself into something big when she could work on these occasional pieces? Unless it was a question of money . . . No, she wasn't strapped, Anita replied, "but a girl has to look out for her old age"—in other words, while she wasn't pressed for cash, it always came in handy.

Since the costly trips to Italy were over, Anita's expenses were relatively modest. Her rent was now over nine hundred dollars a month. Miss Moore, now in the final year of high school, needed tuition, and there were food and clothing and entertainment expenditures, wages for a cleaning woman, a typist, and Gladys.

As she was eligible for Social Security benefits, Gladys was paid the maximum she could earn without forgoing her stipend. And there was a monthly bonus, matching her salary; on the check Anita wrote "A Gift."

Gladys's welfare was a matter of grave concern for Anita as she grew older. In 1972 she transferred $10,000 from her personal savings into a joint account with Gladys that already held a balance of $13,000. Three years later, she gave her companion a gift of $30,000, asking her financial advisor, Edgar Scott, to invest the money as soundly as possible. Scott later sent a letter listing the stocks and securities obtained for Gladys.

But Anita remained "obsessed with money," says Avis Klein, a secretary employed at the time *Kiss Hollywood Good-by* was reaching completion. "At first she made a joke about it — stuff like 'I've got to bring home the bacon,' that kind of thing." Klein remembers an occasion when she and Gladys were telling Anita what they thought she should do about some trivial matter; she listened patiently for a while, then stamped her foot. "I'll do as I please," she announced. "Remember, I'm the breadwinner around here!"

Then it got to be not so much of a joke. "I think she lost some money on an investment," Klein recalls. "And it was also my impression that the drive for money clouded Anita's judgment about her writing. She picked up things she thought would bring in money, not because she was so fascinated with the idea."

That Anita was scared because of a bad investment is true; that she chose a project simply because she thought it would bring in money is open to question. Certainly, commercial viability was never far from her mind — she prided herself on being a pro — and a few ideas she latched on to do smack of trendiness, like a musical about a bag lady she toyed with in the late seventies. Bag ladies were then much in the news, but that doesn't necessarily imply she wasn't genuinely fascinated with them, or that she might not have worked something witty or whimsical out of such grubby subject matter.

Arnold Weissberger told her the bag lady idea was dreary, and this coming not long after the rejection of *The Hollywood Nobody Knows* made her wonder whether (the phrase is repeated several times in the diaries for these years) "I am of any use to anyone."

Her mind was as supple as ever, but her perception was limited by both failing hearing (only marginally corrected by the hearing aid she finally had agreed to wear) and deteriorating eyesight. There were days, weeks at a time, when she gave in to her depression and thought of herself as an invalid, no longer capable of taking care of her family.

On graduating from high school, Miss Moore had lost interest in pursuing a theatrical career. She was "boy crazy," Anita wrote in a moment of bitter distress. That Miss Moore didn't live up to either Gladys's or Anita's expectations is a comment made again and again by confidants, though Anita was wise enough to know the girl had to choose her own life. She had provided the best education she could. Miss Moore would have to make her own choices, though she had never expected early marriage to be one of them.

Too many of the boys Miss Moore was crazy about were white, which made both Anita and Gladys nervous, since both had their suspicions about why white boys dated black girls. But then young Gladys started seeing Jerome Clarke, a black only a few years older, nice looking, well groomed, with perfect manners. He was frequently asked for dinner, and when the young couple quarreled, as they often did, Gladys and Anita always sided against Miss Moore.

"Miss Moore was basically a nice kid," remembers Avis Klein. "But she grew up in this weird environment with two elderly aunts, and the only people coming in and out of the apartment paid attention to her because Anita expected them to. It was an artificial situation."

Klein recalls an evening when after typing late, she was asked by Anita to dine out with the three of them. She requested a rain check, but when Anita and Gladys went to put on their coats, Miss Moore asked her to reconsider: she'd like to have someone her own age to talk to once in a while. "That was very touching," says Klein, "because I'm not Miss Moore's contemporary by a long shot."

Clarke and Miss Moore became engaged in the summer of 1976. She was nineteen, he only a few years older, but Anita made no protest against the marriage. Jerome was steady, holding down a good job with an electronics manufacturer, and he was obviously devoted to Miss Moore. Did she share his feelings? Avis Klein is inclined to feel she married him mainly to escape her two aunts, just as Anita once had married Frank Pallma to get out of Minnie's clutches.

On September 9, 1976, Miss Moore became Mrs. Clarke. After the ceremony there was a reception at the Americana Hotel, with dance music provided by Peter Duchin and his orchestra. After a Caribbean honeymoon, the Clarkes took an apartment in Queens. It was charming, Anita wrote after her first visit.

Jerome went to his job every morning, and Mrs. Clarke, while looking for a job in modeling, worked at a laundromat managed by one of Gladys's friends and located only a few blocks from her old home on

Fifty-seventh Street. Afterward she regularly stopped by her foster mother's for dinner.

Six months after the wedding, the unexpected happened in the worst of all possible ways. One day in March 1977 Anita was gossiping on the phone with Morty Gottlieb when Gladys interrupted to say that another call had come through, with distressing news about Jerome. She was rushing to pick up Miss Moore and get her to the Queens hospital where Clarke had been taken after collapsing on the street. Gladys was so visibly distraught that Anita picked up her mood, and Avis Klein, finishing up a typing job, offered to stay until the situation was clarified.

It was several anxious hours before Gladys called with less than reassuring news: Jerome's condition was grave, and none of the doctors who examined him seemed to know what was wrong. There was a huge swelling in his neck, and the pain was all too obvious. His condition deteriorated, and forty-eight hours later he was dead.

Of what? The cause of his death remains mysterious. Because he was a young black, many of Anita's friends jumped to the conclusion that he died of a drug overdose. Avis Klein disagrees. "Jerome was very straight ... actually he was kind of square." Gladys hinted to a few people, Ray Corsini among them, that Jerome died from complications of sickle-cell anemia.

Miss Moore acted bravely until the funeral, when she fell apart and insisted that she was going to the grave with her husband. She stayed with Anita and Gladys for a few weeks, then moved in with Clarke's parents. Though sympathetic, Anita couldn't admit to being sorry to see her go. It was one less problem.

35

Gladys

O N   N O V E M B E R   2 0 ,   1 9 8 0 ,   nine months before her death, Anita jotted in her diary, "Gladys has sex urge and calls Dr. Aronson." Then, lapsing into pidgin French as she occasionally did, often (though not consistently) in moments of stress, she continued:

> J'ai peur de la condition de G. qui est feu [fou] de temps de temps. C'est un condition qui est dangereuse pour elle, pour moi, et pour cet terrible situation. J'ai peur. [I am afraid of the condition of Gladys who is mad from time to time. It is a condition that is dangerous for her and for me, and for this terrible situation. I am afraid.]

Though Anita's written French was always inexact, rarely did she commit so many schoolgirl faux pas in one short passage as here. Obviously she was writing in a state of high anxiety. What had happened?

Not since the early 1950s, when there were similar, though less drastic, comments about Gladys's behavior, had Anita had anything except praise for her dear companion. Gladys's common sense, her fortitude in times of adversity, her spirituality—these wonderful qualities were inspiring and sustaining. And yet it is clear that the "condition" that so frightened Anita on November 20 had been going on for some time—which suggests that at some point in the past Anita started censoring her own diary.

Gladys's "sex urge," according to Avis Klein (who later heard about it from Anita), was nothing very serious. Apparently Gladys was alarmed that at her age she was still strongly attracted to men, and Anita shared her concern. She consulted Dr. Aronson who brushed the matter aside as nothing important. Certainly it doesn't explain why Anita worried for her friend or why she herself felt threatened.

Her fears were spelled out in a letter dated November 21, 1980 (the day after the diary entry), written to Ruth Dubonnet. It was typed by Florence Weintraub (the Florence referred to in the text), who had replaced Avis Klein as part-time secretary. One sentence is whited out and written over, suggesting there was no opportunity for a fresh copy to be typed; obviously it was put together and mailed on the sly:

Dear Pal,

I cannot talk to you on the phone because Gladys overhears everything, but affairs here are in a frightening condition. Gladys has developed periods of being irrational: behaving and talking in a way that is disturbing to an alarming degree. She is euphoric on the subject of my health, for I am not going better— my sight and hearing have deteriorated to the point that I am incapable of carrying out the simple affairs of a daily routine, and I afraid of what could happen when I am alone with Gladys.

So please phone me frequently . . . but don't say anything alarming because Gladys chooses to believe all is going well . . . she isn't even aware of her own irrational condition.

Because Ted Peckham has more free time than most of my friends I would like him to know the true situation . . . and I would like him to phone the truth to Mary in California since I haven't been able to talk to her freely on account of Gladys. Mary should be alerted that I may have to send for her to fly to New York and take charge.

. . . I feel terribly guilty of being one more burden on your already overburdened shoulders. I don't know anyone in the world who can take your place as an angel of strength and support to helpless weaklings like us. . . . Don't tell anyone of the problems except Ted . . . My other pals have enough problems of their own, so why bother them with mine?

The letter was addressed to Gladys's worst enemy. Ruth Dubonnet had never trusted Gladys and accused her of causing a breach in her friendship with Anita during the 1950s. Ruth felt that entirely too much authority had been delegated to Gladys, a view shared by Mary Loos and Ted Peckham.

In confiding in people ill disposed to Gladys, Anita may in a funny way have been trying to shield her friend. Her "other pals" weren't to know because she didn't want to lower Gladys in their estimation. She could barely admit it to herself — putting it down in her diaries was tantamount to betrayal.

Intensely loyal, Anita blinded herself to the failings of the people closest to her heart. She glamorized them, transforming Mizner into a dashing wit, Aldous Huxley into a modern-day Tiresias. She never quite admitted that R. Beers was a perfectly dreadful husband, that Emerson was a common philanderer until proof jumped out at her from a wardrobe drawer. And now came Gladys, who wasn't the paragon Anita had created for herself and her friends.

To hold on to that image, Anita chose to believe that Gladys held no responsibility for her behavior. A personality change had taken place over which she had no control. Gladys was "euphoric" — in other words, a late-blooming manic-depressive like Mr. E. There *were* similarities, except that Gladys's mood shifts were intensified, perhaps induced by alcohol. She was "a secret drinker" — at least it was a secret from Anita; though many of her friends knew about Gladys's drinking.

"As soon as I started to work, I knew Gladys drank," says Avis Klein. "I grew up in an Irish family, so I learned quick who's having a snort early in the morning, and there's nothing to take the smell away. But it never affected Gladys until around the start of 1980, when I realized that what looked like cute tricks were actually hallucinations."

Around this time Frank Sinatra was appearing in a series of concerts at Carnegie Hall, across the street from Anita's apartment. Gladys claimed to have bumped into "Ol' Blue Eyes" and he had invited her to the opening night. And, Gladys went on, every time Sinatra entered Carnegie Hall, he looked up and waved.

Well, maybe, Klein thought; but then Gladys confided that she had recently returned from Rome, where she went horseback riding with the Pope. That was just after a trip to London, where she and Prince Charles drove through Regents Park in a carriage.

In winter 1980 Anita invited Avis to a fashion show at Halston. "In the cab, I realized she just wanted to get out of the house and talk about

Gladys," Klein says. Avis broached the problem delicately. "People can drink a lot over the years, and then all of a sudden they hit an age and it's very damaging."

Anita shook her head. "Oh, no, that's not it! Gladys doesn't drink. I've dealt with mental illness before, and there's nothing that can be done."

Klein was dumbstruck. "Here was this very sophisticated lady ready to believe Gladys was psychotic rather than admit she had a drinking problem."

"I can be devious, if I must," Anita said. "And now I feel I *must.*" She knew Gladys needed help but would never cooperate, so she had formulated a plan which was about to go into action. Arnold Weissberger would arrange for Gladys to be hospitalized or institutionalized, whichever was necessary. If she recovered, she could live in Teaneck or possibly with relatives in Tennessee. Once Gladys was gone, Anita would find a replacement, preferably a friend rather than a paid companion.

Weissberger promised Anita that Gladys would be properly cared for and then suggested that she consider moving to Los Angeles, where Mary could take care of her. Mary was willing, and Anita tentatively agreed, though the proposal unnerved her. She was too set in her ways, too old to make the adjustment easily.

She consented readily to a change in her will. Earlier, Gladys had been named sole beneficiary and executor. Under the terms of the new will, Gladys remained sole beneficiary, but the estate was placed in trust, a safeguard against Gladys tearing through her inheritance if it came to her before she was again stable. As added protection, Mary was named executor.

Before any of these changes were made, Weissberger went to Acapulco for a winter holiday, and three days after his return to New York, he died from an embolism in the lungs. Losing him was a double blow for Anita: she lost both a dear friend and the only person she trusted to manage this unpleasant business with compassion for all involved.

There were periods when Gladys seemed her old self, but ugly incidents continued to occur. Ruth Dubonnet says she saw Gladys shove Anita into a bentwood rocker with such force that her head hit the back of the frame with a resounding thud. And she had lost a dramatic amount of weight. Was Gladys feeding her properly? She was spending more and more hours in bed. Was her medication correctly administered?

Stanley Simmons, among others, doesn't believe Gladys was ever intentionally cruel. "It was the sad result of a seventy-year-old woman, incapacitated herself, trying to take care of a woman in her nineties."

The diary entries for 1980 show signs of diminishing vitality. Anita's handwriting, formerly bold and easily legible, becomes faint and cramped; spelling errors become more frequent; names of even close friends elude her and are left blank. Sometimes there is only a single entry: "I feel dizzy" . . . "Utterly confused."

Many of the final diary entries concern a new will, which was signed on July 2, 1981. It was drawn up by Jay Harris, Arnold Weissberger's partner, and its terms were not so different from what is known about those of earlier wills. Everything went to Gladys outright, no trust. Gladys and Mary were named joint executors. The will was witnessed by two of Gladys's friends. Anita's signature is easily legible—significant in the light of later developments.

By July Anita was in such poor health that, after many arguments, Gladys agreed to make an appointment for her to see Dr. Aronson. A day later Avis Klein dropped by unexpectedly, and Anita suggested they take a walk in Central Park. Outside, she asked Avis to take her to Aronson immediately.

Aronson found nothing seriously wrong, but advised that if she continued to feel unwell, she check into the hospital for a thorough checkup. Avis suggested that a nurse might come in to look after Anita in her apartment, and Aronson found someone ready to start work later that week.

Leaving Aronson's office, Anita became agitated. Gladys, she fretted, would be beside herself with worry over her prolonged absence. Gladys lived up to her worst expectations. "She was a madwoman," Klein says. "I was so alarmed that I *insisted,* not asked, that Anita treat me to dinner at the Russian Tea Room."

Getting Anita to the restaurant drained Avis of her resourcefulness. Anita was too dazed to offer help, so Klein called Stanley Simmons, who lived a few blocks away, asking him to join them immediately. Simmons suggested they call Mary and ask her to take charge. She was, after all, Anita's only kin. The call was placed from the apartment of Earle McGrath (Fred Coe's assistant on the aborted *King's Mare*), who then lived in the same building as Anita. Though on the tag end of a novel and arranging corrective surgery for her son, Mary said she'd leave for New York the next day.

Avis and Stanley then took Anita to her apartment. Avis volunteered to spend the night. "That's not necessary," Anita said. "Gladys will take care of me." And by then Gladys had calmed down.

Though forewarned, Mary was not prepared for what she saw on her arrival. Anita weighed no more than seventy-five pounds. And Gladys, unkempt and wearing a soiled house dress, suddenly fell to the floor, shouted, rolled about, tore at her clothes. Mary was convinced she was having an alcoholic seizure.

It was not the first. Ruth Dubonnet had witnessed others, and Anita herself related how Gladys had once passed out in the bathtub and might have drowned if Anita hadn't gathered the strength to pull her out.

Mary stayed with her friend Claire Trevor at Trevor's apartment in the Hotel Pierre. Anita went there for lunch the day after Mary's arrival and "ate as though she had never seen food before," says Mary.

Dr. Aronson told Mary he thought Anita should enter Doctors Hospital for tests, though he implied that Anita was deteriorating physically, as people far younger than she naturally do, and nothing was going to delay the inevitable for very long.

On their way to the hospital on July 28, Mary and Anita stopped at Claire Trevor's, where by prearrangement Jay Harris was waiting with a revised will. The major difference between this will and the one signed on July 2 was that Gladys received her inheritance in trust, the income to be paid in quarterly installments. Should Gladys die before Anita, the estate was to go outright to Mary and her son, Edward, in equal shares. Mary was appointed executor; Jay Harris was named trustee. Anita's signature—witnessed by Trevor, Avis Klein, and Trevor's friend Mary Jane Connell—is so feeble it is barely visible on the photostat copy filed with the New York Surrogate Court.

Gladys refused to visit the hospital, not while Mary was around, which of course wounded Anita far more than it disturbed Mary. Other friends came, including Ray Corsini bearing flowers and glad tidings from abroad. Gallimard in Paris wanted to reprint the French editions of *Blondes* and *Brunettes,* and Pan, the leading paperback publisher in England, offered to renew its license for both books.

It didn't mean much money, but that her books were still in demand cheered Anita. She was so alert, in such high spirits, that Mrs. Corsini was sure she was going to pull out of this decline. But as she was leaving, Anita said, "Please keep in touch with Gladys"—not tomorrow or next week, but when the time came when she was no longer around to look after her beloved companion.

B A C K at home, Anita spent most of the day reclining on the living-room couch, but she was eager to get back to work. Some time before, Ed Kennebeck, an editor at Viking, had suggested she do another book about

Lorelei, bringing the Little Rock siren's story up to date. Anita liked the idea—through the years she had written several short pieces about Lorelei's progress, and they were always well received—but she had never gotten around to it. Now she decided to go ahead.

Ray Corsini feared she would drive herself too hard and might not be able to sustain a whole new book. Corsini proposed as an alternative a collection of the many magazine articles Anita had written during her seven decades as a professional writer. (In terms of creative longevity, she is in a class with Bernard Shaw, P. G. Wodehouse, and only a few others.) Anita liked the proposal; she said she'd check through her files and send Avis to the library to see what she could find.

Though she was physically fragile, Anita's mind remained strong—the confusion and disorientation she had experienced earlier in the year had vanished. An art gallery had put together a show, "Anita Loos and Her Friends," a hodgepodge of sketches and paintings of people she had bumped elbows with during her long life. It was a bit of a fraud—some of her "friends," she laughed, were about as familiar to her as Jack the Ripper—but definitely she would be at the opening, even if Gladys had to take her in a wheelchair.

But on August 17, three days before the opening, the event was jeopardized when the building housing the art gallery, the once-grand Biltmore Hotel, was suddenly, unexpectedly, struck by the wrecker's ball. A good portion of the hotel, so steeped in 1920s lore, was demolished before anyone could complain about, let alone halt, the disappearance of another New York landmark. But the gallery was as yet unscathed. The owners said the show would go on, and Anita was ready to walk or ride over the debris to get there.

But after lunch that day, Anita got up from her couch bed, took a few steps, and fell over. Gladys called for assistance, and Anita was taken by ambulance to Roosevelt Hospital on West Fifty-ninth Street. She had suffered a heart attack.

The next day, August 18, 1981, Dr. Aronson moved her to Doctors Hospital, where he felt she would be more comfortable. Her condition was serious but stable. Mary called her from California to say she had finished her book and was dedicating it to her. Anita was pleased and they chatted normally, Mary recalls, as they did every week. So Mary was surprised when, a few hours later, Ruth Dubonnet called to say Anita had died not long before.

Epilogue

A NITA'S friends heard of her death by early evening, just before the TV news shows broadcast the first obituaries. Later that summer there was a memorial service, arranged by Morty Gottlieb, at Mary Loos's request.

Gottlieb opened the ceremony by recalling something Anita had said when the two of them were in charge of a similar service for Sandor Incze: "Sandor was so funny—let's remember him that way." Morty felt that Anita would want her tribute to be joyful, too.

Other speakers included Ruth Gordon, Joshua Logan, Lillian Gish, Leo Lerman, Mary Loos, and Helen Hayes, who closed by saying, "I do hope heaven is chic; otherwise Anita isn't going to be happy there."

Mary Loos had planned to stay on in New York to sort out the estate, but Gladys was so hostile that she decided to return to California. In her will Anita had requested that Gladys be permitted to remain in the Fifty-seventh Street apartment until the lease expired almost a year later. Until then, or at least until the will was probated, Mary expected no cooperation.

As was to be anticipated, Gladys was incensed when she learned that the July 2 will had been superseded by a later one, less favorable to her, drawn up and signed under circumstances she considered conspiratorial. Anita had promised that her inheritance would come to her outright; and only troublemakers, taking advantage of Anita's feebleness, could have persuaded her to break that promise. In September 1981 Gladys filed a petition asking that the July 28 will be overthrown in favor of the one signed three weeks earlier.

Mary eventually decided to settle out of court. She did so for three reasons. New York gossip columns were printing items about the battle, and she felt Anita would have been distressed about such unsavory publicity. She also had been advised that New York judges had a record of favoring blacks over whites in such cases. Finally, the legal fees entailed threatened to eat up what was a modest estate, under $125,000.

A compromise agreement, worked out by Mary's and Gladys's lawyers, divided the estate into "two equal shares . . . Trust A and Trust B." From Trust B Gladys was to receive $25,000 once the document was approved by the court. She was also permitted to draw on Trust A, as long as the withdrawals were approved by Jay Harris, the trustee, and never exceeded $7,500 in any one year. On her death, what remained of the estate would go to Mary and her son.

Gladys stayed on in the apartment until the late spring of 1982. Then she moved to Teaneck, where she still lives. Friends say she has given up drink, and on the phone she sounds fine, though she doesn't want to talk about Anita. Someday soon, she says, but not just yet.

FATE KEEPS ON HAPPENING, the collection of articles Anita only had started to assemble at the time of her death, was completed by Ray Corsini and published in America and England in 1984. In one of the late pieces in the volume, "On Growing Old Disgracefully" (first published in *Vogue* in 1978), Anita writes: "All that anybody really needs to learn are two short words: Behave Yourself. And life can be as sweet as pie, if you just don't allow it to upset your stomach. Any questions?"

Yes: How do you avoid the bellyache? Anita answers this earlier in the article, when she reveals what was disgraceful about her old age:

> You might feel that, at my age, I should look at life with more gravity. After all, I've been privileged to listen, firsthand, to some of the most profound thinkers of my day: Aldous and Julian Huxley, H. G. Wells, Bertrand Russell, Arnold Bennett and H. L. Mencken, who were beset by gloom over the condition the world had gotten into. Then why can't I view it with anything but amusement?

In *Blondes* Dorothy Shaw comments, "Fun is fun, but no girl wants to go on laughing all the time." British poet William Empson paraphased Dorothy's quip in a poem, "Reflections from Anita Loos," the final line of each stanza ending by saying "A girl can't go on laughing all the time." Anita was flattered, but the poem was just a bit pretentious, a little menacing. Prolonged study of Empson's reflections, she feared, might turn her into "a weeper."

That never happened.

In one diary, Anita jotted down and marked with double asterisks and underlined a maxim by La Bruyère, the seventeenth century moralist and satirist: "You must *learn to laugh* before you are happy for fear of dying without having laughed at all." (The italics, and presumably the translation, are Anita's.) In telling of her life, Anita rather implied that "a star danced" at her birth, and like Beatrice in *Much Ado About Nothing,* she had been blessed at that moment with the gift of laughter. More likely, as the La Bruyère quote suggests, it was a lesson hard-learned. But once mastered, it sustained her over a very long life. It was a message she passed along both in the way she presented herself to the world and through the wit and double-edged sophistication of her writing.

Index

Abbott, George, 222, 225
Actors Equity, 82–3, 122
Adair, Yvonne, 227
Adams, Diana, 284
Adams, Maude, 56
After Many a Summer Dies the Swan,
    192
Akins, Zoe, 64
Alcazar Stock Company, 12
Alexander, Cris, 268, 283, 284–5
Algonquin Hotel, 38, 64
Algonquin Round Table, 65
Alice-Sit-by-the-Fire, 209
Allen, W. H., 297
Alstone, Fred, 218, 269
Amazing Adele, The, 245, 247, 248–50,
    252, 268
Ambassador Hotel, 65
American Academy of Dramatic Arts,
    49
American Tragedy, An, 95
Ami-Ami, 245
Anastasia, 254–5
Anderson, Judith, 197
Anderson, Maxwell, 273
Anderson, Sherwood, 77, 78, 79, 87
Anne of Cleves, 273–4
Annie Get Your Gun, 209, 213, 216
Another Part of the Forest, 216
Anouilh, Jean, 256
Armstrong, Paul, 126
Arno, Peter, 205, 248, 290
Aronson, Shephard, 301–2, 307, 308,
    311, 312, 313

Arthur, Jean, 248
Asquith, Anthony (Puffin), 106
Asquith, Margot, 106
Astaire, Adele, 85, 152, 193, 194, 196,
    233, 277
    dancing of, 107–8
Astaire, Fred, 107–8, 152
Atkinson, Brooks, 215–16
Auden, W. H., 277
Austen, Jane, 27
Autobiography of Alice B. Toklas, The,
    279
Avedon, Richard, 232

Babes in Arms, 181
Bachardy, Don, 277
Bache, Julian, 235, 266
Baker, Josephine, 86, 218
Balanchine, George, 284–5, 290
Balenciaga, 284
Ballet Theatre, 223
Balmain, 234
Balzac, Honoré de, 99
Band Wagon, The, 152
Bankhead, Tallulah, 107, 111, 159, 225,
    257, 283, 290
    character of, 64–5
Bara, Theda, 46
Barbarian, The, 158
Barillet, Pierre, 245, 281
Barrie, Sir James, 109, 209
Barrymore, Diana, 266
Barrymore, Ethel, 64, 130, 203, 204, 205
Barrymore, John, 153

Barrymore, Lionel, 203
Barton, Ralph, 95, 101, 227
Bates, Blanche, 12
Bautzer, Greg, 235
Beaton, Cecil, 3, 215, 242
  in California, 135-8, 196
  in London, 134, 298
  Loos's correspondence with, 139, 193, 194
  in New York, 215, 277, 284
Beerbohm, Max, 77, 105
Behrman, S. N., 158, 174
Belasco, David, 12
Bemelmans, Ludwig, 252
Bennett, Arnold, 106, 315
Berenson, Bernard, 105
Berg, Phil, 171, 174
Bergen, Edgar, 178
Bergman, Ingrid, 192, 216
Berkeley, Busby, 250
Berlin, Ellin, 122
Berlin, Irving, 61, 64, 122, 136, 209
Bern, Paul, 147, 156
"Bernice Bobs Her Hair," 232
Bernstein, Leonard, 223
Better Things in Life, The, 141, 269
Biltmore Hotel, 313
Biograph Company, 21, 22, 23, 28-9, 31, 32
Biography, 158
Birth of a Nation, 23, 31, 32-3, 35, 39
Black Pirate, The, 50
Blaine, Vivian, 226
Blair, Janet, 226
Blake, William, 189
Blane, Ralph, 290, 291
Blithe Spirit, 299
Blondell, Joan, 221
Bloomer Girl, 225
Blossoms in the Dust, 195
Blue Lounge, 207; *see also*
  Happy Birthday
Blum, Daniel, 266
Blythe, Betty, 84
Bogart, Humphrey, 159
Bolm, Adolph, 66

Bonfils, Helen, 274
Boothe, Clare, 184
Bordoni, Irene, 177
Born Yesterday, 216, 272
Boston Transcript, 95-8
Bow, Clara, 138, 181, 197, 270
Boyd, Ernest, 87
Brecht, Bertolt, 160, 280
Brice, Fanny, 175, 181
Bristol Old Vic, 274
Brooks, Louise, 296
Brown, Josephine, 241
Brown, Vanessa, 237
Brush, Katharine, 147
Bryan, Dora, 231
Brynner, Yul, 220
Buchholz, Horst, 258, 259, 260-1
Buchholz, Myriam, 259
Burke, Billie, 53, 198
Burns, George, 274
Burton, Richard, 256
But Gentlemen Marry Brunettes, 65, 66, 87, 105, 116-17, 118, 139, 312
  narrative style of, 116, 279, 296
Butterworth, Julie, 244, 254

Cabanne, Christy, 32
Cactus Flower, 245
Caesar and Cleopatra, 232
Cagney (Loos's dog), 150, 205, 217
Cagney, James, 150
Campbell, Stella (Mrs. Patrick), 181
Candide, 99
Cannery Row, 161
Canolle, Jean, 272-3, 281
Capote, Truman, 283
  masked ball given by, 284
Carnaval de Venise, 80
Caron, Leslie, 242
Carousel, 208
Cartland, Barbara, 298
Caruso, Enrico, 105
Case, Frank, 38
Castle, Irene, 76
Cast of Thousands, A, 301, 302, 303
Cavendish, Charles, Lord, 233

Chaney, Lon, 198
Channing, Carol, 245, 247, 248, 256
  King's Mare and, 273, 274, 277, 278,
    280
  as Lorelei Lee, 227-32, 297
Chaplin, Charles, 42, 153, 186-9, 296
Charleston, 86, 107-8, 181
Charlot's Revue, 107
Chekhov, Anton, 273
Chéri (Colette) (novel), 257
Chéri (Loos) (play), 257-61
Cherries Are Ripe, 139, 140
Cheruit, 109
Chevalier, Maurice, 221, 242
Chiang Kai-shek, Madame, 198
Christian Science, 101, 170
Churchill, Clementine and Sir Winston,
  246-7
Cineograph, 16, 21
Citizen Kane, 95
Clair, Bronja, 196
Clair, René, 196
Claire, Ina, 136, 158
Clansman, The, 32-3
Clark, Nathan Gibson (Gibbie), 65-6
Clarke, Jerome, 305, 306
Clarke, Mae, 88
Coca, Imogene, 303
Coe, Fred, 273
  King's Mare and, 273, 274-5, 276-7,
    278, 280, 311
Coe, Peter, 281
Coe, Richard, 259-60
Cohan, George M., 53, 83
Cohn, Harry, 235
Colbert, Claudette, 266
Colefax, Sybil, Lady, 105-6, 134
Colette, Sidonie-Gabrielle, 39, 239, 261
  Anita Loos compared with, 234
  Chéri novels by, 257, 258, 260, 261
  Gigi adaptation and, 234, 237, 239
Collier, Constance, 159-60, 181, 236,
  240, 241
Colt, Alvin, 247
Comden, Betty, 297
Connell, Mary Jane, 312

Conspiracy, The, 49
Conway, Jack, 148, 158-9, 170
Cooper, Diana, Lady, 298
Cooper, Gary, 171, 173, 174
Corn Is Green, The, 203
Corsaro, Frank, 291
Corsini, Ray Pierre, 269, 277-8, 302,
  306, 312
  as Loos's agent, 291-2, 295, 303, 313,
    315
Cosmopolitan, 141, 269
Couéism, 44, 243
Covarrubias, Miguel and Rosa, 78
Coward, Noel, 105, 106, 196, 225, 226,
  281, 299
Cowboy and the Lady, The, 171-2, 174
Crawford, Joan, 196, 215
  film career of, 147, 150, 181, 185,
    186, 192, 194, 198
Creeland, James Ashmore, 77-8
Crowninshield, Frank, 39, 78, 94, 102,
  108
Cukor, George, 158, 169, 192, 287
  casting ideas of, 194, 196, 236, 261
  as host, 159-60, 217
  projects rejected by, 197, 236, 239
  Women directed by, 183-6
Cunard, Emerald, 3
Curtis, Tony, 261
Cyrano de Bergerac, 40

Daily Word, 243, 244, 258, 302
Daisy, 252-3, 254, 255, 256,
  258, 266
Dandridge, Dorothy, 218
Daniels, Bebe, 175
Darling-Darling, 245
Davenport, Marcia, 203
David Copperfield, 160
Davies, Marion, 55-7, 85, 137, 175,
  186-7, 231
  impishness of, 56-7, 137, 138
Davis, Bette, 150
Davis, Mae, 88
Déclassée, 64
Deep Purple, The, 126

Del Rio, Dolores, 135
Del Ruth, Roy, 198
Del Santo, Marcel, 147, 148
Devoe, Dorothy, 270
de Wolfe (Mendl), Elsie, 79-80, 123,
    252, 258
Diary of a Chambermaid, 208
Dietrich, Marlene, 258
Dietz, Howard, 218, 269, 275
Dill, Max W., 104
Doll's House, A, 12
Don d'Adèle, Le, 245
Doro, Marie, 81
Doubleday, 233
Dougherty, T. E., 28-9
Douglass, Kingman, 277
Dramatic Event, 11, 16
Dramatic School, 181
Dreiser, Theodore, 87, 99
Dubonnet, Ruth Obré Goldbeck
    de Vallambrosa, 176, 245
  on Emerson, 110, 129-30
  Loos's correspondence with, 159,
    165-8, 194, 196, 308-9
  Loos's travels with, 130, 244
  in New York, 135, 247, 283, 302
  in Paris, 108-9, 233, 234
  Styne and, 228-9
  on Tipton, 309, 310, 312
Duchin, Eddy, 182, 287
Duchin, Peter, 182, 305
Duncan, Isadora, 136
Duse, Eleanora, 35
Dwan, Allan, 55, 56

East Lynne, 12
Eastman, Max, 41
Ecole des cocottes, L', 277, 280
Eddy, Nelson, 165, 197, 198
Edwards, Florence (Eddy), 245, 247,
    265
Eisenstein, Sergei, 160
El Cholo, 136
Eliot, T. S., 95
Emerson, John (Mr. E) (Clifton Paden)
  background of, 49

Blondes dedicated to, 102
  Broadway career of, 49, 84-5, 90-1,
    139
  correspondence of, 243-5
  death of, 253-4
  divorce of, 173, 178, 199, 206
  Dubonnet on, 129-30
  Fairbanks-Pickford affair and, 47-8
  as film director, 32, 34, 43-4, 48-9,
    50, 55, 57, 67-8, 73
  finances managed by, 52, 88, 138-9,
    173
  Goldwyn and, 171, 172
  health of, 55, 67, 68, 104-5, 106-7,
    110, 119, 120-1, 129, 130, 147,
    253
  infidelities of, 77-8, 85, 140, 152, 153,
    282, 309
  jealousy of, 135, 138
  at Las Encinas, 172-3, 178, 182, 209,
    210, 217, 244
  marriage of, 68-70, 74, 140, 150-2,
    200-1
  Mencken vs., 87
  mental illness of, 172-3, 178, 182,
    210, 230, 309
  M-G-M and, 141, 152-3, 158-9, 164,
    165, 168, 169
  Mizner and, 153-4
  political activities of, 82-3
  screenplays by, 67, 82, 152, 158
  social ambitions of, 122, 128
  on stock market crash, 134
  as traveler, 75, 81, 107, 108, 117,
    119-21, 122-3, 130, 133, 139
Empire, 19, 21
Empson, William, 316
End of Chéri, The, 257
Etna Weekly Post, 7
Evans, Dame Edith, 298

Fairbanks, Beth, 46, 47, 85
Fairbanks, Douglas, 32, 73, 83, 85, 106
  Loos's scripts for, 43-6, 48-9, 50, 53,
    55, 56
  Pickford and, 46-8, 89, 101

popularity of, 42, 46, 270
Fairbanks, Douglas, Jr., 298
Fall of Eve, The, 90, 91, 92
Famous Players-Lasky, 46, 52, 53, 54, 55
Fancy Free, 223
Fate Keeps on Happening, 187–9, 315
Faulkner, William, 95, 98
Feldman, Charles, 236
Felix Krull, 258
Fellows, Dorothy Gordon (Dickie), 81, 107, 135, 181, 196, 282
Feuchtwanger, Lion, 160
Fields, Fritz, 16, 17
Fields, Joseph, 224–5
Fields, W. C., 173
Fifty Million Frenchmen, 177
Fine Arts-Triangle Productions, 31, 32, 49
    Fairbanks and, 43–6
Fiske, Minne Maddern, 49
Fitch, Clyde, 49
Fitzgerald, F. Scott, 145, 150, 184, 219, 225, 232
    Redheaded Woman and, 147–8
Fitzgerald, Zelda, 148
Fitzmaurice, George, 75
Flagg, James Montgomery, 64
Flanner, Janet, 284
Flaubert, Gustave, 106
Fleming, Victor, 73
Flying Blonde, The, 201
Folies-Bergère, 67, 228
Follow the Girls, 226
"For Me and My Gal," 177
Fortune Teller, The, 13
Fortuny, 250, 251
Forty Carats, 245
Foundling, The, 48
Four Horsemen of the Apocalypse, The, 80
Fowler, Gene, 128
Foyles, 298
Francis, Kay, 173
Franklin, Sidney, 67–8

Frankovich, Mike, 287
Freed, Arthur, 181
Freud, Sigmund, 94, 98
Frohman, Charles, 48
Fryer, Robert, 300

Gable, Clark, 73, 162, 289
    MacDonald and, 164–5
    roles for, 156, 157, 164, 169, 179, 182–3, 201, 203
    temperament of, 164–5, 196–7
Gabor, Jolie, 266
Gallimard, 312
Galsworthy, John, 106
Gam, Rita, 237
Garbo, Greta, 150, 160, 177, 192, 261, 289
Garland, Judy, 181, 287
Garson, Greer, 194–5
Gentlemen Prefer Blondes (film), 231
Gentlemen Prefer Blondes (musical), 104, 298
    backers' auditions for, 228
    planning of, 222–7
    productions of, 227–31, 276
Gentlemen Prefer Blondes (novel)
    admirers of, 213, 247, 295
    comedic themes of, 98–100
    critical response to, 95–8, 100, 108, 148
    Dorothy in, 66, 316
    Emerson and, 102
    French edition of, 312
    Mencken and, 88, 93, 94, 95, 98, 101–2
    plot of, 3, 92–3
    publication of, 92–3, 94, 95, 102, 103
    sequel to, *see But Gentlemen Marry Brunettes*
    sources for, 66, 67, 88, 100–1
Gentlemen Prefer Blondes (play), 86, 104, 110–11, 192, 207
George, Gladys, 170–1
Gershwin, George, 173
Getting Mary Married, 56–7
Gibson, Dana, 64

Gielgud, John, 105
Gigi (Colette) (novel), 234
Gigi (film), 242, 297
Gigi (Loos) (play), 234, 235–42
Gigi (musical), 297
Gilbert, John, 136
Girl from Missouri, The, 158
Girl Like I, A, 27, 281, 283–4, 289, 291, 297
Gish, Dorothy, 28, 32, 35, 282, 290
Gish, Lillian, 35, 101
  in films, 32, 37, 270
  later years of, 249, 282, 314
  popularity of, 36, 50
Glas, Emile, 120–1, 130
Glass Menagerie, The, 253, 262
Glaum, Louise, 46
Goddard, Paulette, 186–9, 202, 208, 232, 283, 302
  Loos's collaboration with, 295–7
  Loos's travels with, 237, 238, 240–1
Goetz, F. Ray, 177–8, 197, 199, 217
Gogo, I Love You, 280
Goldbeck, Ruth, see Dubonnet, Ruth Obré Goldbeck de Vallambrosa
Goldbeck, Walter, 109
Goldwyn, Samuel, 171–2, 173, 174, 176
Goldwyn Follies, The, 173
Gone With the Wind, 179, 183, 185
Good Earth, The, 164
Goodman, Ruth, 98
Gordon, Max, 272
Gordon, Ruth, 90–2, 215, 245, 249, 314
Gordon, Stanley, 283, 284
Gottlieb, Morton
  Loos's friendship with, 266, 268, 290, 306, 314
  as producer, 236–7, 241, 245, 250, 273, 274
Goudeket, Maurice, 239, 261
Goya, Francisco de, 137, 266
Gramercy Park, 85
Grand e La Pace, 245–6, 282
Gray, Timothy, 299–300, 303
Great Canadian, The, 179, 182–3
Great Ziegfeld, The, 165

Grédy, Jean-Pierre, 245
Green, Adolph, 297
Gregory, James, 290, 291
Griffith, D. W., 23–5, 28–9, 106
  at Fine Arts-Triangle, 30–1, 41–2, 43–4
  Intolerance and, 31, 37, 38–9
  last film of, 141
Grimes, Tammy, 248–9, 250–1
Grosset and Dunlap, 301
Guerlain, 276
Guilbert, Yvette, 134
Guinzburg, Harold, 278
Guinzburg, Tom, 278, 291

Hagman, Larry, 266
Haight, George, 203
Hall, Peter, 242
Halston, 284, 309
Hamilton, Edith, 100
Hamilton, Hamish, 289
Hamlisch, Marvin, 303
Hammerstein, Dorothy, 209
Hammerstein, Oscar, 208, 209, 213, 215, 218, 228, 262
Hampden, Walter, 40
Handl, Irene, 298
Happy Birthday, 217, 221, 224, 258
  film version of, 235
  musical version of, 256, 271–2, 290, 298–300, 303
  planning of, 208, 209, 210
  production of, 213–16
Harcourt Brace Jovanovich, 292, 295, 296–7
Harding, Ann, 158
Harlem, 86
Harlow, Jean, 147, 150, 156–7, 158, 161–2, 169, 289
  death of, 170–1
Harper's Bazaar, 92, 94, 95, 102, 103, 105, 111
Harriet, 208
Harriman, Averell, 215
Harriman, Marie, 182, 215
Harris, Jay, 311, 312, 315

Harris, Julie, 232
Harrison, Rex, 291
Harron, Robert, 32, 35
Hart, Lorenz, 181, 196, 225
Hayes, Helen, 287
    Daisy written for, 252–6, 258
    in *Happy Birthday*, 208, 209, 213,
        214, 215–16
    Loos's collaboration with, 292–5
    Loos's friendship with, 207, 265–6,
        283, 290, 314
Hearst, William Randolph, 55, 56–7,
    137
Held, John, 61
Hellman, Lillian, 216
Hello, Dolly!, 278
Hemingway, Ernest, 95, 253
Henry VIII, King of England, 273
Hepburn, Audrey, 237–8, 240, 241, 242,
    244, 248
Hepburn, Katharine, 160, 192, 204, 217
Herald Tribune, 119, 261
Herbert, Victor, 13
Hergesheimer, Joseph, 87, 100, 122
High Button Shoes, 224
High Spirits, 299
His Picture in the Papers, 44, 84
Hitler, Adolf, 121, 202
Hit-the-Trail Holiday, 53
Hofmannsthal, Hugo von, 257
Holden, William, 283
Hold Your Man, 156–7
Hollerith, Charles, 248, 290
Holliday, Judy, 235, 271–2, 290, 298,
    300, 303
Holloway, Sterling, 126–8
Hollywood, 135–6, 159–61, 287
Hollywood Hotel, 32, 41, 65
Hollywood Nobody Knows, The, 303,
    304
Hopkins, Arthur, 203, 204, 205, 207
Hopkins, Robert (Hoppy), 162–4, 165,
    170, 171, 179, 183, 200, 201
Hornblow, Arthur, 162
Horne, Lena, 86, 218
Hotel Del Coronado, 19, 20, 25–6

House of Mirth, The, 108
Howard, Frances, 171
Howard, John, 164
Howland, Jobyna, 64
Hubble, Edwin, 160–1, 217
Huff, Louise, 54, 55
Huxley, Aldous, 98, 189–92, 194, 199,
    217, 254, 309, 315
Huxley, Julian, 189, 315
Huxley, Laura Archera, 254
Huxley, Maria, 189–92, 194, 199, 217,
    254
Huxley, Matthew, 189
Hyman, Bernard, 164, 165, 169, 170–1,
    174, 179, 182–3

Iceman Cometh, The, 216
"I Don't Want to Walk Without You,"
    224
Iles, Margaret, 18, 20, 21
I Married an Angel (film), 197–8
I Married an Angel (musical), 196
Ince, Thomas, 31
In Colorado, 21
Incze, Sandor, 236, 237, 314
Ingraham, Lloyd, 32
In Our Time, 95
Intolerance, 28, 31, 33, 35, 42, 76, 93
    actors in, 36, 37, 57
    opening of, 37, 38–39
Irène-Dana, 109
Irma la Douce, 280
Isherwood, Christopher, 192, 217, 254,
    277, 284

Jack Dunstan's Cafe, 124–6
Jacqueline, 218–19, 268
Jeffers, Robinson, 95
Jelliffe, Alfred, 104–5, 120
Joan of Lorraine, 216
Johns, Glynis, 281–2
Johnson, Charlie, 30
Johnson, Nunnally, 275
Johnson, Rita, 170
Johnson, Samuel, 215
Josephine, Empress of France, 230

Joyce, James, 98
Judith of Bethulia, 28, 29
Jument du roi, La, 272–3
Junior Miss, 224

Kanin, Garson, 215, 245
Keaton, Buster, 60
Keaton, Natalie Talmadge, 60, 68
Kelly, Emmett, 244
Kelly, Grace, 237
Kelly, Mark, 154–5
Kennebeck, Ed, 312–13
Kern, Jerome, 104, 209
Kerr, Walter, 261
King's Mare, The, 273–4, 276–7, 278, 280, 281–2, 290, 311
Kinsey Report, 233
Kirkland, David, 68, 73
Kiss Hollywood Good-by, 105, 292, 297, 304
Kiss Me, Kate, 225
Klein, Avis, 304, 305, 306, 308, 309–10, 311, 312, 313
Knight, Arthur, 283
Knopf, Edwin, 203–4
Kolb, C. William, 104

La Bruyère, Jean de, 316
Lady, Be Good!, 107
Lady Audley's Secret, 21
Lamb, The, 42
Lane, Kenneth, 284
Lanvin, 75–7, 109
La Pace, 245–6, 282
Lardner, Ring, 148
Las Encinas Sanatorium, 172–3
Lasky, Jesse, 100
Laugh and Live, 46–7
Laughton, Charles, 273
Lawford, Patricia Kennedy, 272, 277
Lawford, Peter, 272
Lawrence, Gertrude, 107, 192
Lederer, Charles, 137, 138, 231
Lederer, Francis, 287
Leigh, Vivien, 261
Leighton, Margaret, 274, 281

Le Jardin de ma soeur, 80–1
Lelong, Lucien, 226
Lend an Ear!, 227
Lerman, Leo, 266, 314
Lerner, Alan Jay, 242, 297
LeRoy, Mervyn, 175, 181
Les Seizes, 268, 280
Let's Get a Divorce, 53, 54
Léveillée, Claude, 269, 280
Levin, Herman, 223–31
Lewin, Albert, 169, 170, 172, 199
Lewis, Robert, 257, 258, 259, 261
Lewis, Sinclair, 87
Life of Christ, The, 16
Lillie, Beatrice, 107
Lindsay, Vachel, 35–6, 37, 40–1, 68–70
Little Caesar, 147
Liveright, 95, 102, 104, 105, 111
Loew, Marcus, 61
Logan, Joshua, 213–15, 218, 228, 261, 314
Lola (fortune-teller), 203
Lombard, Carol, 248
London, Jack, 11–12
Long Day's Journey into Night, 5, 294
Look Homeward, Angel, 258
Loos, (Corinne) Anita
    as actress, 12–13, 16, 19, 20, 29
    black culture admired by, 86
    childhood of, 9–10, 12–17, 19–20
    death of, 313–14
    diaries of, 258, 307
    divorce planned by, 173, 178, 199, 206
    enforced retirement of, 103, 105, 121, 130–1
    Fairbanks vehicles written by, 43–6, 48–9, 50, 53
    families as seen by, 99, 268
    fashion and, 28, 39–40, 75–7, 109, 234, 309
    finances of, 52, 88, 102, 173, 267, 269, 276, 278, 288, 289, 291–2, 296, 297, 303–4

health of, 117–18, 120–1, 122, 130,
151, 245, 246, 254, 255, 291,
301–2, 304, 308, 310–12, 313
love as seen by, 98, 207
marriages of, 30, 49–50, 68–70, 74,
85, 91–2, 104–5, 140, 150–2, 178–9,
200–1, 219
politics of, 82
professionalism of, 150, 304
publicity for, 50, 77, 106, 232, 283–4,
297–8
religious faith of, 243–4, 268
residences of, 39, 41, 64, 65, 74–5,
85, 139–40, 159, 170, 175–6, 202,
217, 232, 247, 267
romances of, 176, 178, 205–6, 221
screenwriting of, 43, 48–9, 53–4, 56,
150, 161, 204
self-assessment of, 84
size of, 17, 19, 26, 228, 266
suitors of, 26, 30, 40–1, 68
as traveler, 67, 75–81, 105–10, 117–21,
122–3, 130, 133, 139, 233–4, 255–6,
275–7, 281–2, 303
war efforts of, 201–2
will of, 310, 311, 312, 314–15
on women's rights, 73–4
work methods of, 48–9, 219, 279–80
Loos, Anita Johnson (sister-in-law),
30
Loos, (Harry) Clifford (brother), 7–8,
135, 136, 182, 229, 254, 278
Anita Loos's vacation with, 197
death of, 269
as doctor, 29–30, 269
education of, 16, 17
Emerson and, 150, 172–3, 206
health of, 170
marriage of, 30, 41, 135, 287
Loos, Gladys (sister), 10, 12, 15,
268
Loos, Mary Anita (niece), 41, 135, 195,
201, 254
Anita Loos's relationship with, 286–7,
313
on Emerson, 153, 206

as executor of Anita Loos's will, 310,
311, 314, 315
marriage of, 216, 269, 286
Santa Monica house and, 175,
217, 278
on Tipton, 309, 310, 311–12
Loos, Minerva (Minnie) Smith
(mother), 25, 41, 135, 151, 197
as chaperone, 28, 29, 30, 32, 38
children of, 7–8, 9, 10
death of, 173–4
father's legacy to, 16
marriage of, 5–7, 8, 10, 13–15, 85, 89,
140
Loos, R. Beers (father), 116, 123, 135,
150, 170, 309
Anita Loos's career and, 12–13, 20, 21
death of, 207
extramarital affairs of, 13–15, 85
in Hollywood, 41
later years of, 174
marriage of, 5, 7, 30, 89, 140
mother of, 25
in newspaper business, 7–9, 10–11, 25
theater and, 7, 11, 12–13, 16, 18–19,
21
Lopez, Vincent, 219
Lorelei, 297
Lorraine, Lillian, 48, 100–1
Losch, Tilly, 152, 196
Loudon, Dorothy, 300
Love from Judy, 299
Lowe, Charles, 256, 277, 278, 297
Lubin Company, 23
Lubitsch, Ernst, 158, 287
Lute Song, 220
Lyceum, 19, 21
Lyon, Ben, 175

MacArthur, Charles, 207–8, 252–3,
254
Macbeth (film), 33–5, 159
Macbeth (Shakespeare), 33, 34, 255
MacDonald, Jeanette, 164–5, 197, 198
MacLaine, Shirley, 298–9
Macmillan, 278, 292

Madame Curie, 192
Mainbocher, 109, 215
Make a Wish!, 299
Mama Steps Out, 169
Mamoulian, Rouben, 207, 208, 209–10, 213, 217, 218, 287
Maney, Richard, 227, 242
Mankiewicz, Herman J., 95
Mann, Thomas, 160
Mannix, Eddie, 174, 201, 203
Man of the Hour, The, 44
Marbury, Elisabeth, 79–80
Margo, 201–2
Marion, Francis, 219–20
Marlborough, Duchess of, 246
Marsh, Mae, 32, 35–40, 42, 61, 290
Marsh, Oliver, 67
Martin, Elliott, 303
Martin, Hugh, 299–300, 303
Martin, Mary, 217–18, 220, 266, 300
Marx, Karl, 41
Marx, Sam, 147, 148, 150, 151, 162, 171
Mascot, 8–9, 10
Masses, 41
Matrimaniac, The, 61
Maugham, W. Somerset, 106
Maxwell, Elsa, 80–1, 107, 135, 181, 196, 282, 284
Maxwell, Marilyn, 226
Mayer, Louis B., 175, 187, 194, 201, 234
   actors and, 164, 170, 196
   M–G–M executives and, 158, 169, 174, 181
McCarey, Leo, 171, 174
McGrath, Earle, 274, 275, 277, 278, 311
McGraw-Hill, 269
McGuire, Dorothy, 204, 205, 206
Meade, Fred, 18, 21
Mencken, H. L., 104, 128
   Blondes and, 88, 92, 93, 94, 95, 98, 102
   on *Brunettes,* 117
   Loos's friendship with, 64, 86–8, 200, 315
Mendl, Elsie de Wolfe, 79–80, 123, 252, 258

Mendl, Sir Charles, 252
Meredith, Burgess, 208, 237
Merman, Ethel, 209, 226
Methot, Mayo, 159
Metro-Goldwyn-Mayer(M–G–M),61, 141, 147, 179–81, 182–3, 209, 289
   actresses with, 150, 156, 219
   Emerson and, 141, 152, 158–9, 164, 165, 168, 169
   executives at, 158, 168, 181, 203
   Loos's dissatisfaction with, 171, 172, 200–1, 202–3, 204
   San Francisco produced by, 163–8
   writers at, 145, 148, 160, 162, 179–81, 183, 192, 194
Michell, Keith, 281, 282
Mielzener, Jo, 213
Miller, Arthur, 262
Miller, Gilbert, 236–42, 244, 265, 266
Miller, Henry, 12
Miller, Kitty Bache, 236, 244, 265, 266
Miller, Marilyn, 75, 85
Millionairess, The, 277
Mineo, Sal, 261
Minnelli, Vincente, 210
Mitchell, Grant, 84
Mitchell, Maxie, 16–17
Mizner, Addison, 123, 126, 154
Mizner, Wilson, 138, 156, 309
   background of, 123–6
   characters based on, 163, 196, 270
   Emerson and, 153–4
   friendships of, 128–30, 162, 174, 178, 200
   health problems of, 146–7, 154–5
   in Hollywood, 135–6, 146–7, 150, 153–4
   in memoirs, 290
   physical appearance of, 126–8, 146–7
   wit of, 128, 309
Molnár, Ferenc, 139
Molyneux, Edward, 80, 81
Monroe, Marilyn, 231
Montand, Yves, 258, 261
Montecatini Terme, 245, 246, 255–6, 275, 282, 292, 296

Montparnasse, 218, 268-9
Moore, Charles, 268
Moore, Colleen, 141
Moore, (Annette) Gladys
  childhood of, 268, 276, 280, 286,
    287-8, 302
  as dancer, 284-5, 290
  Loos's travels with, 275, 276, 281,
    282, 297
  marriage of, 305-6
Moore, Grace, 164
Moore, Owen, 46
Moore, Willie, 268
Mosheim, Grete, 120
Mother Was a Lady, 219-20, 222, 225
Motion Picture Association, censorship
  by, 185
Mouse Is Born, A, 145-6, 233, 234-5,
  243-4
Much Ado About Nothing, 316
Mulligan, Gerry, 271-2, 290, 298-300,
  303
Mumford, Lewis, 95
Muni, Paul, 165
Murfin, Jane, 184
Museum of Modern Art, 270, 284
Music and Drama, 10-11
Mussolini, Benito, 117, 118-19
My Fair Lady, 291
"My Friend Irma," 192
"My Rose, My Rose," 30
My Sister Eileen, 224

Naked Genius, The, 222
Nathan, George Jean, 87
Nation, 283
Nazimova, Alla, 181
Neighborhood Playhouse, 248, 249
Nesbitt, Catherine, 237-8, 240, 241,
  242, 266
Neutra, Richard, 170, 175
Newlands, Anthony, 276-7
New Republic, 36
New York City, guide to, 292-5, 296
New York City Ballet, 284-5
New Yorker, The, 184-5, 236, 283, 289

New Yorkers, The, 177
New York Hat, The, 23-5
New York Morning Telegraph, 21
New York Times, The, 95, 215-16,
  232, 261, 283
New York Tribune, 98
Nicolson, Harold, 105
Nielsen, Alice, 13
Niesen, Gertrude, 226-7
No Mother to Guide Her, 47,
  269-71, 277
None but the Lonely Heart, 205
Northanger Abbey (Jane Austen), 27
No Strings, 219
Novarro, Ramon, 158
Nutcracker, The, 284-5, 299

Oberon, Merle, 171, 174
O'Brien, Shaun, 285
Oelrichs, Marjorie, 109-10, 122-3, 181-2
Oklahoma!, 208
Old Buddha, 203, 204, 205, 207
Oliver!, 281
One Hundred Men and a Girl, 176
O'Neill, Eugene, 256
One Way Passage, 147
"On Growing Old Disgracefully," 315
On the Town, 223
Our Dancing Daughters, 181
"Over There," 83

Paden, Clifton, *see* Emerson, John
Pair o' Fools, 104
Palisades Park, 60
Pallma, Frank, 30
Pallma, Frank, Jr., 30, 33
Pan, 312
Pandora's Box, 296
Paramount Pictures, 172, 238, 242
Paris, 177
Parker, Dorothy, 128, 208
Paul, Grand Duke of Russia, 225
Pearl Harbor, bombing of, 139
Peckham, Ted, 268, 283, 302, 308, 309
Percy, Eileen, 137-8
Perfect Woman, The, 73

Perils of Paulette, The, 295-7
Perkins, Anthony, 259
Philadelphia Story, The, 192
Piaf, Edith, 268
Pickfair, 89
Pickford, Charlotte, 48
Pickford, Jack, 48, 54, 75
Pickford, Lottie, 48
Pickford, Mary, 26, 83, 106
   Fairbanks and, 46-8, 89, 101
   film career of, 23-5, 52, 219
   popularity of, 35, 36, 42, 50, 270
Pidgeon, Walter, 195
Pirate, The, 210
Pisani, Dr., 246, 255
Pitts, ZaSu, 219-20
Plummer, Amanda, 250
Poiret, 257
Poland, Baron, 227
Police Gazette, 11
Polly of the Follies, 82, 84
Porter, Cole, 108, 176, 177, 178, 196,
   284
Porter, Linda, 108, 215, 233, 284
Pound, Ezra, 95
Powell, Dick, 221
Powell, Eleanor, 196
Powell, William, 164
Pride and Prejudice (Jane Austen), 194
Prince, Harold, 262
Prince Chap, The, 19
Pringle, Aileen, 102
Proust, Marcel, 134
Public Enemy, 88

Quo Vadis?, 12

Rafferty, Frances, 202
Rainer, Luise, 181
Rambeau, Marjorie, 205, 207
Ramshackle Inn, 219
Rapf, Henry, 162
Rattigan, Terrence, 257
Reaching for the Moon, 44
Reagan, Nancy, 220
Red Boy, 266

Redheaded Woman, 147-50, 158
Reed, Florence, 241
"Reflections on Anita Loos," 316
Reliance-Mutual, 28
Remarque, Erich Maria, 295
Reynolds, Sir Joshua, 123
Riffraff, 16-2
Road to Plaindale, The, 22
Robbins, Jack, 223
Robbins, Jerome, 223
Roberts, Rachel, 291
Robin Hood, 50
Robinson, Horace, 17
Robinson, Nina Smith, 17, 29
Rodgers, Richard, 219, 262
   Hammerstein and, 208, 209, 213,
     215, 218, 228, 262
   Hart and, 181, 196, 225
Roman Holiday, 241
Room at the Top, 258
Rooney, Mickey, 181
Roosevelt Hotel, 135
"Rosary, The," 201, 203
Rose, Billy, 224, 228
Rosen, Lucy, 250-1
Rosenkavalier, Der, 257
Ross, Diana, 86
Rouleau, Raymond, 239-40, 242
Russell, Bertrand, 315
Russell, Rosalind, 185, 186, 196

Sale, Edward, 269, 312
Sale, Mary, *see* Loos, Mary Anita
Sale, Richard, 216, 217, 254, 269, 278,
   286
San Francisco, 163-8, 169
San Simeon, 136-7
Santayana, George, 98, 107
Saratoga, 169, 170-1
Sardou, Victorien, 53
Saturday Review, 283
Saud, King of Saudi Arabia, 275
Schenck, Joseph, 68, 73, 301
   background of, 60-1
   marriage of, 60, 61, 75
   New York residence of, 64, 65

Talmadges' careers and, 61, 64, 82, 141
 at Twentieth Century-Fox, 204, 206, 207
Schenck, Nick, 60–1
School of American Ballet, 284
Schwartz, Arthur, 215
Scott, Edgar, 287, 304
Scott-Moncrieff, C. K., 95
Selden, Albert, 248, 250
Sell, Henry, 94
Selwyn, Edgar, 104, 110, 111
Selznick, Irene Mayer, 302
Sennett, Mack, 31, 43
"Sex Can Make a Dunce of You," 105, 207
Shakespeare, William, 33, 34, 214
Shaw, George Bernard, 105, 277, 313
Shearer, Norma, 150, 175, 185–6
Shelley, Gladys, 280
Shepard, Eugenia, 284
Sherwood, Madeleine, 265, 278, 283
Sherwood, Robert E., 265
She Stoops to Conquer, 217
Short, Bobby, 298
Shubert Organization, 250
Signoret, Simone, 258, 259, 261
Sills, Beverly, 291
Silsbee, Esta, 219, 220
Simmons, Jeffrey, 297
Simmons, Stanley, 247, 265, 266, 268, 283, 284, 290, 291, 310, 311
Sims, Hilda, 218
Sinatra, Frank, 224, 309
Sklar, Robert, 283
Smart Set, 86
Smith, Cleopatra Fairbrother, 5, 25
Smith, George, 5, 8, 16, 17
Smith, Oliver, 223, 224, 225, 226–7, 234, 248
Smith, Tommy, 95, 102
Social Register, The, 139, 140–1
Social Secretary, The, 61
Soldier's Pay, 95
Something About Anne, 290, 291

Sondheim, Stephen, 262
Soul Sinners, The, 21
South Pacific, 217–18, 228, 230
Spaeth, Sigmund, 95
Stanley, Kim, 259, 260, 261, 273
Stanwyck, Barbara, 195
Star and Garter, 222
Stein, Gertrude, 78–9, 276, 279
Steinbeck, John, 161
Steinem, Gloria, 74
Stendhal, 95
Stokowski, Leopold, 176–7
Stone, Fred, 53
Story of Louis Pasteur, The, 165
Stowe, Harriet Beecher, 207
Strauss, Richard, 257
Streetcar Named Desire, A, 266
Strickling, Howard, 236
Stromberg, Hunt, 184, 195–9, 200–1, 214
Struggle, The, 141
Sturges, Howard, 108, 176, 177, 178, 199, 205, 233, 245
Styne, Jule, 224, 226, 228, 229, 247, 256, 297
Sugar (Loos's boyfriend), 205–7
Sullavan, Margaret, 204, 274
Susan and God, 192–3
Sutherland, Donald, 276
Suzy, 284
Swanson, Gloria, 61, 136
Swarthout, Gladys, 275

Tallon, Ninon de, 234, 257, 273, 274, 281
Talmadge, Constance (Dutch), 65, 68, 171
 character based on, 100
 in films, 32, 35, 37, 57–9, 60, 61–4, 67, 73, 82, 88, 141
 later years of, 285–6, 287, 302
 Loos's friendship with, 65–6, 85
 McGuire vs., 204
Talmadge, Natalie, 60, 68

Talmadge, Norma, 32, 66, 68, 85
  film career of, 57-9, 61, 64, 141
  marriage of, 60, 61, 75
Talmadge, Peg, 59-60, 67, 85
Talmadge family, 59-60, 65, 67, 75,
  78, 301
Talmadge Girls, The, 300, 301, 302, 303
Taste of Honey, A, 231
Teahouse of the August Moon, 257
Tell it to the Marines, 198-9
Temperamental Wife, A, 61-4
Tender Buttons, 78, 79
Tent City, 25, 30
Terrail, Claude, 240
Terry, Ellen, 56
Thalberg, Irving, 141, 162, 170, 181,
  185, 195, 214
  books on, 89, 145-6, 234
  health of, 158, 168-9
  at M-G-M, 141, 147, 148, 152, 156
  San Francisco and, 163-4
Theatre Arts, 232
Theatre World, 266
They Knew What They Wanted, 107
They Met in Bombay, 196-7
Thompson, Peter, 28
Thomson, Virgil, 283, 284
Three Musketeers, The, 50
Time Remembered, 256
Times Square, 294
Tincher, Fay, 28
Tipton, Gladys, 232, 234, 266, 272, 277,
  279, 302, 313
  background of, 248
  charity work of, 268, 280, 286
  financial arrangements for, 303-4,
    310, 311, 314-15
  irrational behavior of, 307-10,
    3-12
  Jerome Clarke's death and, 306
  Loos's dependency on, 267-8, 269,
    302
  as Loos's sister substitute, 247-8,
    267-8
  Loos's travels with, 205, 217, 275,
    276, 281, 282, 297

  mother of, 255-6, 266, 267, 290
Todd, Mike, 22-2, 224
Toklas, Alice B., 79, 276
To the One I Love the Best, 252
Touch of the Poet, A, 256, 259
Toulouse-Lautrec, Henri de, 123
"Town Talk," 21
Tracy, Spencer, 16-2, 164, 165
Tree, Sir Herbert Beerbohm, 33, 34
Tree Grows in Brooklyn, A, 206
Trevor, Claire, 312
Triangle Pictures, 31, 32, 4-2, 49
  see also Fine Arts-Triangle
    Productions
"Trolley Song, The," 290
Truex, Ernest, 53
Tsarskoe Selo, 28
Tuesday Widows, 85-6, 98, 171
Turner, Lana, 181, 201
Tushingham, Rita, 231
Twentieth Century-Fox, 204, 206
20,000 Years in Sing Sing, 147
Twice Over Lightly, 292-5, 296

United Artists, 172
Unity, 243-4

Valentino, Rudolph, 80, 138
Vallambrosa, Paul de, 129, 130,
  135
Vallambrosa, Ruth de, *see* Dubonnet,
  Ruth Obré Goldbeck
  de Vallambrosa
Valley of Decision, The, 203-4
Van Dyke, W. S., 165, 198
Vanity Fair, 39, 41, 74, 94
van Loon, Hendrik, 95
Van Vechten, Carl, 98
Victoria, Queen of England, 207
Victoria Regina, 295
Vidor, King, 158
Viertel, Salka, 160
Viking, 278, 283, 289, 29-2, 293, 297,
  301, 312
Villa Trianon, 80, 252
Virtuous Vamp, A, 64, 205, 303

Vogue, 315
Voltaire, 99

Wagg, Kenneth, 274
Wagner, Robert, 261
Walker, June, 111
Walpole, Hugh, 160
Warner, Jack, 147
Warren, Whitney, 282
Washington *Post,* 259–60
Wayne, John, 282
Weintraub, Florence, 308
Weissberger, Arnold, 281, 299, 304, 310, 311
Wells, H. G., 106, 186, 189, 315
Wendel, Betty, 178, 206, 210, 229–30, 253, 254
Wendel, Sandy, 178, 206, 229–30, 254
Wescott, Glenway, 283, 284
West, Mae, 156
Wharton, Edith, 79, 108
When Ladies Meet, 194
White, Miles, 227, 228, 240
White Collar Girl, 205
Whitman, Walt, 29, 37
Whole Town's Talking, The, 84–5, 104, 107
Why Girls Go South, 102–3, 108
Wild and Wooly, 44–6
Wilde, Oscar, 94, 123
Wilder, Thornton, 257
Wild Girl of the Sierras, 35
Williams, Tennessee, 253, 262, 266
Wilson, Edmund, 268, 271, 283
Wilson, Flip, 86

Wilson, John, 233, 244, 245, 247
    alcoholism of, 227, 248, 265
    Blondes directed by, 225, 226–8
Wilson, Marie, 193, 202, 203
Wilson, Natalia (Natasha) Paley, 225–6, 233, 244, 265, 268, 283, 284, 290
Windsor, Duke of (Prince of Wales), 106, 107
Witness for the Prosecution, 257
Wizard of Oz, The, 198
Wodehouse, P. G., 313
Wolff, Helen, 293
Woman's Place, A, 73
Women, The (Boothe), 184–5
Women, The (film), 184–6
Woods, Ella, 37, 38
Woods, Frank (Daddy), 32–3, 37, 38, 42
Woollcott, Alexander, 65
World War II, 193–4, 196, 199, 200, 20–2, 242
Worth, 7, 109, 257
Wyler, William, 174

Yerkes, Myra, 124
Young, Robert, 164
Yurka, Blanche, 74

Zanuck, Darryl, 175
Zen Buddhism, 295–6
Ziegfield (theater), 224, 231
Ziegfield, Florenz, 104, 222
Zola, Émile, 99
Zorina, Vera, 196
Zukor, Adolph, 53

A Note on the Type

The text of this book was set in a film version of Fairfield, a typeface designed by the distinguished American artist and engraver Rudolph Ruzicka (1883-1978). Fairfield displays the sober and sane qualities of a master craftsman whose talent has long been dedicated to clarity.

Rudolph Ruzicka was born in Bohemia and came to America in 1894. He designed and illustrated many books and was the creator of a considerable list of individual prints in a variety of techniques.

Composed by Superior Type, Champaign, Illinois
Printed and bound by Halliday Lithographers,
West Hanover, Massachusetts
Designed by Iris Weinstein